A Critical Study of the Rule of Benedict

A Critical Study of the Rule of Benedict

Volume 2, Prologue, Chapters 4, 6, 7, and 73

Adalbert de Vogüé

Translation by
Colleen Maura McGrane, OSB

New City Press
of the Focolare
Hyde Park, New York

Published in the United States by New City Press
202 Comforter Blvd., Hyde Park, NY 12538
www.newcitypress.com
©2014 Benedictine Sisters of Perpetual Adoration (English translation)

This book was first published in France as La Règle de Saint Benoît: Commentaire Historique et Critique (Parties I-III) par Adalbert de Vogüé, No.184 dans la collection Sources chretiennes by Les EDITIONS DU CERF, Paris, France. © 1971, EDITIONS DU CERF.

Cover design by Leandro de Leon

Library of Congress Cataloging-in-Publication Data

Vogüé, Adalbert de.
 [La Regle de Saint Benoit. English]
 A Critical Study of the Rule of Benedict / Adalbert de Vogüé, ; Translation by Colleen Maura McGrane, OSB
     volumes cm
 Includes bibliographical references.
 Summary: "The work of Dom Adalbert de Vogüé, OSB (1924-2011) serves as the basis of all serious study of the Rule of Benedict. Vogüé, uses literary criticism to show how the Rule of Benedict developed. He establishes the dependence of the Rule of Benedict on the Rule of the Master"-- Provided by publisher.
 ISBN 978-1-56548-480-1
 1. Benedict, Saint, Abbot of Monte Cassino. Regula. 2. Monasticism and religious orders--Rules. I. Title.
 BX3004.Z5V6313 2013
 255'.106--dc23
                                                    2013047935

ISBN: 978-1-56548-494-8 (vol. 2)

Printed in the United States of America

Contents

Part One: The Prologue and the Epilogue

Chapter One

The Introductions of RM 9
    Endnotes 33

Chapter Two

The Prologue of Benedict 41
    Endnotes 55

Chapter Three

The Epilogue (RB 73) 59
    Endnotes 72

Part Two: The Spiritual Art

Chapter Four

The Treatise of the Master (RM 3–6) 79
    I. The Group and Its Connections 79
    II. The Details of the *Ars Sancta* (RM 3) 89
    III. The Additions (RM 4–6) 107
    IV. The Geneses of the Treatise and the *Ars* 110
    Endnotes 113

Chapter Five

The Treatise of Benedict (RB 4) 123
    Endnotes 150

Part Three: Silence and Humility

Chapter Six

Silence... 157
    I. The Treatise of the Master (RM 8–9) 157
    II. The Treatise of Benedict (RB 6) 169
    III. Theory and Practice of Silence 174
    Endnotes 187

Chapter Seven

Humility 195
    I. The Treatise of the Master 195
    II. The Treatise of Benedict 227
    III. The Meaning of the Treatise:
        The Fear of God and Humility 230
    Endnotes 245

Part One

The Prologue and the Epilogue

Chapter One

The Introductions of RM

Ordinarily, authors most clearly articulate their intention in the introductions and conclusions of their work. Thus, we will begin by successively examining the Prologue and final chapter (RB 73) of the Rule of Benedict, two passages that are clearly complementary. The Prologue of RB corresponds to a series of introductions four times longer in RM. In contrast, the Epilogue of RB has no parallel in RM.

Benedict literally draws almost the entire Prologue from the last part of the introduction of RM (Ths). Only two short passages at the beginning and end are his own (Prol 1–4 and 46–49). We will see that both have clear connections with other preliminary passages from RM. Therefore, we must begin by considering the entire series of introductions from the Master.

The Conclusion of the Rule of the Four Fathers

This series of the Master consists of an initial Prologue, followed by a *Thema* in three parts. But in manuscript P*, the Prologue seems to echo what it follows, that is to say the conclusion of the *Rule of the Four Fathers (RIVP)*.[1] A parallel version of the two texts has been arranged by H. Vanderhoven and G. Penco.[2] According to Penco, *RIVP* inspired the beginning (*qui legis ... qui obscultas*) and principal ideas of the Prologue of the Master, as well as the appeal to unceasing prayer that rings out at the end of his homily on the Our Father. In fact, as Vanderhoven rightly understands,[3] the dependent relationship is exactly the opposite: RM inspired the edited conclusion of *RIVP*. We must not forget that this small final passage is read only in manuscript P*. Absent from recension E*, which all the other witnesses of *RIVP* belong to, it is clearly meant to bind the latter to RM.

Moreover, it could be that the same hand that added this ending to the text of *RIVP* also inserted the words *primo tibi qui legis deinde et tibi*, read in the first line of the Prologue of the Master. This interpolation does not fit the context grammatically[4] or logically.[5] When removed, the introduction of the Master becomes lucid: *O homo qui me obscultas dicentem*. Therefore, it is likely that the first paragraphs[6] of the Prologue were originally addressed only to the "listener." The reference to the "reader" would have been rather awkwardly added at the time when the conclusion of *RIVP* was edited. In the latter, the formula *qui legit ... qui audit* forms part of a beautiful blessing taken from the Book of Revelation. When the editor introduced this formula, removed from its scriptural context, into the Prologue of the Master, it was undoubtedly to create an artificial link between the two Rules.

The Prologue of the Master

Having extricated the Prologue of the Master from its additions, we can now consider it in and of itself. It is composed of six paragraphs, each of whose beginning is clearly indicated by the recurrence of a word pertaining to hearing (*obscultas, auditor, audis, auditus, audi*) and, from the second paragraph forward, *ergo*. These appeals to the listener punctuate the entire passage and are accompanied by insistent imperatives, calling first for understanding and attention (*cognosce, percipe, intende, intellige*), then for obedience and action (*ingredere, sequatur, obserua, age, adinple*). Listeners must first recognize that it is God who speaks, then, understand the divine message, and finally let this message sink into their hearts and make efforts to follow it. This progression observed in the first three paragraphs is interrupted in the fourth, which returns to the initial invitations to recognize the word of God and apprehend his warning. But the progression returns in the last two sections: one must practice what one hears; it is not only a matter of listening, but also of doing.

Therefore the exhortation achieves real progress, which must not be hidden by its many obvious repetitions. If one considers the eschatological terms that appear in each paragraph, one again observes what was noted in following the series of imperatives. The first paragraph focuses on death; the second passes beyond, speaking of rendering an account to God; and the third mentions "damnation." As with the imperatives, the fourth paragraph pauses: it repeats death, judgment, and damnation, although, for the first time, and insistently, it depicts this damnation as eternal punishment. In the fifth paragraph, one finds the resurrection, with its consequences of eternal glory in the company of the saints, or eternal fire, in company with the devil.

After this complete evocation of the last things, the sixth paragraph has nothing to add: it speaks no more of eschatology. Nevertheless, one can say that the Master has progressively unveiled a painting of the *nouissima*, from death to a blessed or wretched eternity, via the judgment. First, the progression follows the course of events that leads to eternal damnation. Then, after the recapitulation of the fourth paragraph, it opens onto a vast contrasting tableau, where death is followed by resurrection and beatitude is contrasted with the fire of Gehenna.

Thus, two parallel progressions run together, supporting one another throughout the Prologue. As the formidable picture of the last things unfolds, the demands of the preacher will become more detailed and specific. In both cases, the fourth paragraph marks a pause after the regular progression of the first three paragraphs. One then resumes the march to the end.

Two remarks will complete these formal considerations. We note first the curious fluctuation of persons in the first three paragraphs. Each time, the author begins by distinguishing himself from the listener, — "I" and "you" — then identifies himself with the listener, using "we." The fluctuation ceases with the fourth paragraph, appearing once again as a break in the development.

Two unique phenomena also occur at the beginning of the fourth paragraph: "you" plural replaces "you" singular, and "we" replaces "I."[7] It is no longer a matter, as previously, of what one could call a predicatory or human "we," which unites author and reader in their shared human condition. This new "we" is a simple plural of author, a literary equivalent of "I." The "you" plural may be a plural of this same genre, literary rather than actual, equivalent to "you" singular.[8] However, it may also be that the Master inadvertently switches from his supposed single "listener" to the assembly of *fratres* whom he usually addresses.

In any case, after this double variation, the Master consistently uses "I" and "you" singular in the rest of the Prologue, except for citations. Therefore, the predicatory "we" that ends each of the first three paragraphs does not reappear in the last three. This is not an insignificant change of tone. It serves to make the warnings of the second half even more insistent. From now on, it is the listener, and he alone, who is involved. The speaker presents him with a personal choice that will decide his very fate.

Our second remark concerns scriptural citations and allusions. There are none in the first two paragraphs. It is only at the end of the third that one finds the exposition on the "two ways" that presents some unequivocal, although implicit, allusions to the Gospel maxim regarding the broad and narrow ways.[9] Subsequently, the fourth and fifth paragraphs are once again devoid of scriptural references. Scripture reappears in the last paragraph, this time in a series of citations illustrating the words *regula* and *uirga*.[10]

Thus, recourse to Scripture occurs only twice, in the third and sixth paragraphs, at the end of each half of the text.[11] This restraint is undoubtedly connected with the purpose of the passage, wholly intended to present the Rule as a quasi-inspired work. The proper name of the latter—*regula*—will not appear until the final paragraph (Pr 23–24). Prior to this, the Master uses only the ambiguous name of *scriptura*.[12] Even paired with the demonstrative *haec*, this name unquestionably calls to mind Holy Scripture, especially as it continually affirms that it is God who speaks. This intended ambiguity is probably involved in the absence of any formal citation of canonical Scripture until the final paragraph. To cite Scripture too soon would destroy the prophetic atmosphere, the sacred aura that envelops such an apocrypha, the mysterious *scriptura*. It is only when it is shown for what it is, a simple monastic Rule, that the flood of scriptural citations begins to flow. And these citations are specifically aimed at linking the name *regula* and its synonym, *uirga*, to inspired Scripture.[13]

This collection of formal analyses and, in particular, our last remark, has introduced us to the purpose of the great overture of the Master. It is nothing other than a solemn presentation of the Rule. The written work appears as the speech of a man and, through the latter, as the speech of God. The messenger of God urges the hearer to give him his full attention. In fact, the message concerns the listener's present and future destiny. Death is imminent and meeting with the divine judge inevitable. The hearer must move toward it willingly, by acting correctly. He has been granted a limited lifespan in which to amend and progress toward the good. This journey of amendment and progress toward God can only be made on the narrow way of the Gospel where one observes the divine precepts. The hearer must set out and run with all his might! From now on, he will have no excuse since he has heard the divine warning and recognized the way that God has mapped out for him. There is no salvation for him except in fulfilling the Rule.

Therefore, the Rule is presented as the map for the journey to God, the program of good works required for salvation, and an explanation of the demands of the Gospel. It is not only a solemn, but also a dramatic presentation, since it calls for a choice with eternal consequences. In each paragraph, a threat accompanies the exhortation and a frightening prospect appears alongside the designated path. Death by surprise, rendering an account, damnation, the absence of any excuse on the day of judgment, eternal remorse without remedy, the never-ending fire of Gehenna—this series of misfortunes is so well highlighted that any positive hopes pale in comparison. The tone of the passage is severe and even somber. Its principal motive is fear. There is a reason that the author ends by brandishing the *uirga*, a symbol of chastisement and rectitude. Since the Rule cannot be the instrument of God's wrath on the Day of Judgment, it is that of his justice here below![14]

The Thema and Its Three Parts

The chain of citations that ends the Prologue is continued by two citations from the Psalms that open the following passage. The first concerns the *uirga-regula*. Now it is "parables" that are involved. This expression clearly points to the symbolic character of the narration that follows in which baptism is depicted using the image of a spring that exhausted travelers discover along the way.

The author speaks in first person for the last time in these two citations from the Psalms: "I will open my mouth in parables.... For them I have become a parable." From now on, he will disappear, except to implicitly distinguish himself from the brothers to whom the homilies on the *Pater* (Our Father) and the Psalms are addressed. "You" singular disappears at the same time as "I." The parable of the spring is written completely in "we" and this predicatory "we" also prevails in the commentaries on the *Pater* and the Psalms, except for brief and frequent digressive statements of the "See, brothers" type. If "you" singular is occasionally retained, it is only in some clearly interpolated phrase[15] or where it is imposed by the scriptural text on which it is commenting.[16] Therefore, one no longer finds the tone of the Prologue. One has advanced from the discourse of the author/speaker to a single individual to some homilies addressed to a group of brothers. In the Prologue, the Master undoubtedly speaks to a postulant to whom he is about to read the Rule.[17] In the subsequent passages, he seems to address the entire community whom he also intends to hear the Rule daily (RM 24.15).

While this new series is enigmatic in more ways than one, the phrase *Incipit Thema* that appears at the beginning is especially so. A corresponding *Explicit Thema Regulae* appears before Chapter One in P*, but is missing in A*. Following J. Froger, we first held this *Explicit* to be inauthentic and thought that the phrase *Incipit Thema* applied only to the psalmic citations involving "parables." However, this interpretation begs discussion. The two initial citations indicate the parabolic genre of the narrative rather than its theme. Moreover, the parable concludes at the end of the first passage. This latter obviously continued with the commentaries on the *Pater* and the Psalms. The announcement of the only parable does not constitute a very appropriate *thema* for such a series. Finally, in spite of its absence from A*, the *Explicit Thema regulae* of P* is not easily eliminated. An *Incipit* normally calls for an *Explicit*. This principle is verified four times in RM.[18] Moreover, there is a striking parallelism between the indications *Incipit Prologus* and *Incipit Thema* on one hand, and *Explicit Prologus regulae* and *Explicit Thema regulae* on the other. In both, the word *regulae* appears only in the *Explicit*.

These various indicators seem to prove that, in the mind of the author, *thema* designates the whole of the three passages in P that conclude with the *Explicit*. As this latter says, it is a matter of the *Thema regulae*, of a passage that announces the theme of the entire Rule. Indeed, the last lines, culminating the entire *Thema*, describe the intent of the work quite satisfactorily: "to establish a school for the Lord's service."[19] One finds several examples of smaller works having a Prologue and *Thema* in succession in the *Discourses* of Ennodius of Pavia.[20] This would be the case here. It is true that in the *Discourses*, the *Thema* is a simple formula of a few words or a very brief passage.[21] The two psalmic citations of the Master correspond better to the model in this regard. But the *Discourses* of Ennodius are themselves brief little works. In several of them, the connection of the *Thema* to the whole is not very different from that of the *Thema* of the Master to the entire Rule.[22] Given the length of RM, there is nothing exorbitant about it being preceded by a *Thema* of several pages.[23]

Whatever the significance of the word *thema*, it is certain that the three passages included under this title in P* form a whole. The first (Th) is a commentary on the call of Christ in Matthew 11:28–30: "Come to me, all you who labor…. Take my yoke upon you and learn from me…. " The beginning of this text is included as an appeal to baptism, where Christ "re-creates" sinful and mortal persons who lay their burden of sin at his feet.[24] The rest of it applies to a new invitation from Christ, subsequent to baptismal regeneration: the heavy burden of past faults must be exchanged for the yoke of the Lord, which is light and brings "rest."[25] Henceforth, instead of Adam and Eve, the "voice of the Lord" and the "Christian law" will be their father and mother. In other words, they give themselves totally to Christ and the Gospel.

The transition to the second part (Thp) occurs by means of the repetition of the terms "father" and "mother." This time "our father" is designated in all clarity: it is the Lord himself, meaning Christ. Our mother is the Church.[26] The parents according to the flesh are designated with the same clarity: one no longer speaks of Adam and Eve, but of "our earthly father" and our "human mother," who must now be abandoned. The Master opens his own commentary on the Lord's Prayer with this familiar theme of African commentators on the *Pater*.

Chapter 1: The Introductions of RM

One sees that this new section is closely tied to what precedes it. The idea of paternity, present at both ends of the baptismal parable, is found at the beginning and end of the homily on the *Pater*. In both passages, supernatural paternity is not attributed to the First Person of the Trinity, but to Christ. Some additional parallels confirm the unity of intent and authorship: in both cases, life prior to baptism is presented as a "descent" in this world;[27] in both cases, "birth" and "generation" are linked;[28] in both cases, one speaks of the "knowledge of baptism,"[29] "the invitation of the Lord,"[30] and our "discovery" of him.[31] These parallels, whose list could be lengthened,[32] suffice to demonstrate that the same thought and writer are at work in both passages. The commentary on the Lord's Prayer is clearly the continuation of the parable of the spring. Coming from the baptismal font, the neophytes have the *Pater* explained to them. Nothing is more natural, if one recalls the *Catechesis mystagogica* of Cyril, the *De Sacramentis* of Ambrose, and the *De cognitione baptismi* of Ildephonsus, where the Lord's Prayer is also explained to the newly baptized.[33]

The homily of the Master on the *Pater* cannot be original in every respect, as it belongs to a rather long and vast tradition. However, in each of the expositions connected with the first four petitions, one finds what can almost be considered signature traits: "good works," "accounts to be rendered," "self-will," and the *annona* of servants. They are accentuated to varying degrees, some discrete, others very blatant. All of this will be abundantly demonstrated in the Rule, if it has not already been so in the Prologue.[34]

A clearly indicated transition moves one from this second passage to the next (Ths): after prayer, it is time to discuss action. The latter is presented as "service." This is because our new status as sons and daughters has not taken away that of servants.[35] Our heavenly Father is also our Master.[36] These two aspects of the relationship with Christ, touched on here and there in the homily on the *Pater*, are joined in a beautiful and striking formula at the beginning of the fourth passage. The schema for divine service will require two psalm texts: first some verses from Psalm 33, then Psalm 14 in its entirety. Each of these lists of good works is concluded with a call to progress, to act. The second time, the conclusion is more extensive and serves as a peroration to the entire passage: we must "run and act" now. It is this imperative that prompts the establishment of the "school of the Lord's service."

Therefore, while announced at the beginning, the ideas of action and service actually inform this entire third passage. Is that to say that it adequately distinguishes itself from the second passage, the latter discussing prayer, the former, action, as the transition announced? Actually, the commentary on the *Pater* was already full of exhortations to good deeds. In fact, its moralizing manner hardly differs from that of the commentary on the Psalms. If it is to be distinguished, it is by its formal invitation to action and its choice of scriptural texts directly linked to this intent.

The relationship that the themes of prayer and action and Father and Master establish between the two passages is apparent at the beginning of Ths. It is found again toward the end when the author invites readers to "ask the Lord to grant us the help of his grace."[37] This phrase is reminiscent of the commentary on the two final petitions of the *Pater*, where we previously found the key words.[38] As we have said, the homily on the *Pater* generally focuses more on action than prayer. It is only toward the end that it recommends unceasing prayer to obtain grace. Therefore, the commentary on the Lord's Prayer and that on the Psalms concur in discussing prayer at the end.

Such are the primary connections between the second and third passages.[39] As solid as they may be, they are still not as strong as those that unite the first and third passages. The commentary on Psalm 33 is clearly connected to the parable of the spring. In both, the divine voice proclaims: "Come!" and this is followed by a second appeal, which the "one who hears" responds to with actions or words.[40] In both, one begins by seeing before hearing.[41] In both, one exults in having heard "the voice of the Lord who invites us."[42]

These similarities establish an obvious parallel between the "Come" of the Gospel and that of the Psalm, between the call to baptism and the call to learn the fear of the Lord. In both, this "come" rings out at the beginning of the passage. Both divide the passage in two: the Gospel pericope becomes the object of two distinct citations, the second longer than the first; the commentary on the Psalms also revolves around two texts, of which only the second is cited completely and is therefore longer. From all evidence, the same author is at work in the commentary on the Gospel and that on the Psalms. Less constrained by the text on which he comments than in the homily on the *Pater* and freer to compose as he wishes, he spontaneously constructs diptychs, which will be found a number of times in the Rule, especially in the chapter on the abbot.[43]

Two diptychs frame the vast homily on the *Pater*, which is itself constructed around a long middle section containing commentary on the third petition. In its own way, this harmonious construction attests to what our analysis has continually emphasized: the homogeneity of the entire discourse contained between the Prologue and Chapter One.

Each of the three parts is linked to the other two. The group forms a well-organized trilogy, in which, without being forced, everything clearly connects and corresponds. We no longer need to justify the *Explicit Thema regulae* of P*. Authentic or not, this *Explicit* at least has a certain basis in the literary reality that we have just analyzed. Even if one had to reject the title *Thema regulae*, the group thus delineated definitely forms a compact whole and represents the reflective work of quite an accomplished writer.[44]

Thema *and Prologue*

But it is not enough to simply confirm the unity of authorship of the *Thema*. One can go a step further and suggest that the author of the *Thema* is also that of the Prologue. In fact, there are a number of expressions common to both passages: "good deeds," the "negligence of the sinner," the "listener," "ignorance," the "way" or "ways," "running," the "light," of this world or of this life, and the "propitious" God.[45] But the most decisive fact is that two entire phrases of the Prologue appear almost unchanged in the commentary on the Psalms. According to the first, our present life is only a limited time span in which God, in his goodness, waits daily for us to amend our ways.[46] According to the second, we must take advantage of this respite and run now, while we are still alive and have the time![47] One sees that these two phrases are connected, the second drawing its conclusion from the first. It is even more striking that they are both in the same order and a few lines apart: in the second and fourth paragraphs of the Prologue, the conclusion of Psalm 14, and the general conclusion of the commentary on the Psalms. Therefore, a single redactor worked on the Prologue and the *Thema*. He intentionally preserved a clear echo of the former at the end of the latter.

This sort of inclusion shows that the Prologue and the *Thema* were conceived as a whole.[48] Together they constitute a single introduction in two parts, the one ending with the formal presentation of the Rule, the other with the presentation of its objective: to establish a school of the Lord's service. Just as the Rule has been equated with and joined to Holy Scripture, the school is connected to baptismal rebirth and the Church. In both, the author is concerned with grounding his literary and institutional work in Christian revelation.

The continuity of the Prologue and *Thema* is even more apparent if one considers their shared theme of "hearing." The first thing that struck us in approaching the Prologue was the constant return of a verb of attention, followed immediately by a verb of action, at the beginning of each of its six paragraphs. But the *Thema* is equally abundant in words of this sort. In the parable of the spring, the travelers "hear" a twofold citation of the Gospel.[49] The commentary on the Psalms opens with *Venite filii audite me*, and one continues to "listen to" the divine word.[50] Clearly, this hearing must lead to action. Each of the three parts of the *Thema* affirms this in its own way, the homily on the *Pater* no less than the others. One recalls that the Lord's Prayer is presented as a source of moral teachings, of exhortations to action.

Thus, the entire *Thema* can be summarized in the Gospel formula that serves as the conclusion to Psalm 14: "hear the word and put it into practice."[51] Therefore, a single thread runs through and unites the two introductions. The Prologue calls the reader to listen to the Rule and observe it, the *Thema* to listen to Scripture and put it into practice. The Rule is first suggested to its hearer and, in its turn, proposes the Gospel, *Pater*, and Psalms. Its message does not pretend to be original or independent. To listen to the Rule is, above all, to listen to Scripture.

An appeal to hear and to act, to go to the Lord and run toward him—an appeal based on the imminence of death and the eternity of its consequences—here, in brief, is what one finds in the *Thema*, as well as in the Prologue. This identical starting point, often expressed in the same words, attests to unity of authorship in this double introduction. This preliminary observation is of great importance in setting forth the delicate problem that we must still resolve, that of the literary sources and *Sitz im Leben* of the *Thema*.

Thema *and Baptismal Catecheses*

In fact, at first glance, it appears that this unusual passage is a baptismal catechesis that has been refashioned into the Prologue of a monastic Rule.[52] The parable of the spring speaks of itself in this way. The homily on the *Pater*, which is based on it and refers directly to baptism, calls to mind many citations from the Fathers on the same subject addressed to *competentes* or to the newly baptized. In itself, the commentary on the Psalms is less clear but, taken in this context, it brings to mind the tradition and explanation of the Psalms that one finds at Naples and perhaps in Africa among the preparatory rites of baptism.[53] Consequently, one can ask if the Master has not drawn the three parts of his *Thema* from some collection of episcopal homilies for baptismal candidates or neophytes. By a simple adaptation, he could use these long passages to extend his introduction with little effort.

A preliminary remark will enable us to clarify the question. In the *Thema* of the Master, the reference to baptism precedes the commentaries on the *Pater* and the Psalms. In spite of the intentional obscurity of

Chapter 1: The Introductions of RM

the parable, it seems that the author addresses those who have already been baptized. Therefore, he explains the Lord's Prayer and the Psalms to the baptized, not to catechumens. The significance of this remark becomes apparent if one recalls that not all early churches arranged the various rites of Christian initiation in the same order. While the tradition of the Psalms does not seem to have occurred before baptism, the explanation of the Lord's Prayer was sometimes placed beforehand, other times afterward. Above, we cited the texts of Cyril, Ambrose, and Ildephonsus that made the commentary on the *Pater* the subject of a postbaptismal homily.[54] But there are a greater number of other witnesses that show that the tradition of the *Pater* and its explanation could be addressed to the *electi ad fidem*, to the *competentes*. Whether it preceded the handing over of the Creed, as at Naples, or followed it, as at everywhere else,[55] this tradition of the *Pater* took place during Lent, before baptism. This is attested to by Theodore of Mopsuestia,[56] Augustine,[57] Pseudo-Chrysostom, the Lectionary of Naples,[58] the early Gelasian, and the *Missale Gallicanum uetus*.[59]

It is apparent that the Master does not concur with these witnesses. He seems to depend on the liturgical practices of Jerusalem, Spain, Milan, and perhaps fourth-century Rome,[60] rather than those of Syria, Africa, Naples, seventh-century Rome, or Gaul. This may provide a clue for locating and dating RM. In any case, this observation makes rather problematic the connection that, following J. Froger, we have sketched between the *Thema* of the Master and the Lectionary of Naples or the Sermons of Pseudo-Chrysostom. If the Master is referring to an actual liturgical practice, it is not to the handing over of the Psalms and *Pater* to the *competentes*, as was practiced in Naples and Africa.[61] The sermons of the *Thema* do not suppose such a rite, where the bishop gives those to be baptized the text to learn by heart. They are simple postbaptismal homilies, utilizing the *Pater* and the Psalms to complete the instruction of the faithful.

Furthermore, today, we possess only two homilies for the handing over of the Psalms,[62] and both comment on Psalm 22, the classic text for baptismal catechesis.[63] Pseudo-Chrysostom adds Psalm 116 only out of compassion for poorer memories that could more easily retain a relatively short psalm. Therefore, it seems that Psalm 22 was the standard text for the rite of handing over. Yet, the Master comments not on this psalm but on Psalms 33 and 14. Moreover, he makes very different use of these psalms than do the ceremonial homilies in the handing over of Psalm 22. In RM, the psalm gives rise to extensive mystagogical commentary, while in the homilies, the psalm is most often only called upon and cited as a moral teaching.

In this regard, the end of the *Thema* instead brings to mind some sermons of Augustine for the conclusion of Easter week. When the neophytes are stripped of their white clothing to return to ordinary life and mingle with the crowd of the faithful and unfaithful, the Bishop of Hippo reminds them of the permanent moral demands of their baptism. Like the Master, he composes or borrows from Scripture short lists of good works to be accomplished and wrongs to be avoided.[64]

It is true that the situation of the listeners is not the same. In Augustine, they are Christians who will live in the world, while in RM, they are men who will "establish a school of the Lord's service." However, among the neophytes of Augustine, there are some persons who, after baptism, "vow perfect continence," while others intend to live in marriage. In its turn, Pseudo-Chrysostom testifies that baptism was an opportunity to choose a state of life, a means to practice Christian chastity: to enjoy marriage or remain in virginity, continence, widowhood, or even to "live the life of a monk" or "enter into a community of consecrated daughters."[65]

These references from Augustine and Pseudo-Chrysostom are connected with a well-known tendency of the Patristic Age to link baptism more or less closely with the practice of continence.[66] They are valuable to anyone seeking to catch a glimpse of the concrete situation of the hearers of the *Thema*. One can well imagine that some neophytes of the fifth, and perhaps even of the sixth century may have decided to together embrace monastic life after baptism. The *Thema* would have been the exhortation from the priest or bishop who was preparing to serve as their director. This "master" would have drawn up a sort of introductory course to the *scola dominici seruitii* from the classic elements of baptismal catechesis.

Obviously, this is only a hypothesis. One would like to be able to corroborate it from western texts witnessing to a situation of this sort.[67] While proposing it conditionally, we have done our utmost to find an existential basis for it in the *Thema* of the Master and to concretize the direct passage, which it apparently intends to occur, from baptismal font to monastery gate.

However, one must not deny that this enigmatic passage may have an entirely different thrust. The evocation of baptism and recourse to the catechetical genre of the explanation of the *Pater* could well be simple literary devices. The intent of the *Thema* would be more theoretical than practical. Without aiming at a specific situation, the Master would seek only to make plausible the spiritual bond that links the monastic vocation to baptism and the monastery to the Church. This intent would correspond rather well to two trends that one finds in the

Rule as a whole: an affinity for images and an interest in the monastery-Church parallel. Moreover, it would account for several particularities of the text. First, the *Incipit Thema*, which one would hardly expect to find at the beginning of a sermon. Whatever its exact significance, it reminds one of an academic exercise. Next, the parable of the spring bears no resemblance to any of the known sermons for catechumens and neophytes. Its obscure and symbolic genre contrasts with that of these simple and direct addresses. Its allusions to liturgical rites are rare and unspecified.[68] One has the impression of being in the presence of a spurious fantasy, an artificial creation, rather than in the presence of a discourse connected with life and responding to actual needs.

One will recall that the *Thema* is closely tied to the Prologue, a passage that is apparently unconnected to baptism and bears the mark of the Master. Moreover, we have seen that the commentary on the *Pater* announces several favorite themes of the author, especially in the third and fourth petitions. All of this suggests that the *Thema* is, in large measure, the personal work of the author of the Rule. While it seems plausible that the Master used some texts from catechetical homilies and clear that he had in mind some liturgical and homiletic conventions related to baptism, the whole of the *Thema* is nonetheless the fruit of his imagination and reflection, a passage especially created to serve as an introduction to his Rule.

The Beginning of the Commentary on the Psalms

The last part of the *Thema* is of particular interest to us since it will appear practically unchanged in RB. Thus, we will at least quickly review it. As we have seen, its first two sentences connect it to the commentary on the *Pater*. They do this not only by a series of contrasting terms: prayer/action, father/master, sons/servants, but also by the final antithesis: *poenam ... gloriam*. In fact, this last pair previously resounded in the commentary on the third petition of the *Pater* (Thp 53). It is interesting to compare the two passages. While both contrast hell and glory, the commentary on the *Pater* does so with a tone of encouragement and hope, that on the psalms with one of fear and apprehension. This emphasis placed on the somber side of the alternative coincides with what precedes it: the entire beginning of Ths is a severe warning in the style of the Prologue. The author chooses to surround his invitation to service of God and obedience with negative motives and alarming views: we must not grieve God by evil actions, irritate him, or provoke him to disinherit us and hand us over to eternal punishment.

The Paraphrase of Psalm 33

Next, the presentation of Psalm 33 begins with a summons to shake off sloth and sleep. Only verses twelve to sixteen of the psalm will be cited. The Master is not alone in showing particular interest in this little section. One finds it reproduced in 1 Peter and in the sermons of Augustine, Peter Chrysologus, and Pseudo-Chrysostom, with slight variations as to its beginning and end.[69] The section of the Master includes verse sixteen and is longer than those of these patristic authors. Therefore, it does not seem that the Master depends on any of them, although he comes close to Augustine and Pseudo-Chrysostom when he has the listener respond, "*Ego*."

But it is another passage of Augustine, the second *Enarratio in Ps 33*, that may have inspired the *Thema*.[70] It contains both the dialogical presentation and the *Ego* response uttered by the listener. Moreover, Augustine joins the New Testament phrase "*Qui habet aures audiendi audiat*" to the "*Venite filii audite me*" of the psalmist. A little earlier, he combined two passages of Isaiah into a single citation, which the *Thema* also does, albeit differently.[71] These and other details[72] prove that Butler and Delatte are right: the Master and Benedict have clearly borrowed from this homily of Augustine rather than that of Pseudo-Chrysostom, as proposed by Morin.[73] Nonetheless, the sermon of the latter retains a certain amount of interest for us, both because it comments on these verses without the rest of the psalm and because it depends on Augustine, two characteristics that connect it to RM and RB.

The final verse that the Master cites speaks of God turning his "eyes" and "ears" toward those who act according to his commands. The phrase that introduces the entire citation parallels this finale of the psalmic text. Here again, it is a matter of "opening the eyes" and "listening with attentive ears," but this time it is a matter of we who act. The light of God shines on us; the divine voice calls to us each day. Therefore, we are invited to open our eyes and ears, to act on what we hear. Then God, in turn, will pay attention and respond to our prayers.

In this dialectic, one cannot say that the initiative belongs to us, since the light and the call of God exist prior to our perception of them. However, the two parallel phrases speaking of "eyes" and "ears" indicate a sort of precedence of human action. If we wish God to listen and act, we must do so first. One recognizes here the idea that the Master will later develop: "*Conuertimini ad me et ego conuertar ad uos*."[74] Elicited by the divine call, human "conversion" in its turn invites the "conversion" of God, that is to say his gift of grace.[75] It is this gift of divine grace that the Master has in mind when he puts into God's mouth the words, "I will keep watch over you and I will listen to your prayers, and before you call me, I will say, 'Here I am.'" Those who do good see their prayers immediately answered, even anticipated, by the Lord and thus obtain the help of grace.[76]

Therefore, one discerns an unambiguously Christian meaning at the end of this citation of Psalm 33. In the same spirit, the first phrase of the psalm (*Venite filii* ...) is framed by two citations from the New Testament, the first, an invitation to "listen with one's ears,"[77] the second, to "run while there is still light." Thus, the psalmic text appears as a word "from the Spirit to the churches." It is the same voice of Christ that rings out in the psalm and in the Gospel, crying successively *Venite* and *Currite*.

Although the two New Testament texts emphasize the Christian interpretation of the psalm, it must be acknowledged that they do not perfectly fit the context. The first is an invitation to listen to "what the Spirit says to the churches," while Psalm 33 is presented as an appeal from the "Lord" (Christ) to his "sons." Augustine only cited the words of Christ here: *Qui habet aures audiendi audiat*, which fit better. The Master seems to have been ill-advised in adding the words from Revelation (*quid Spiritus dicat ecclesiis*) to this citation from the Gospel.

The second text (*Currite* ...) is even less in context than the first. In the language of the Master, "to run" is synonymous with "to act."[78] Yet, the sentence from the psalm that it comments on speaks only of listening. To speak here of running is to anticipate the conclusion of the paragraph, where one will be spurred on to progress and action (*pergamus itinera eius*). Moreover, *lumen vitae* inopportunely recalls *lumen deificum* from the phrase in the introduction. In fact, the "divine light" that the listeners were then asked to open their eyes to is something altogether different than the physical light that shines on all human beings, good or evil.[79] Moreover, the "life" of which we speak here, that is to say life here below, before death, is not the same as the "true and eternal life," which will be discussed later.

Therefore, these two citations from the New Testament are rather untimely, especially the second. It may be that they were the work of a second hand that altered the original text of the commentary on Psalm 33. The *Qui habet aures audiendi audiat* undoubtedly belonged to the original (Augustine certifies it). The rest is probably due to a later redactor, that is to say, to the Master himself. Thus, one again catches a glimpse, through the *Thema*, of the literary source that the Master seems to have drawn from.

This commentary on Psalm 33 presents several other traits that tend to Christianize the teaching of the psalm. While juxtaposition of the "multitude of people" with "the worker who pays heed" is primarily a means of passing from the plural (*Venite ... uos*) to the singular (*Quis et homo*), the phrase *quaerens Dominus ... operarium suum* calls to mind the Gospel parable of the *paterfamilias* who goes to the marketplace in search of workers for his vineyard.[80] The *Ego* response expresses the free commitment of the elect, although this fictive dialogue between God and the hearer is, for both the Master and Augustine, chiefly a means of animating their text. The phrase *Si uis habere ueram et perpetuam uitam* reflects a concern to give the "life" promised by the psalmist its true eschatological dimension. Undoubtedly, this also stems from Augustine who is equally insistent on this point: *Non hic quaerat dies bono*. Likewise, to say that "the voice of the Lord invites us" and "shows us the way to life" is to suggest that this life is not found here below. Correctly understood, our present existence is only the way. Some supernatural means correspond to this transcendent goal. Just as life is transported to eternity, the "good" that the psalmist referenced is described in Christian terms: "faith" must be the source of good works, and one progresses toward the kingdom under the guidance of the Gospel.

These touches, and the Paulinian phrases that they echo, conclude the psalm on a definite Christian note. One understands the enthusiastic exclamations of our author: "What could be sweeter ... ? See in his goodness.... " He pours all the sweetness of the Gospel, all the divine goodness manifested by Christ, into the aged text of the Old Testament. Thus Christianized, the *Venite* of the psalmist seems as intoxicating to him as that of the Lord himself in the parable of the spring.

The Paraphrase of Psalm 14

Therefore, the Master has constructed quite a program of Christian ethics around these few verses of Psalm 33. Its main point, *Diverte a malo et fac bonum*, will later appear as the foundational axiom for conversion.[81] Apart from this very important maxim, the practical teaching of Psalm 33 is rather meager, since it is reduced to avoiding the sins of the tongue. That is why a second, more developed, list of good and evil actions will be sought from Psalm 14. In both psalms, the author has woven a web of connections: the "Lord shows us the way" to the "kingdom"[82] that one reaches by a course of "good actions." The dialogical presentation is also similar, although it is only in Psalm 33 that the Lord takes the initiative and the person is supposed to respond; here it is the person who asks and receives a response from the Lord. The fact that Psalm 14 follows Psalm 33, in reverse of the numerical order of the Psalter, is definitely atypical, but the commentary on the psalms had to begin with *Venite*, both to recall the first part of the *Thema*[83] and to give God the initiative in the dialogue.

Psalm 14 contains ten precepts, which led Arnobius and Cassiodorus to consider it a "decalogue." According to these two commentators, it is Christ, the perfect one, who fulfills the law and lives in the tent.[84] None of this interpretation is reflected in RM. For the Master, it is we who act, we who ask the Lord, and we who receive his response and must put it into practice. However, we will see that his commentary has several parallels with that of Cassiodorus.

Psalm 14 is cited by the Master almost completely without commentary. Only the beginning of verse four elicits a paraphrase. Instead of interpreting it as regarding duties toward one's neighbor, like the rest of the psalm, the Master seeks there the attitudes that should be adopted toward the devil and God. *Ad nihilum deductus est in conspectu eius malignus* teaches resistance to the suggestions of the devil; *timentes Dominum magnificent*, the humility that connects good works with divine grace.

This last exegesis supposes that one reads *magnificent* in the plural, a rare reading that one finds in Cassiodorus. However, the latter has only an insignificant commentary on these words. Everything the Master says about humility and the acknowledgment of divine grace is totally original. Cassiodorus and the Master are closer to one another in their exegesis on *Ad nihilum deductus est ... malignus*. Both use the active form of the verb (*deduxit*) and recognize the devil in *malignus*. However, for Cassiodorus, it is Christ who conquers the devil, while for the Master, it is the Christian. Furthermore, the paraphrase of the Master adds several traits that tend to internalize the scene: the devil "suggests" and he and "his suggestion" are repelled by the glance of the "heart."

This internalized exegesis is extended by a paraphrase from the last verse of Psalm 136: the thoughts inspired by the devil are shattered against the rock that is "Christ." Of course, there is nothing more commonplace than this use of Psalm 136. Also, nothing dearer to our author: it appears twice more in the Rule (RM 3.56 and 8.23). Moreover, the entire passage on the struggle against the suggestions of the devil announces one of the favorite themes of the commentary on the *Pater*, as well as the Rule as a whole, where *suadere* and *suasio* are frequently applied to the devil.

While this development on evil thoughts contrasts with the simple citation that precedes it, it is only half as long as the development on grace that follows. The insistence of the *Thema* on this last point is truly remarkable. One finds several terms here that echo the citation of and commentary on Psalm 33: *timentes Dominum, bona obseruantia, ipsa in se bona*. It is not simply a matter of fearing the Lord, doing right, and accomplishing good works. One must also recognize the work of the Lord in this edifying conduct. In the last verse cited from Psalm 33, the gift of grace appears as God's response to our conversion, good works, and prayers. Here the emphasis is on the power of grace without which we can do no good. As in the previous case, this theme reappears several times in the Rule, especially in the *Ars Sancta*.[85]

Psalm 14 not only provides a much longer series of precepts than Psalm 33, but also deepens its moral teaching by entering into the interior realm of thoughts. It also reveals the two conflicting origins of human action. It is the devil who suggests the evil from which one must turn away; it is God who gives the power to do good.[86] Thus far, grace has been glimpsed only in the images of eyes, ears, and the divine *Adsum*. Here it is referenced by name and its role is clearly defined. All of these new elements of Christian ethics appear in the paraphrase on verse four. Thanks to it, Psalm 14 not only prohibits sinful words and actions but also addresses evil thoughts, even the most pernicious of them all, pride.

The House Built on Rock

Both glosses on verse four end with one or several Paulinian expressions: the first with the "Christ-rock,"[87] the second with two citations from the Letters to the Corinthians, arranged in proper order. The conclusion of the psalm engenders some Christian touches of the same sort. The author combines the *Qui facit haec* of the psalm with the *Qui audit haec uerba mea et facit ea* of the Gospel, while *non mouebitur in aeternum* is explained by the rest of the Gospel text: the parable of the man who built his house on rock.[88]

This way of proceeding from the psalm to the Gospel, from the Old Testament to the New, is reminiscent of the end of the commentary on Psalm 33. Owing to some Paulinian allusions, the Gospel was also expressly referenced there (Ths 17). However, here the author is not content with a simple reference, but enlarges it to an actual citation. Thus both the commentary on Psalm 33 and that on Psalm 14 have New Testament conclusions in keeping with their length. Furthermore, the entire commentary on the psalms emerges in full Christian light, in the presence of Christ. The concluding text of the Gospel is reminiscent of the Gospel *Venite* at the beginning of the *Thema*. The citations from the Psalms have been only an occasion to indicate the chief tenets of a purely Christian ethic, which is now unambiguously revealed as such.

In yet other respects, the parable of the man who built his house on rock makes an excellent conclusion to the commentary on Psalm 14.

We previously encountered Christ the "rock." The image takes on only a slightly different twist in its modification here. According to Psalm 136, it is a matter of smashing evil thoughts against the rock at their conception. According to the text of the Gospel, it is a question of building an indestructible edifice on the rock, against which the wind and rain pound in vain. In both cases, Christ appears as the strength by which the soul resists the attacks of the devil.

Beyond this parallel, one will note that the Gospel parable serves as the conclusion to the Sermon on the Mount. It plays this same concluding role in the *Thema*.[89] The Master can then skillfully portray the Lord "finishing his discourse" and "keeping silent," as, according to the Gospel, he did on the mountain. If need be, this connection in and of itself would suggest that it is none other than Christ who has spoken throughout the citations of the Psalter.

The Conclusion of the Thema

In the Gospel, the image of the man who builds on rock has its counterpart in the man who builds on sand. It is this latter who actually ends the Sermon on the Mount. However, one will note that the *Thema* does not include him. In the context of Psalm 14, it wishes to present only a hopeful and successful view. This focus on the positive aspect of the dilemma is characteristic of the entire commentary on the Psalms. All that it proposes of the last things are life and happy days, dwelling in the tent and resting on the holy mountain. There is no subsequent reference to the eternal punishment that the first sentences presented in such a threatening manner. Perhaps the author so emphasized fear in this beginning only in anticipation of its absence in the psalm text and commentary.

However, in the final paragraphs of this passage, the joyous momentum toward the kingdom will be tempered by gravity. While the "punishment of hell" is only mentioned in passing[90] and the gaze remains turned toward eternal blessing, it is now a matter of moving into action, of putting into practice what one has just heard. Having nothing more to say, the Lord falls silent, and this expectant silence has something formidable about it,[91] like that of an adjudicator about to render judgment. The preacher that we have just listened to is also the Master of our lives. His patient goodness grants us the days of our lives only so that we will amend according to his teachings, do penance, and experience conversion. One finds here the severe warning of the Prologue, corroborated by two scriptural citations.[92]

A little later, the author becomes even more insistent: while there is still time, we must "run and act."[93] This time, the evocation of the

Prologue is accompanied by a clear allusion to the Johannine text that was cited at the beginning of the commentary on the Psalms: "run while you have the light of life."[94] Thus, by echoing both the first paragraph of the introduction and the beginning of the last, this ending of the *Thema* achieves a double inclusion. A solemn note resounds in these key passages: death is near, time is short, and our actions are eternally binding.

Along with this theme of the urgency and gravity of the task, the invitation to ask the Lord for the help of his grace in what is impossible to our nature[95] appears a final time in the conclusion of the *Thema*. In speaking thus, the author does not only repeat the theme of prayer that appears at the end of Psalm 33 and those of divine grace and human potential that are developed around Psalm 14. He also returns even more clearly to the commentary on the last two petitions of the *Pater*.[96] Only the role attributed to grace is described differently. According to the *Pater*, it should free us from the temptations of the devil. Here, as in the commentary on Psalm 14 but with greater detail, it comes to the aid of the powerlessness of human "nature."[97] Thus, the end of the commentary on the Psalms echoes that of the commentary on the *Pater*. In this conclusion of the *Thema*, several of the most characteristic notes of not only the last passage, but also of the entire introduction, are brought together in rich harmony.

A final characteristic will complete our evidence. The concluding sentence on participation in the sufferings and glory of Christ essentially reproduces the last sentence of the first paragraph of commentary on the words *Pater noster*.[98] Therefore, just as there were two allusions to the Prologue in this conclusion, there are also two allusions to the commentary on the *Pater*, the former alternating with the latter. A table will demonstrate this fact:

	Pr	**Thp**	**Ths**
This life is a reprieve so that we may amend.	6–7		36–38
Pray to obtain the help of grace.		69–79	41
Run while there is still time.	16		43–44
Participate in the sufferings of Christ and in his kingdom.		11	46

Perhaps this recapitulative function of the end of the *Thema* at least partially explains and excuses a certain confusion and disorder that become apparent. Injunctions accumulate from one sentence to the next (*praeparanda sunt, currendum et agendum est, constituenda est*), accompanied by the triple repetition of *ergo* that is reminiscent of the cumbersome structure of the Prologue. Moreover, the first of these *ergos*[99] picks up rather clumsily on the commentary on Psalm 14 that one was diverted from by a digression about the "silence" of the Lord following the parable of the house built on rock.

The Presentation of the Monastery

In concluding this commentary, we highlight the final sentence of the text, not so much because of its final position as because of its intrinsic importance. In fact, the author has waited until the last moment to divulge two decisive words that explain everything that precedes them: *scola* and *monasterio*. Up to this point, he has carefully avoided any reference to things monastic. Certainly, some characteristic notions of the Rule, such as self-will, the service of God, and the *annona*, were recognizable here and there. However, the text never diverged from vocabulary that one could find in any baptismal catechesis. After having kept the rules of this borrowed literary genre for so long, the Master now reveals his true colors. *Scola* and especially *monasterium* finally make it clear. This *in extremis* apparition of the proper term or keyword is reminiscent of that of *regula–uirga* at the end of the Prologue. The same reserve in monastic terminology and concern to be rooted in the common ground of Christian revelation and catechesis delayed the decisive words that clearly distinguished its focus until the final lines.

The monastery appears as "the school of the Lord's service." Whatever the significance of *scola*—it perhaps extends beyond our notion of "school"[100]—and of the genitive *seruitii*,[101] it is certain that they reveal two aspects of the Person of Christ that correspond to two attributes of monastic life. He is Lord (*Dominus*) and Master[102] (*magister, doctor*), the one who is served and the one who teaches this service. Therefore, we have to both serve him and learn from him how to serve him. These two ideas are brought together in that of obedience to Christ.

This obedience will be perpetual—we must practice it until death. It will be costly and involve suffering. But the difficulty that it causes will reveal a new face of Christ and a new aspect of our relationship with him. He is not only the Lord who commands and master who teaches, but also the man of suffering with whom we suffer, the Redeemer whose passion leads us to his kingdom. More precisely, as the last word (*consortes*) of the Prologue says, he enables us to share in his inheritance. This term, "co-heirs," wonderfully concludes a phrase that began with that of "service." One repeats the journey in reverse that, at the beginning of the passage, led from the condition of sons to that of servants, from the loss of inheritance to eternal punishment.[103] Then, everything was threatening; now, everything is hopeful.

To conclude, one will note how this first and very belated definition of the monastery remains unassuming. Everything is defined in relationship to Christ, and to him alone. It is true that service can only be in relationship to him. But, without a doubt, "master" and "teaching" bring to mind the one to whom the Rule constantly gives the title of master and teacher: the abbot. Yet the latter is not named. It is only on the following page, at the beginning of Chapter One, that he will appear alongside the Rule in the definition of the cenobite. Later we will learn that he is the teacher appointed by Christ to direct his *scola*, the representative of Christ in the monastery,[104] and the one who, by his teaching, takes the place of the Master of the apostles.[105] But here we are still required to disregard the human intermediary[106] and to stay focused solely on Christ, the only Master and Teacher, with whom the great introduction of the *Thema* both opens and closes.

*The Order of Texts in Florilegium E**

At least this is the meaning of the conclusion for those who rely on the complete manuscripts. But we know that Florilegium E* presents it differently. It places the end of the *Thema* (Ths 40–60) after RM 1, without a break. Dom Vanderhoven wished to see the remains of an original version of the Rule in this sequence.[107] Before the insertion of *De generibus monachorum* (1.1–75), the order of the texts would have been as follows:

Ths 1–39
1.76–92
Ths 40–46

The obvious affinity of the conclusion of Chapter One with the two passages that would have originally framed it supports this hypothesis. In fact, this exhortation addressed to some *fratres* is similar to the *Thema*. One may even note that its first scriptural citation from Zechariah connects easily with the last citation of the *Thema* from Ezekiel, which it is supposed to have preceded in the original redaction: both speak of "conversion."[108]

However, one must not overlook the fact that the witness of E*, on whom this entire theory depends, is uniquely suspect. In fact, in several instances, this florilegium arbitrarily assembles passages from different authors, or various chapters from the same work, under a single title.[109]

It is true that nowhere else does one find two passages assembled under the same title opposite their normal sequence, as is here. But one must take into account the fact that the florilegium continually backtracks in the series of excerpts from the Master that precede those of RM 1 and the *Thema*.[110] Given that Chapter One follows Chapter Two, what is so surprising about the *Thema* following Chapter One?

This situation may be explained in two ways. First, by a literary motif: placed between RM 1 and RM 10, the excerpt from the *Thema* becomes part of a series of discourses, of a sort of homiletic centon. Second, by a doctrinal reason: affirming that one must "persevere in the monastery until death," the passage is undoubtedly meant to correct the praise of hermits who leave their monasteries,[111] conforming to the cenobitic, even anti-eremitical, tendency of the author of E*.[112]

Far from representing the original state of the Rule, it is likely that the position of the conclusion of the *Thema* after Chapter One resulted from a shift made by the florilegium. In support of this interpretation, one will note that Ths 40–46 does not make a good sequel to the end of Chapter One. In fact, the latter ends with a solemn conclusion, which begins with: *Ergo* and ends with the antitheses *gehenna ... gloria*.[113] One hardly expects to next see the text continue with a paragraph that also begins with *Ergo* and ends with a new eschatological clausula.[114]

Therefore, the 1.92–Ths 40 sequence that E* attests to is not very convincing. We must now say more about Ths 39–1.76, the correlative sequence that Vanderhoven's theory supposes. In fact, 1.76 definitely seems to be the beginning of a new discourse rather than the continuation of one already in progress. Not only is this sentence strikingly similar to the opening section of the treatise on humility,[115] but the initial position of *Fratres* indicates the beginning of an autonomous section, like the commentary on a petition of the *Pater* or a chapter of the Rule.[116] A beginning of this sort presupposes a break and an announcement, such as the wording of a new clause of the Lord's Prayer, a title of a chapter, or even the phrase *ad ipsum regulam reuertamur* that one reads in 1.75. Yet, nothing resembling this is found in Ths 39.

Therefore, it is not likely that 1.76–92 followed Ths 1–39 in the original. The order of texts in the complete manuscripts is more acceptable than what E* witnesses to or suggests.[117] We will retain from the testimony of this florilegium and the hypotheses that it has elicited only the obvious fact that the end of Chapter One extends the *Thema* beyond *De Generibus*. The similarity of the two passages is confirmed when one compares them with Chapter Fourteen, where the prayer of the excommunicated brings together Scripture citations from both:

RM 14		Th	Ths	**RM 1**
41	Ez 33:11		38	
43	Rom 2:4		37	
57	Mt 7:7			79
59	Zec 1:3			76
60	Is 58:9		14	
62	Mt 11:28	10		

In spite of this certain similarity, the second passage was undoubtedly never part of the *Thema*. It has always been separated, either by *De generibus*, if one holds it to be original, or at least by a title such as *Incipit*, which is read at the head of the first chapter.[118]

Moreover, not only is the order of the complete manuscripts confirmed by the literary facts that have just been indicated, it also agrees perfectly with the doctrinal content of 1.76–92. This passage is clearly intended to introduce the treatise on the abbot. It does so with the same bias toward discretion in the use of monastic vocabulary and desire to remain as long as possible on the scriptural and ecclesiastic foundation that characterize the *Thema*. Beginning with the *scola*, as defined by the *Thema*, it carefully presents the "teacher," "shepherd," and "superior" who must rule it in the name of Christ, without even mentioning the name *abbas*. This very unassuming presentation is reminiscent of that on the monastery at the end of the *Thema*. Both passages seek to introduce the realities of monastic life little by little without setting aside those of the Christian life. And they follow the same method: linking these two ways of life, in which monastic life stems from and is the gate of perfection of baptism, they draw a parallel between the call to baptism and that to the monastery, the *ecclesia* and the *scola*,[119] and the bishop and the abbot.

Chapter 1: The Introductions of RM

Endnotes

1 *Reg. IV Patrum* 6.1–4 in Jean Neufville,"*Régle des IV Pères* et *Seconde Régle des Pères.* Texte Critique," *Revue Bénédictine* 77 (1967): 90.

2 G. Penco, *S. Benedicti Regula*, Biblioteca di Studi Superiori Series 39 (Florence: 1958), 193. The parallel texts of the Master are Pr 1–2, 19, 40–41; Thp 71 and 79.

3 H. Vanderhoven, "Les plus anciens manuscrits de la Règle du Maître transmettent un texte déjà interpolé," *Scriptorium* 1 (1946–1947): 194. Penco, who claims to represent Vanderhoven, does not seem to have correctly understood.

4 *Tibi* is difficult to explain. See Philip B. Corbett, *The Latin of the Regula Magistri with Particular Reference to its Colloquial Aspects: A Guide to the Establishment of the Text*, Recueil de travaux d'Histoire et de Philologie IVe Series 17 (Louvain: 1958), 63–64, whose explanation is unsatisfactory.

5 There is a contradiction between this *qui legis* and the assertion of Pr 21: *quam ego tibi lecturus sum*: the author is distinguished from the reader, then identified with him or her.

6 See Pr 5, 8, 16, 19, 22. Cf. n. 17 below.

7 Pr 15–16: *Ergo uaciuus uester auditus sequatur meum eloquium. Et intellege tu, homo, cuius admonemus intuitum....*

8 On the plural of "courtesy," see A. Blaise, *Manuel du Latin Chrétien* (Strasbourg: Le Latin Chrétien, 1955) § 171. This scarcely seems to be the same case here. But in the same way that this form of plural corresponds to the plural of "majesty," perhaps the "you" plural here corresponds to the "we" of the author.

9 Pr 9–14 (Mt 7:13–14).

10 Pr 23–27. Note how the text alternates between the Apostle and the Prophet and then concludes with "the Lord." This last text is taken from a psalm (therefore, from the Prophet), but put in the mouth of the divine author.

11 This observation, like those that precede it, justifies the appreciation of F. Renner, "Die Genesis der Benediktus-und Magister-regel," *Studien und Mitteilungen zur Geschichte des Benediktiner-Ordens und seiner Zweige* 62 (1950): 120–125. Judged solely on the basis of its harmonious proportions, the Prologue appears to be a carefully crafted passage, a work of art.

12 Pr 5, 16, 21. Perhaps the first two occurrences of *scriptura* specifically designate the Prologue, but the third definitely designates the entire Rule.

13 The first two citations concerning the *uirga* are found (in reverse order) in Pseudo-Chrysostom, *Serm.* 27 and 30, PLS 4.804 and 827 (= Morin, *Serm.* 13 and 3). According to this author, the *uirga* represents the "law" and the "word of God" (*uigor legis ... praecepta legis ... uerbum Dei*). If the Master had this interpretation in mind when he called his Rule *uirga*, he intended to suggest that it could be equated with Scripture.

14 Cf. RM 93.15–19.

15 Thp 50: *Vides ergo....* "I" also reappears in this phrase, but it is an impersonal "I."

16 Thp 59 (Tob 4:16. Cf. RM 3.9: *quis ... uult ... faciat*); Thp 62–65 (Rom 7:24; *Visio Pauli* 40); Ths 12–13 (Ps 33:13–15). Likewise, the "I" in Thp 62 and 79–80 comes from the cited text.

17 Pr 21 (cf. 87.3; 89.8, 90.5). Perhaps the divergent indication of Pr 1 is interpolated (see nn. 4–6 above). If one holds that it is authentic, one could understand it in the sense that by a sort of division, the author-reader applies the words that he has written and read to himself.

18 See Cap 1 and 95; Pr T and 27; 1.T and 10.123; 51.T and 53.65. Only the *Incipit* of 11.T remains without a corresponding *Explicit*. However, it may have been connected to the final *Explicit* (95.24) before the expression *Expl. Regula sanctorum Patrum* was written, which was probably later.

19 Ths 45.

20 See Ennodius, *Dict.* 12 and 21 (*Thema ... Praefatio*); 22 (*Praefatio ... Thema*).

21 Two words (*Dict.* 12); eleven lines (*Dict.* 21); ten words (*Dict.* 22); six verses (*Dict.* 24).

22 The work is around thirty times longer than its *Thema* in *Dict.* 21, ten times in *Dict.* 24, seventeen times in RM.

23 Paulinus of Nola, *Ep.* 28.6, says that he placed the letter of his friend Endelechius, who had requested the panegyric for Theodosius, at the beginning of this work as its *Thema* (*pro themate praescribitur*). Here again, the *Thema* undoubtedly goes beyond a few words.

24 Th 10 (Mt 11:28). *Reficiam* is next interpreted by *renouati* (11), *recreauerit* (13), and *recreationem* (17). Cf. Paulinus of Nola, *Ep.* 32.2: *in loco refectionis humanae* (the baptistry).

25 Th 14–15 (Mt 11:29–30).

26 Thp 1–2 (Mt 6:9). The beginning (*inuenimus*) is more reminiscent of Augustine, *Serm.* 57.2: *inuenimus Deum patrem et matrem ecclesiam*, than the texts of Cyprian and Tertullian cited in the notes of RM. One finds *inuenimus* in the same context in Augustine *Serm.* 58.2; 59.2.

27 Th 3: *in saeculi huius descendimus uiam*; Thp 4: *natio nostra in mundum ... descenderat.*

28 Th 3: *nati ... generati;* Thp 4–6: *natio ... generatio.*

29 Th 19: *cognitione ignoranti baptismi;* Thp 10: *propter agnitionem baptismi.*

30 Th 17: *Domini inuitantis nos uocem* (cf. Th 24); Thp 8: *nos non desinit inuitare.*

31 Th 25 and Thp 2: *inuenimus.*

32 Cf. *diuina ... uox* (Th 9) and *uox dominica* (Thp 9); *audemus* (Th 25 and Thp 10). One will note that all of these parallels with Th are found only in the first paragraph of Thp. However, the "voice of the Lord" is found in Thp 36 and 60.

33 Cyril, *Myst.* 5.11–18; Ambrose, *Sacr.* 5.18–30 (cf. 6.24); Ildephonsus, *De cogn. bapt.* 133–135, PL 96.166. In Cyril, the explanation of the *Pater* forms part of the teaching on the Mass; in Ambrose and Ildephonsus, it is attached to a series of teachings on prayer.

34 See Adalbert de Vogüé, *La Règle du Maître*, Sources Chrétiennes 105–107 (Paris: Cerf, 1964–65) I.108, n. 2.

35 Thp 50, 56, 69.

36 Thp 17, 21, etc.

Chapter 1: The Introductions of RM

37 Ths 41.

38 Thp 69, 71, 79.

39 One can add to this the very similar eschatological conclusions from Thp 11 and Thp 46. See also n. 42.

40 Compare Th 9–11, 13–16, and Ths 6–12.

41 Compare Th 8 (*conspicimus*), 13 (*intuentes*), and Ths 6 (*apertis oculis*).

42 Compare Th 17, 20, 24 and Ths 13. Cf. Thp 8 (*nos ... inuitare*).

43 RM 2. See Adalbert de Vogüé, *La Communauté et l'Abbé* (Brussels: Desclée des Brouwer, 1961), 78–85; ET: *Community and Abbot* (Kalamazoo, MI: Cistercian, 1979 [I] and 1988 [II]).

44 This again confirms the conclusion reached by F. Renner, *Die Genesis*, 136–138 (cited in n. 11), based on a brief consideration of the length of each passage.

45 Compare Pr 3 with Thp 4.22 and Ths 16 (*bona acta*), Pr 4 with Ths 5 (*neglegentia peccatorum*), Pr 5 with Ths 10 (*auditor*), Pr 9 with Th 19 (*ignorantia*), Pr 10 with Th 3, 12, 22, and Ths 16, 20, 29 (*uia*), Pr 16 with Ths 9, 18, 44 (*currere*), Pr 19 with Ths 43 (*lux*), Pr 22 with Thp 23 (*propitius*).

46 Pr 7 and Ths 35–37.

47 Pr 16 and Ths 43–44. Cf. Pr 18 and Ths 44 (*in aeternum ... in perpetuum*).

48 Therefore, with F. Renner, *Die Genesis* 136–137 (see n. 11 above), one can consider a triptych in which the homily on the *Pater* is at the center and the Prol and parable of the spring form a first section that is almost symmetrical to the third (the commentary on the psalms). The parable itself is rather brief in order to balance Ths. From a quantitative point of view, Pr and Th better correspond to the last part when combined. Also, without wishing to use what is probably coincidental as an argument, we note that *Aperiam in parabolis os meum* (Ps 77:2), cited by the Master at the beginning of Th, is preceded in the text of the psalm by a verse that could summarize the entire Prologue: *Attendite popule meus legem meam, inclinate aurem uestram in uerba oris mei* (Ps 77:1).

49 Th 11, 13, 16.

50 Ths 6, 12, 20, 31, 39.

51 Ths 39 (Mt 7:24).

52 Following the title of an article by E. Manning in *Revue Mabillon* 52 (1962): 61–74.

53 See note on Ths 1 and *La Règle du Maître* I.229. The Lectionary of Naples analyzed by Dom Morin attests to the existence of the rite in this Church. According to J. P. Bouhot, the Sermons of Pseudo-Chrysostom, which Morin also placed in Naples, seem instead to be of African origin: "La collection homilétique pseudo-chrysostomienne découverte par Dom Morin," *Rev. des Études augustiniennes* 16 (1970): 139–146 (cf. PLS 4.651).

54 See nn. 33 and 60. The testimony of Cyril concerning Jerusalem is indirectly corroborated by that of Etherius, *Pereg.* 45–46, who does not indicate the tradition of the *Pater* before Easter. According to Chrysostom, *Hom. VI in Colos. 4*, the baptized recited the *Pater* when they emerged from the font. Is that to say that they learned it only at this moment, or that they had done so previously? In

any case, it seemingly figures no more in the *Pater* of the *Catéchèses baptismales* (meaning postbaptismal), edited by A. Wenger (SC 50), than it does in the other Paschal homilies of Chrysostom.

55 See G. Morin, "Étude sur une série de discours d'un évêque du VIᵉ s.," *Revue Bénédictine* 11 (1894): 400–401. If, as J. P. Bouhot thinks (see n. 53 above), the Sermons of Pseudo-Chrysostom are African, certain churches of Africa would have agreed with that of Naples on the *Pater*–Profession of Faith sequence.

56 Theodore of Mopsuestia, *Hom. Catech.* 11.

57 Augustine, *Serm.* 56–59.

58 Ps.-Chrys., *Serm.* 28, PLS 4.817 (= Morin, *Serm.* 23). On the origin of this text, see n. 53 above. As concerns the *Lectionary of Naples*, see G. Morin (cited in n. 55 above).

59 *Sacram. Gelas.* I.36; *Miss. Gall. uet.* 17.

60 According to Ambrose, *Sacr.* 3.5, Milan followed the practice of the Roman Church in every respect except for the rite of the washing of the feet. Therefore, at this time, Milan would have had the explanation of the *Pater* after baptism. It is seemingly the same at the beginning of the sixth century, since John the Deacon, *Ep. ad Senarium* 3, does not mention the tradition of the *Pater* among the rites of preparation for baptism.

61 While they clearly agree on the prebaptismal character of the tradition of the Psalms and the *Pater*, the Lectionary of Naples and the Sermons of Pseudo-Chrysostom diverge somewhat as regards the respective position of these two traditions. At Naples, the tradition of the Psalms comes before that of the *Pater*. In contrast, in Pseudo-Chrysostom, the *Expositio Psalmorum* (*Serm.* 30), comes after the Homily *De oratione dominica* (*Serm.* 28). It is true that one cannot rely entirely on the order of these Sermons to reconstruct that of the rites. In this regard, it is significant that one of the two Sermons for the tradition of the Profession of Faith (*Serm.* 27 and 29) is found before the Homily *De oratione dominica*, the other after. From a phrase at the beginning of *Serm.* 29 (PLS 4.822), it is clear that the tradition of the Profession of Faith came after that of the *Pater*, which coincides with indications of the Neapolitan Lectionary and confirms the position of *Serm.* 29, but weakens that of *Serm.* 27. One therefore remains hesitant as concerns the place that the manuscripts assign to the homily on the Psalms *after* the homily on the *Pater*. If it would turn out that this position corresponds to the order of the rites, there would be disagreement between Ps.-Chrysostom and the Lectionary of Naples. The order of the *Thema* of the Master, which is opposite that of the Neapolitan Lectionary, would then find an interesting parallel in Ps.-Chrysostom.

62 Pseudo-Chrysostom, *Serm.* 30, PLS 4.825 (= Morin, *Serm.* 3); Pseudo-Augustine, *Serm.* 366, PL 39.1646.

63 See Ambrose, *Sacr.* 5.13, and the witnesses cited by J. Daniélou, "La Messe et sa catéchèse chez les Pères de l'Église," *La Messe et sa catéchèse:* Vannes, 30 avril–4 mai 1946, Lex Orandi 7 (Paris: Éditions du Cerf, 1947), 49 ff.

64 Augustine, *Serm.* 260 and 353.

65 Augustine, *Serm.* 260, PL 38.1201; Pseudo-Chrysostom, *Serm.* 24, PLS 4.804 (= Morin, *Serm.* 13): *alius constituit monachi uitam tenere, aliae in choro sacrarum puellarum permanere.* Some lines earlier, one finds the passage on the *uirga*

Chapter 1: The Introductions of RM

from *Serm.* 30 (see n. 13 above). Commenting on Psalm 22, it sees in *semitas iustitiae* "the different paths of humankind:" virginity, continence, and marriage. Therefore, this sermon, intended for catechumens, also alludes to chastity at the baptismal commitment. Note also the interpretation *semitae = semiuiae id est angustae*, which brings to mind Pr 14 (similar interpretation in Ps.-Augustine *Serm* 366.4).

66 For example, see Gaudentius, *Serm.* 8, PL 26.890; Orientius, *Commonitorium* II.327–328. In the Pachomian Lives there is even question of making "monastic profession" at baptism. See Louis-Théophile Lefort, *Les Vies Coptes* (Louvain: Bureaux du Muséon, 1943) 201.12–13 (*Bo* 186) and the *Vita Prima* (*G¹*) 140 (p. 88.9–10), with the commentary of A. Veilleux, "La Liturgie dans le cénobitisme pachômien au IVᵉ siècle," *Studia Anselmiana* 57 (Rome, 1968): 218 and 222–223. Some general information on this matter is found in J. Leclerq, "Genèse et évolution de la vie consacrée," *Cahiers de la Revue diocésaine de Tournai* 7 (1967), 2–27. See especially J. Gribomont, "Le monachisme au sein de l'Église en Syrie et en Cappadoce," *Studia Monastica* 7 (1965): 2–24, in particular 12–16.

67 Although similar, this is a different situation than that attested to by *Les Vies Coptes de S. Pachôme* 141.27–29, *Bo* 81 (cited n. 68) and the *Ep. Theodori*, in Armand Boon, *Pachomiana Latina* (Louvain: Bureaux de la Revue, 1932), 106.11–16: some catechumens were received into the Pachomian monasteries and baptized there at Easter. See also *Les Vies Coptes* p. 21.20 (S^{1o}) and 344 (S^{3a}. Cf. *Bo* 193), as well as Pachomius, *Reg.* 49, with the commentary of A. Veilleux (cited above in n. 68) 198–212. On the other hand, nothing indicates that it is a matter of catechumens in Pachomius *Reg.* 1 and 139, in spite of A. Veilleux, 199 and 215, who reads too much into the meaning of *rudis*.

68 One finds only *abrenuntiauimus* and *renuntiemus* (Th 18 and 21); *sapientiam accipientes* (Th 20). These last words probably allude to the "salt of wisdom" that catechumens "received" in the mouth. See John the Deacon, *Ep. ad Senarium* 3, PL 59.402ab; *Sacram. Gelas.* I.31–32; Ildephonsus, *De cogn. bapt.* 26 (rite not used at Toledo), etc.

69 1 Peter 3:10–12 (Ps 33:13–17); Augustine, *Enar. in Ps. 143*.9 (Ps 33:12–15); Peter Chrysologous, *Serm.* 62 (Ps 33:12–14); Ps.-Chrysostom, *Serm.* 5, PLS 4.752–756 [= Morin *Serm.* 6] (Ps 33:12–14).

70 Augustine, *Enar. in Ps. 33*.II.16–20.

71 Augustine, *Enar. in Ps. 33*.II.9: *ipsum Dominum quaere et exaudiet te, et adhuc te loquente dicet: Ecce adsum* (Is 58:9 and 65:24). See Ths 14.

72 One finds the question *Et quid dicit?* in Augustine (cf. Ths 8: *Quid?*). Pseudo-Chrysostom has nothing like this.

73 However, *clamat* and *si uis* (Ths 10 and 13) are found in Pseudo-Chrysostom, not in Augustine. Is this enough to assume dependence?

74 RM 1.76 (Zec 1:3).

75 RM 1.77–81. One will note that to "be converted" is to "turn away from evil and do good." This recourse to Psalm 33 emphasizes the parallelism of this passage with Ths.

76 On the apparent Semi-pelagianism of this doctrine, see *La Règle du Maître* I.90, n. 9.

77 Rev 2:7. Cf. Augustine, *Enar. in Ps. 33*.II.16 citing Mt 11:15.

78 See Pr 16: *curras*; Ths 44: *currendum et agendum est*.

79 RM 91.33 confirms that this is the interpretation that the Master gives to Jn 12:35. — The variant *currite* (for *ambulate*) is found not only in the *Praedestinatus* (see note on Ths 9), but also, as *curramus*, in Faustus, *Hom. ad. monach.* 1 and 10, PL 50.833a and 853c (= Eusebius, *Hom.* 35 and 44), from where it passed to Caesarius, *Serm.* 130.2; 168.8; 197.4; 209.1). The gloss *uitae*, noted in a Pseudo-Augustinian sermon by P. Delatte, *Commentaire sur la Règle de saint Benoît* (Paris: 1913), 10, n. 2 (ET: Paul Delatte and Justin McCann, *The Rule of Saint Benedict; A Commentary* [London: Burns, Oates & Washbourne, 1921]) is not part of the authentic text of this sermon, such as one reads in Faustus, *Hom.* 10 and Caesarius, *Serm.* 197.4. Therefore, until proven otherwise, it remains proper to RM and RB.

80 Mt 20:1–16. In the Latin version, the parable ends with *Multi enim sunt uocati, pauci uero electi*. Does *in multitudine populi* refer to this *multi*? The author seems to be thinking specifically of a religious vocation in which a member of the Christian community is called forth for special service.

81 RM 1.77. See n. 117 below.

82 This image of the way by which one arrives at a goal was suggested by Ps 14, where the "mountain" and the "tent" are its destinations. From this, the Master extends these localized images to the commentary of Ps 33 that, in and of itself, does not suggest them.

83 Not only do the two *Venite* at the beginning of the two passages correspond, but both the second part of the Gospel citation (Th 14) and the second psalm (Ths 19) speak of "rest." However, this term is only emphasized in the commentary on the Gospel (Th 20, 23), while that of the psalm prefers "dwelling in the tent" (Ths 18, 20, 39). The agreement between Th and Ths on this point may be incidental.

84 See B. Egli, *Der Vierzehnte Psalm im Prolog der Regel des Heiligen Benedikts* (Sarnen: 1962). The *Enarratio in Ps.* 14 of Augustine is very brief and offers nothing of note.

85 Ths 41; 2.51; 3.46.

86 Cf. RM 3.46–47: to attribute good to God, evil to the devil and oneself.

87 1 Cor 10:4: *petra autem erat Christus*. Add the reference in the apparatus.

88 Mt 7:24–25. *Assimilabitur* is replaced by *Similabo eum*; *uenerunt flumina* is omitted. It is the same Lord who speaks first in the psalm and then in the Gospel (cf. Ths 8–9 and our commentary in *La Règle du Maître*, cited in n. 34).

89 However, the image of the "house that one builds" does not agree with that of the "tent toward which one runs" (Ths 18–20). Moreover, the Master is probably not intending to compare the "mountain" on which the Lord gives his sermon and the "holy mountain" where one will find rest.

90 Ths 42: *Et si fugientes gehennae poenam*....

91 Cf. RM 10.41; 13.27; 14.46: *Haec fecisti et tacui* (Ps 49:21).

92 Ths 36–38. Cf. Pr 6–7.

Chapter 1: The Introductions of RM

93 Ths 43–44. Cf. Pr 16.

94 Ths 9: *Currite dum lumen uitae habetis* ... (Jn 12:35). This Gospel text was previously alluded to in Pr 16.

95 Ths 41.

96 Thp 69–71 and 79.

97 The word *natura* appears here for the first time (cf. 7.11; 23.56; 53.9).

98 Thp 11. Therefore, this sentence is at the beginning of Thp, while the passages on prayer are at the end. Thus, both ends of Thp are recapitulated (in reverse order) in this finale of Ths.

99 Ths 39: *Cum ergo interrogassemus Dominum* ...

100 See note on Ths 45. Here, however, *magisterio* and *doctrina* clearly suggest an educational institution. Cf. 1.83 and 92.96 where *scola* reappears in company with *doctrina* and *magister*.

101 It is unclear what type of genitive *seruiti* is. Elsewhere, *scola* is followed by a genitive of possession (1.83: *Christi*; 90.12, 46: *Domini*; 92.26: *Dei*. Cf. 92.29: *diuinae*) or a genitive of identity (90.29, 55; 92.64: *monasterii*). It is perhaps a matter of this latter here. In fact *seruitium* and *scola* are almost interchangeable, as is evident in comparing *dominici scola seruitii* and *seruitio sanctae scolae* (87.9) where the two words exchange functions. Therefore, it seems that the *scola* is identified with service or that, at most, it is distinguished as the place where service is taught and carried out.

102 One can ask if *ipsius* and *huius* do not represent *scola*, the school being considered as the dispenser of education. However, while the Master may sometimes personify the monastery, personification of this sort does not occur in any of the nine other instances of *scola*. Therefore, *ipsius* and *huius* more probably refer to Christ, previously implied by *dominici* and then portrayed by *Christus* and *Dominus*. In fact, Christ is called *magister* in 13.14 and 14.13.

103 Ths 2–4. However, Christ appears there as Father and we as his sons. In contrast, here we become his coheirs, therefore his brothers.

104 RM 1.83 and 2.2.

105 RM 14.13–14.

106 This requirement appears even more clearly since *in ... doctrina ... perseuerantes* brings to mind Acts 2:42 where it is a matter of the teaching of the Apostles. Here the author has substituted Christ (*huius*) for the Apostles.

107 *Les plus anciens manuscrits*, 201–212 (cited in n. 3 above). One advantage of this ingenious theory is that, to a certain extent, it accounts for the double version of the end of the Prologue in the manuscripts of RB. In fact, the passage of the *Thema* moved by E* (Ths 40–46) begins exactly where the "interpolated" text of Benedict (Prol 39 = Ths 39) stops. Vanderhoven infers from this that the "interpolated" Benedictine text depends on an E* version of RM (earlier), while the "pure text" evidently depends on a P*A* version (later). This reconstruction of Vanderhoven implies the precedence of the "interpolated" text of the Benedictine Prologue over that of the "pure" text, a thesis that F. Masai and E. Manning openly support (See "Les états du chapitre premier du Maître et la fin du Prologue de la Règle bénédictine," *Scriptorium* 23 [1969]: 399–411).

According to the latter, Benedict would have found the short Prologue ending with the clause *erimus heredes regni caelorum*, which would have been indispensable to its meaning, in his source. I believe that my two confreres are mistaken. Undoubtedly, the original text of Ths 39 ended with *sed si compleamus habitatoris officium*. This method of ending a phrase with a conditional that begins with *sed si* is found not only in Cornelius Nepos (see R. Hanslik, "Zur Sprache der Cornelia, der Mutter der Gracchen, und des hl. Benedikt," *Wiener Studien* 79 [1966]: 304–307), Augustine, and Gregory (B. Linderbauer, *S. Benedicti Regula Monachorum herausgegeben und philogisch erklärt* [Metten: 1922], 140), but also two or three times in the preceding pages of the *Thema* (Thp 61 and 76. Cf. Thp 73). Therefore, the long or "pure" Prologue of RB is certainly original, and the short or "interpolated" Prologue, certainly later.

108 *Conuertatur et uiuat* (Ths 38 = Ez. 33:11); *Conuertimini ad me* (1.76 = Zec 1:3).

109 See A. de Vogüé, "Scholies sur la Règle du Maître," *Revue d'Ascetique et de Mystique* 44 (1968): 131 and 141.

110 See A. de Vogüé, "Nouveaux aperçus sur un Règle monastique du vi^e siècle," *Revue d'Ascetique et de Mystique* 41 (1965): 25–26.

111 RM 1.3–5.

112 See *Nouveaux aperçus*, 51–52 (cited in n. 110) and n. 111. Cf. A. de Vogüé, "La Règle de saint Benoît et la vie contemplative," *Collectanea Cisterciensia* 27 (1965): 98. ET: "The Rule of Saint Benedict and the Contemplative Life," *Cistercian Studies* 1 (1966): 54–73.

113 RM 1.90–92. Cf. Thp 53, which ends the commentary on the third petition. Each petition of the *Pater* is entirely autonomous, treated as a distinct chapter (see n. 116 below).

114 Ths 40–46.

115 RM 10.1: *Clamat nobis scriptura diuina fratres dicens....*

116 Thp 58 and 76; 11.1; 15.1; 16.1.

117 Another indicator: *Diuerte a malo et fac bonum* (Ps 33:15), already cited in Ths 13, is again cited in 1.77 (see n. 81 above). This repetition is better understood if the two citations belong to two distinct passages.

118 This *Incipit* seems encumbered by the *De generibus* annotation, which follows poorly from it, as we have highlighted in *Scholies*, 264 (cited in n. 109). Other words could have been added. Only *actus* is definitely original, as the *Explicit* of 10.123 demonstrates. Is that to say that *De generibus* and *monachorum in coenobiis* are interpolations, as well as the 1.1–75 passage to which these words allude? That is not for certain. Instead, we think that the original text included both an *Incipit* announcing Chapters One to Ten and a title announcing Chapter One. The formula that we read today probably results from combining these two announcements. This unfortunate combination would explain both the anomalies of the current formula and the absence of a particular title for Chapter One, also an abnormal occurrence. In this hypothesis, *De generibus* could have very well belonged to the original redaction.

119 RM 1.83: *Christi ... ecclesiae et scolae*.

Chapter Two

The Prologue of Benedict

Benedict and the Master

We are now ready to undertake the work of examining the Prologue of Benedict. Since four-fifths of this passage literally coincides with the commentary on the psalms from RM, we must now ask which of the two Rules the common text belongs to. The answer is unambiguous: this text originates in RM. Our analyses have sufficiently established that the commentary on the psalms belongs to a well-constructed whole that includes not only the *Thema* trilogy, but also the preceding Prologue and subsequent conclusion of Chapter One. In RB one finds none of the harmonious parallels that so firmly join the third part of the *Thema* to the series of introductions that precede it in RM.

Likewise, there are several indications of discontinuity in RB between the common text and the two small passages that are added to it at beginning and end (Prol 1–4 and 46–49). First, it is obvious that these two passages are written in second-person singular, while the common text is in first-person plural.[1] The connections are stylistically and logically unsatisfying. Why speak of prayer and the work of grace at the beginning of a phrase that will call to mind divine adoption and warn against evil actions that sadden the Lord (Prol 4–5)? This second part of the phrase, where the common text begins, corresponds better to the beginning of RM where divine adoption is revealed in the Lord's Prayer that has just been completed and the fear of saddening the Lord is the motive that drives the discussion of the "performance of our service" (Ths 1–2). The rest of the common text will insist on our responsibility for our actions and on the necessity to do good. Clearly, the theme of this passage is action, as the beginning of RM indicates, not the prayer and need for grace required by the sentence of Benedict.

In the last sentence of the common text, the insertion of the second passage proper to Benedict is even more awkward. This sentence is perfectly coherent in the common text: "the school of the Lord's service" is mentioned in its first part and "its master" and "his teaching" in the second.[2] The addition of Benedict interrupts this succession of ideas. Moreover, there is actually a dissonance between the content of the addition and the second half of the phrase. Benedict proclaims his intent to establish nothing that is hard or overwhelming. He clearly gives an impression of severity in the beginning, but he adds that the narrow way will soon expand, at least subjectively, under the broadening impact of love. An "ineffable sweetness" will accompany the disciple on the way of the divine commandments.

It is here that the common text resumes. In a totally different tone, it exhorts the reader not to abandon the teaching of the Lord, to persevere until death, and to participate in the sufferings of the Lord by patience. One now returns to the severe expectations of the addition, but this time with no hope of escaping trial until death. Suffering will mark all of life and only end in the glory of the eschatological kingdom. Therefore, there is disagreement between the text of RB and the final common conclusion. The one foresees a brief period of tribulation opening onto a sunny route, the other a career that will be difficult until the end. Rightly understood, these two views are not irreconcilable, but their rapid succession, without transition or explanation, leaves the reader with an impression of incoherence.[3]

Therefore, the beginning and end of the Benedictine Prologue show quite clearly that it is not the source of the common text. One can add to these facts several observations on the most notable variants that separate the two Rules. We will begin with the citation *Hodie si uocem eius audieritis nolite obdurare corda uestra* (Ps 94:8) that Benedict adds at the beginning of the paraphrase of the first psalm.[4] Repeating three words from the previous sentence (*audiamus, cottidie, uox*), it seems to follow rather naturally. However, this repetition is rather awkward. It asks us to "listen to the divine voice" and repeats, "If you hear his voice," without taking into account the fact it is already God who is supposed to be speaking. Furthermore, this first citation does double duty with the following, where it is again a question of "listening,"[5] and delays the citation of the verse *Venite filii audite me*, which is the objective.

But these minor drawbacks do not suffice to demonstrate the interpolation. Therefore, we turn to a group of later variants: the absence of the appositions *auditorem, iustos,* and *petram* in RB.[6] The omission of the last is particularly suspect. In fact, in the paraphrase of Psalm 14:14 and Psalm 136:9, the common text adds an explanatory gloss to the cited text three times. Thus, *malignus* is accompanied by *diabolum*, *conspectibus* by *cordis sui*, and *paruulos* by *cogitatur*. There is no reason not to treat the fourth word (*petram*) in the same way, and the Master does so by writing *Christum petram*.[7] Benedict only retains the gloss

(*Christum*) and omits the final word from the commentary. The same anomaly occurred above when RB omitted *iustos* in the paraphrase of Psalm 33:16. In these two cases, and perhaps in that of *auditorem* as well, it seems that Benedict has condensed the original text.

A similar but more significant omission occurs at the end of Psalm 14. There, Benedict first omits two verses of the psalm, then the composite citation *Qui audit haec ... non mouebitur in aeternum*, and finally the little dialogue that the Master constructed on these words.[8] This series of omissions eliminates the connection that unites the end of the psalm with the Gospel parable of the house built on rock. Yet, the author of the text certainly made this connection, and it is indispensable for its understanding. In removing it, Benedict makes the text difficult to understand, indeed, completely obscure at first glance. Moreover, the words *Vnde me*, which serve as a conjunction, are meaningless,[9] and the verb *ait* is foreign to the style of the passage. Such evidence clearly does not favor the Benedictine redaction.

However, one can account for its omissions quite easily. The verses removed from Psalm 14 speak of "fraud" and "usury," two sorts of faults that suppose use of material assets. The latter being excluded by cenobitic profession, one understands why Benedict has not preserved these verses, just as he removed a series of precepts connected to the same faults from the *Ars Sancta* (RM 3.20–21, 28, 30).

The subsequent omissions are explained by a constant need to abridge text. This abridgement occurs near conclusions where Benedict has added several lines to the common text. In a previous study, we stated that a similar mechanism accounted for the alternating omissions and additions found in the chapter on the abbot. Whenever Benedict adds text, he cuts an almost equal amount.[10] This is undoubtedly in preparation for the final addition (Prol 46–49) where he omits a slightly shorter passage.[11] Unfortunately, while its beginning (Ps 14:4–5) can be cut without great inconvenience, it is not the same for the rest of the text. It is regrettable that in his desire to shorten the text, Benedict seriously compromises its intelligibility.

The Preamble of Benedict

Since we have established that, at least for the most part,[12] the original content of the common text is found in RM, it is sufficient to examine the beginning and end of the Benedictine Prologue, which are all that actually belong to Benedict. The initial invitation to listen and to put into practice (Prol 1) plunges us immediately into the atmosphere of the Prologue of the Master, where the words *obsculta, o, praecepta, cordis tui*, *admonitionem*, and several others are also found.[13] The phrases "precepts of the Master" and "admonition from a father" obviously reference the Rule, but Benedict does not give it its proper name of *regula*, as did the Master in concluding, or clearly indicate its twofold human-divine origin.

One is often asked who the "master" and "father" is. In the context of the rest of the sentence, one would be tempted to identify him with "the One" who the reader has drifted from and must return to, that is to say, with God himself. This identification is corroborated by the fact that *fili* will be replaced at the beginning of the common text by *filiorum* (Prol 5), this latter representing us in our condition as children of God. Moreover, the words *magister/pater* call to mind those that Prol 6–7 will use in reference to Christ: *Dominus/pater*.

However, this same pair will be employed in the second chapter to designate the abbot.[14] Therefore, one could understand a human progenitor here, which the following phrase, where *mihi* obviously represents the latter, confirms. An additional argument ensues from the fact that, Pseudo-Basil, whom we will later discuss, refers to himself as "father" in a very similar phrase.

In the end, it seems impossible to opt for one meaning at the exclusion of the other. Benedict probably intended to leave it ambiguous. The Master clearly indicated two authors: God and his human spokesperson, such that the Rule appeared as an inspired document, similar to Holy Scripture. Benedict has not preserved this ambitious presentation. The divine and human authors are no longer formally distinguished or explicitly joined. They are merged from vague expressions, applicable to either, into a single evocation, in which the writer appears first, then behind him, his God and Lord.

The first sentence's appeal to listen and act concludes with a reference to the goal that must be attained. This goal is to return to God from whom one has drifted. Here again, Benedict obviously agrees with the Master. One is reminded that the Prologue of RM constantly alternated between appeals to pay attention or act and reminders of the last things. Benedict's exordium reproduces these two movements. In a single short phrase, Benedict says once and for all what the Master repeats in five or six paragraphs.

While this summary is quite complete in the first part,[15] it is less so in the second. Instead of a detailed and progressive recollection of the last things, from death to eternal happiness or damnation, Benedict proposes only the "return to God," which is also a vague and general formula. One finds here not so much a synthesis of the different ends of paragraphs of the Master as a condensed version of the conclusion of the first paragraph. Here, the Master wrote: *Ad quem Dominum Deum ex voluntate nostra per bona acta uel beneplacita iustitiae ire debemus.* More briefly, Benedict writes: *ut ad eum per oboedientiae laborem redeas.* In this formula, instead of "good works and right intentions," the "labor of obedience" is represented as the single means to go to God. Likewise, instead of the "sinful negligence" that the Master will speak of next, the "sloth of disobedience" will be held responsible for our drifting from God.

But this is not the principal difference between RM and RB. More important is the fact that the Master speaks only of going to God (*ire*), while Benedict speaks of returning to him (*redeas*). The source of this divergence appears in the next clause, where the Master, looking toward the future, warns us that, against our wishes, we will have to appear before God burdened with sin (*ne per neglegentiam peccatorum ab inuito rapiamur accersiti per mortem*), while Benedict, looking to the past, reminds us that we have drifted away from God through our disobedience (*a quo per inoboedientiae desidiam recesseras*). It is in consideration of this previous distance that the journey toward God is seen as a "return." The contrast is no longer between approaching God willingly or by constraint, as in RM, but between the previously committed separation and the future reunion. Therefore, Benedict only envisions the divine reunion as a happy event, without reference to the bleak possibility of appearing in a state of sin. Thus, the threatening perspective and motive of fear that dominate the entirety of the Prologue of the Master disappear. In RB, the fault belongs to the past; the future can only be viewed in terms of reconciliation.

However, this approach in which the individual is no longer placed before "two paths" of good and evil, but instead between an aberrant past and a future given to the return, is not proper to Benedict. Although it does not appear in the Prologue of RM, it is found in the *Thema*. One is reminded of the parable of the spring: at a summons from Christ, the journey descending in the "way of this world" is suddenly reversed. After Baptism, one takes the opposite way, the one that leads "to rest." A beautiful formula from the commentary on the *Pater* describes this conversion in terms very close to those of Benedict: *ut ... illum redeat in paradisum generatio nostra per gratiam, unde cum libero arbitrio ceciderat per offensam* (Thp 5–6). Therefore, the theme of exile and "return" already appears in RM, but this return is attributed to grace, not to the "labor of obedience." Moreover, the Benedictine formula is even closer to certain formulas of Cyprian and Augustine, which may have served as models.[16]

Thus far, the object of "obedience" has not been indicated. It appears that it is a matter of reading and obeying the Rule, itself considered the expression of the divine will. The word *oboedientia* is repeated in the phrase that follows, and this time it is no longer contrasted with "disobedience," but with "self-will." This brings to mind the commentary on the third petition of the *Pater*, where the Master warns against *propria voluntas* (Thp 30, 53), as well as numerous passages in both Rules that condemn this vice. In view of the quasi-technical meaning of this term, it would seem that, in comparison, the word *oboedientia* also tends to take on a specifically monastic meaning.

Another parallel emerges: *abrenuntias* is reminiscent of the baptismal "renunciation" that was at issue in the *Thema* of the Master.[17] But there, the newly baptized renounced the burden of their sins, here one renounces self-will. This difference again highlights the shift toward more specifically monastic concepts.

The very common introductory formula[18] of this second phrase demands little attention, while its military metaphor merits much more. The Lord Christ is presented as a "king" for whom one will "take up powerful and glorious weapons" and "go to battle." This image does not appear in the introductions of the Master, since Ths 17 reduces the Paulinian armor to the "belt for the waist." Nor is it found elsewhere in RM, where one searches in vain for the words *rex* and *arma*. Only *militare* is proper to the vocabulary of the Master. Similar to here, one also finds it side by side with *oboedientiae* in one of the last phrases of the *Thema* that Benedict reproduces.[19] This phrase may have influenced the beginning of the Benedictine Prologue. In fact, it is followed by an invitation to prayer, which corresponds to Prol 4. The two passages speak successively of a "service of obedience" and of the necessity of prayer. But even if Benedict is inspired by the common text, he further develops the notion of "armed service" with two new concepts: "Christ the King" and "powerful and glorious weapons." Are these concepts original? We will discuss this when we speak about Pseudo-Basil.

This second phrase of Benedict is clearly along the same lines as the first. It contains the same optimism and way of envisioning the future in a favorable light. The theme of the return to God has even taken on something of a soldierly and triumphant character. It is no longer a labor, but a battle that is viewed enthusiastically. God is not only the ultimate end and object of the return, but the Lord Christ, the King under whom one will henceforth battle. The individual to whom this has been addressed seems to have decided to enter into combat. The words issued here are the same as those that will be spoken to the postulant at the end of the Rule.[20]

Thus, the tone has intensified from the first sentence to the second. This latter finishes on a glorious note that marks the summit and, as it were, the conclusion of the preamble of Benedict. The next phrase simply introduces the common text. It begins with *In primis* in order to indicate a break with the preceding text and a new beginning. Indeed, after having extolled the work to be undertaken, one will now carry out its first step: prayer. Its necessity is affirmed as a general principle, which goes beyond the particular case of entry into monastic life: at the beginning of any good work (*quidquid agendum inchoas bonum*), one must ask God to bring it to completion (*a Deo perfici ... deposcas*).

These words bring to mind two passages of the Master: first, the chapter on work, where he insistently prescribes prayer at the beginning and end of all work,[21] then the *Ars Sancta*, where it is said: *Desideria sua a Deo perfici optare*.[22] But the most important parallels are found in the introductions of the Master. At the end of the Prologue one reads, *Age quod est bonum* (Pr 22). The commentary on the last two petitions of the *Pater* serves solely as an invitation to unceasing prayer to obtain divine assistance.[23] This incessant prayer scarcely differs from the *instantissima oratio* that Benedict calls for. Obviously, he summarizes the end of the commentary on the Lord's Prayer before reproducing the commentary on the Psalms. Moreover, these two clauses of Benedict correspond to a sentence of the Master that begins with the word *oratio*.[24] Therefore, the ties of RB with RM are indisputable.

However, if the idea of recommending prayer comes from the Master, that of connecting this prayer specifically to the *beginning* of monastic life, like that of linking it with the beginning of every good work, belongs to Benedict. Recall that in RM, the connection established between the two parts of the *Thema* is much less explicit. After "finishing the Lord's Prayer" it sets out to "discuss the performance of his service." By these words, does the Master wish to indicate the necessary priority of prayer over action? In any case, this principle is stated implicitly. In contrast, Benedict explicitly affirms it. For him, prayer becomes the obligatory preparation for service, conforming to a doctrine that the Master will only clearly announce midway through his Rule.

Apparently, this prayer is addressed to Christ; *eo* can only represent *Domino Christo* from the preceding phrase. Thus appears a third aspect of our relationship to Christ. He is not only the end of our journey and the king whom we serve, but also the one whose assistance we implore with prayer, as our efforts cannot succeed without him. One will note that Benedict does not seem bothered by the thought, acquired from the Master, that Christ is the one to whom we pray. He no more rejects this than he does the idea that Christ is Father: it is clearly suggested by the first phrase of the common text that immediately follows.

The three phrases of the Benedictine Preamble seem to vary in their similarity to RM. If the first corresponds directly with the Prologue and the last with the end of the commentary on the *Pater*, the one in between reveals only some vague influences, which are perhaps only coincidental. The *Thema* may well suggest exile and return, renunciation, self-will, and the service of obedience, but one would not dare assert this.

In any event, the second sentence is highly original. The "weapons of obedience" replace the "yoke" of Christ that the parable of the spring invites one to shoulder.[25] Thus, entry into the service of God takes on the appearance of military enlistment. This is quite novel. The Master does not ignore the theme of combat, but he considers only its defensive aspect, conforming to the spirit of the last two petitions of the *Pater* that give him occasion to develop it (Thp 67–81). In contrast, in RB, the battle theme further develops that of the return to God. Therefore, it is a matter of initiative and offense. Just as the first sentence of Benedict retains only the prospect of conversion from RM, the second lends something of the bold and exultant to the movement described in the *Thema*. The entire Benedictine Preamble breathes hope. The confident tone with which Benedict addresses the individual and speaks to him of his vocation contrasts with the anxious note that rings out in the first words of the common text.

Benedict and Pseudo-Basil

In order to complete the study of this preamble, we must compare it to a Pseudo-Basilian text that greatly resembles it. Here is the beginning of this *Admonitio*[26] alongside the text of Benedict:

Pseudo-Basil	Benedict
Audi fili admonitionem patris tui	[1]Ausculta o fili praecepta magistri
et inclina aurem tuam ad uerba mea	et inclina aurem cordis tui
et accommoda mihi libenter auditum tuum	et admonitionem pii patris libenter excipe
et corde credulo cuncta quae dicuntur ausculta.	et efficaciter comple …
Cupio enim te instruere	[3]Ad te ergo nunc mihi sermo dirigitur,

Chapter 2: The Prologue of Benedict

Pseudo-Basil	Benedict
quae sit spiritalis militia	quisquis abrenuntians propriis uoluntatibus,
et quibus modis regi tuo militare debeas.	Domino Christo uero regi militaturus, oboedientiae fortissima atque praeclara arma sumis.

It is evident that one of these two texts inspired the other, but which is the earliest? The *Admonitio* definitely existed in the seventh century, as it is cited by the Defensor of Ligugé. But, given that its Basilian authenticity is more than doubtful, nothing proves that it existed in the time of Benedict. Only a comparison of the two texts will be able to reveal their relationship. This comparison demands that one take into account a text from Proverbs that seems to have suggested the first two lines:

*Fili mi, ausculta sermones meos
et ad eloquia mea inclina aurem tuam* (Prov 4:20).

In this text from the Vulgate, the word *ausculta* parallels the phrase of Benedict, but *ad eloquia mea* corresponds to that of Basil (*ad uerba mea*). Taking into account possible variants in the version of Proverbs and the presence of *obsculta* in the Prologue of the Master, it seems to us that Pseudo-Basil has the most chance of directly reading and being inspired by the Scripture text. Therefore, Benedict depends on the *Admonitio*. In support of this conclusion, one will note the greater symmetry of Pseudo-Basil. Its four lines have almost the same number of syllables (14-13-15-15), while Benedict registers many variations, some almost twice as long as others (12-10-17-18).[27] Furthermore, in the first line, *patris* (Basil) corresponds better to *fili* than does *magistri* (Benedict).[28] Therefore, the words *admonitionem patris* seem to have originally been in the first line (Basil) rather than the third (Benedict).

Without overestimating the probative value of the various indicators, one can reasonably say, until proven otherwise, that Basil is the source of Benedict. In this hypothesis, one sees how Benedict has combined the *Prooemium* of Pseudo-Basil and the Prologue of the Master. One will recall that the Master may have provided several words for Benedict, especially *praecepta*, which is missing in Basil, and *magistri*, which perhaps alludes to the response formulas of RM.

But, above all, the Prologue of the Master has suggested the theme of action that is depicted in the last line of Benedict. Benedict finds the theme of attention in both of his models, and it is this that enables us to compare them. Compared to Basil, whose influence is dominant, the Benedictine redaction is more original and vigorous: its form is more varied and less subject to the biblical rule of parallelism. As regards content, one will note the suggestions of interiority (*cordis*)[29] and tenderness (*pii*).

After the second verse, solely influenced by the Master, RB again concurs with the *Admonitio* as regards the "service of the king." Therefore, the *Admonitio* is the source of this metaphor that is completely lacking in RM. It is true that the Preamble of Pseudo-Basil does not speak of obedience or weapons in this sentence. But these two elements, especially the second, appear in its first chapter, which deals entirely with the "spiritual army." Therefore, only the attributive adjectives *fortissima* and *praeclara* are particular to Benedict. The vibrant note with which they resonate corresponds with the emotion that comes through *pii*. While the attributive adjective *uero regi*[30] is not found as such in the *Admonitio*, it reflects the thought of its first chapter: Christ is a "heavenly" king, infinitely superior to the kings of earth.

Is this the extent of the influence of the *Admonitio*? Perhaps it again exerts itself in the next phrase of Benedict that admonishes prayer. In fact, at the end of his chapter *De oratione*, Pseudo-Basil will write: *Quodcumque opus inchoaueris, primo inuoca Dominum, et ne desines gratias agere, cum perfeceris illud.*[31] Although the same idea is found in the Master, the pair *inchoas ... perfici* ties Benedict more particularly to Basil. However, the significance of the second of these terms is different in each: in the first, it is God who "achieves" it; in the second, it is the individual. Therefore, one can only venture to say that Benedict recalls this phrase from Pseudo-Basil, especially since it appears much later in the *Admonitio*.

If we limit ourselves to what seems certain, Basil has still contributed no less than the Master to the birth of the Benedictine exordium. His brief *Prooemium*—we have reproduced almost half—better coincides with the intent of Benedict than do the long introductory passages of RM. Therefore, it serves as a model and framework to summarize the latter. When one compares Benedict and Basil, what is most striking is that the latter was content to simply call attention to his teaching and indicate the theme. Following the Master, Benedict also calls for implementation: *effaciter comple*. Furthermore, he depicts the hearer in the very act of enlisting and taking up arms. Service is no longer only a teaching objective of the Master. It has already inspired the disciple to make a commitment. This engaged stance is reminiscent of that of the newly baptized at the end of the parable of the spring. If the military image comes from Basil, the presumed dynamism of the reader is found only in RM.

The Final Addition (Prol 46–49)

As personal as it may be, the preamble of the Prologue is a summary of RM. In contrast, the final addition (Prol 46–49) is entirely independent of RM. In the middle of the *Thema*, Benedict inserts three sentences that are completely his own. Even the theme of the "narrow way," which serves as a visible link between this passage and the Prologue of the Master, is used by Benedict in an original manner.

The first sentence returns to the idea of "institution," just announced by the common text. It preserves its "we," but somewhat modifies its significance. As the entire context shows, when the Master says, "We are going to establish a school," he uses the "we" of the preacher, encompassing both the listener and himself. In RB, the *nos* drifts toward the "we" of the author. The author of the Rule now speaks in his own name as legislator, distinguishing himself from those subject to the law whom he will address in the following phrase.

The legislator hopes to lay down "nothing harsh or burdensome." The first of these two adjectives is reminiscent of the *aspera* that the novice will be forewarned of.[32] The second brings to mind the efforts of the weekly servers and reader that must not be *graue* because of the fast.[33] These connections suggest that the hope expressed contains both the ideal and the reality. Since one can only go to God by *dura* and *aspera*, the author knows that these hardships cannot be absent from his work. But he is genuinely concerned about taking into account human weakness and not overburdening anyone. Undoubtedly, he first thinks of the delicate balance between fasting and work, which will be the object of repeated and somewhat anxious statements,[34] then perhaps of the measure of food and especially wine, concerning which he mentions his scruples about using his authority to regulate the diet of others.[35]

An idealistic wish, we might say. In fact, the following phrase reintroduces the difficulties that Benedict had hoped to eliminate. However, he only presents them with a host of precautions and justifications. First, it is not for certain that one will encounter them.[36] Second, it is only a question of things being "a little strict." Finally, there are ample grounds to impose them: justice demands it, as the correction of vices and the preservation of charity are at stake. This last reason is decisive. "To rid oneself of vices" is clearly the final word of both the treatise on the abbot and that on humility.[37] This is the only reason that one comes to live in the monastery. The concrete result of this work toward amendment is charity, the queen and sum of all the virtues. To possess it is to have accomplished all the work of the *praktikè*.[38] To "preserve" it is to remain in this state of perfection. Some rather weighty and lofty reasons amply justify the little restrictions imposed by the Rule. If this is required by the "way of salvation" and if, as Benedict will say, the "salvation of souls" (RB 41.5) is at stake in fasting and work, no observance can be too difficult.

Still, when discussing the fast, Benedict is careful to remind the abbot that he must be vigilant that this does not lead to grumbling. Here he appeals to those who are weak and encourages them to stand firm. *Non refugias* echoes a phrase from the directory on the abbot: *infirmi non refugiant*.[39] The "flight of the weak" must be prevented both by the discretion of those in authority and the courage of those who follow. Benedict adds some subjective remarks for the frightened beginner to these objective measures of the Rule, pointing out that the way of salvation is necessarily narrow at the beginning. This statement may seem surprising given that its underlying Gospel text says nothing about a beginning that is necessarily narrow. According to it, the way that leads to life is apparently narrow at beginning and end (Mt 7:14). That is also how the Master presents it in the third paragraph of his Prologue.[40] Benedict boldly limits the narrow passage to the beginning of the journey. In short, it is only a gateway.[41]

This optimistic interpretation is explained in the last phrase of the addition. If the road seems to broaden as one advances, it is not because it has become less narrow, but because the heart of the one who is progressing has expanded. This idea of an utterly interior expansion is suggested by a verse from Psalm 118 from which this expression is derived. Undoubtedly, the pairing of the words *via* and *dilatasti* in this verse was intended to remind Christian listeners of the Gospel saying concerning the Two Ways. Already Hilary and subsequently Ambrose made this connection between the psalm and the Gospel.[42] To harmonize the two texts, they teach that the way is narrow "because one must enter it with diligence and prudence." This closely corresponds to the concept of Benedict that the way is narrow *at its beginning*. Expansion of heart is produced by faith and the indwelling presence of God.[43]

This role attributed to faith makes one think of the Benedictine Prologue: *processu ... fidei*. But where does the (*dilectio*) love that Benedict speaks of come from? He would have encountered it not in Hilary or Ambrose, but in Augustine. When the latter comments on this verse, he contrasts the constriction of fear with the expansion of love. This is because the expansion of the heart is the delight of justice, in other words: charity.[44] This interpretation is very close to that of Benedict, especially as Augustine plays on the words *dilatatio*, *delectatio*, and *dilectio*, a play of assonances that is perhaps echoed in the RB Prologue (*dilatato ... dilectionis*).

However, Augustine does not mention the narrow way. To find a parallel between the psalm and the Gospel like that of Hilary, one must go down past Arnobius[45] to Cassiodorus. The latter has a phrase that is curiously similar to that of Benedict: *cum uia mandatorum eius legatur angusta, nisi dilatato corde non curritur.*[46] But it says nothing about the "beginning" and offers a purely intellectual explanation of the expanded heart. It is accomplished by knowledge, the light of truth, understanding of the virtues, and orthodox faith.

It is evident that the paraphrase of Benedict on this psalm verse brings together scattered elements from other commentators. With Hilary, Ambrose, and Cassiodorus, he contrasts the expansion of the heart with the narrowness of the way. With Hilary and Cassiodorus, he mentions faith, but perhaps, as we will see, in a different sense. With Hilary alone, but more explicitly, he limits the narrow way to the beginning. With Augustine, Benedict speaks of the role of love, and more specifically of *dilectio*. However, one will note that Augustine categorically attributes the outpouring of charity in our hearts to the Holy Spirit. It is God that expands the heart; one runs by the gift of his grace. For their part, Hilary and Cassiodorus mention divine causality, while Ambrose at least speaks of the Trinity and the Word dwelling in the soul. In contrast, Benedict says nothing of the action or presence of God. The restraint of his paraphrase is probably responsible for this omission. On the other hand, it is compensated for in part by the mystical tone of *inenarrabili*, where one experiences the presence of God. Like the joys that he prepares in heaven, the sweetness of the love that he inspires here below is indescribable.

How can one read this word in RB and not think of a saying of Syncletica that Benedict would likely have read in the *Vitae Patrum*: "When the irreligious are converted they have sorrow and many struggles, but then an inexpressible joy"?[47] Indeed, we have already described the two phrases spoken of in this text: the difficult beginning and happy continuation. But this route is a commonplace. To cite only four names chosen at random, Pseudo-Macarius, Gregory of Nyssa, Diadochus of Photice, and Caesarius of Arles have all traced it in similar terms. There are only slight variations from one author to another as to what leads to the change that makes the path easier. Macarius speaks of the help of grace and the synergy of the Spirit;[48] Gregory adds *agape*,[49] along with grace; Diadochus mentions virtuous habit;[50] and Caesarius the same.[51] Without specifically describing the succession of the two phases, Jerome and Augustine also promise an effortlessness that they attribute to love for Christ.[52]

Clearly, the thought expressed by Benedict is widespread. But among all the possible parallels, we must give priority to the finale of the chapter on humility in the two Rules, as well as to the passage of Cassian from which they originate. Here also, here especially, one moves from fearfully keeping the Commandments to observing them "almost naturally, effortlessly."[53] As we will see, the Master and Benedict rather ineptly attribute this ease to "habit," but, with Cassian, they also offer the loftier and truer explanation: it is love that makes it so. This teaching is very close to that of the Prologue. Whether the beginning is called the narrow way or the fear of God, and the middle termed "progress in religious life and faith"[54] or the ladder of humility, there is always the same contrast between two phases in which the first is characterized by effort and anxiety and the second, by ease and expansion.[55]

Overview

The final addition of the Prologue ends on this encouraging note. It is easy to see here the tenderness, fervor, and optimism of the preamble. The similarity of the two passages is not only due to their use of "you" singular. More profoundly, they flow from the same paternal solicitude for postulant and beginner. Benedict lavishes affectionate and encouraging words on these weak souls. He appeals more to hope and good will than to fear. Without brandishing ominous visions of disobedience and death, judgment and hell, he simply proposes returning to God, as if the listener is already converted and ready to set out. He does not hide the fact that this return will be difficult; he immediately transforms it into the service of the true king, with powerful and glorious weapons.

The transformation will be even more striking in the second passage where the difficulty, relegated to the beginning of the way, will give way to the sweetness of a mysterious love. The stated intentions of the legislator could be no more reassuring than this: he wishes to impose nothing difficult; he worries about the fears of his disciple and anticipates them with kindness.

Such are the rays with which Benedict has wished to illumine the austerity of the common text.[56] These touches from the Prologue, especially the second, already foreshadow what will become one of the most constant traits of the entire Rule: compassion for the tempted and weak, particular concern to understand their difficulties and assist them with right teaching, in a phrase, the sense of subjectivity.

Chapter 2: The Prologue of Benedict

Endnotes

1 Apart from a few passages in the singular imposed by scriptural citations (notably, Ths 12–13: see n. 16 in Chapter One).

2 Prol 45 and 50 (= Ths 45–46).

3 It is the same at the end of the chapter of the Master on humility. Fear and humility are represented either as steps toward the love that casts out fear (RM 10.88–91) or as virtues that envelop all of earthly existence and have heaven as their only end (10.87 and 92). The first perspective (spiritual development here below) comes from Cassian, while the second (eschatological reward) belongs to the Master. In spite of the effort of 10.118–122 to synthesize, they remain juxtaposed rather than connected. The clash between source text (RM) and addition (RB) is similar here. When Benedict revised RM, he reproduced the mishap that occurred when the Master revised Cassian.

4 Prol 10. Note that, in both Rules, Psalm 94 serves as the daily Invitatory at the beginning of Night Office.

5 Prol 11 (= Ths 11): *Qui habet aures audiendi audiat...* (Rev 2:7). This *audiat* corresponds to the *audite* imperative from Psalm 33, while the previous citation presented the verb in the conditional (*si ... audieritis*). This is another piece of evidence that mitigates against the first citation being proper to Benedict.

6 Prol 14, 18, 28 (= Ths 10, 14, 24). See Adalbert de Vogüé, *La Règle du Maître*, Sources Chrétiennes 105–107 (Paris: Cerf, 1964–65), I.320, n. 14.

7 It is true that the gloss comes before the word of the psalm here, but this difference from the preceding cases is probably explained by the unusual, slightly awkward, connection between "the rock" and "Christ." The same order is found for another reason in Ths 14: *uos iustos*.

8 Prol 33. Cf. Ths 29–30 (Ps 14:4–5) and 31–33 (Mt 7:24; Ps 14:5).

9 Based on a similar case from RB 5.11 (*unde Dominus dicit*), it would seem that Benedict wishes to use the actual citation to explain the biblical allusion. Perhaps he began by reproducing the composite citation (Ths 31), intending that the words *Vnde et Dominus in euangelio ait* would introduce the exact citation that explains it, and then shortened it even more. However, in RM, the words *Dominus in euangelio* are read in the introduction of the composite citation itself.

10 See Adalbert de Vogüé, *La Communauté et l'Abbé* (Brussels: Desclée des Brouwer, 1961), 86–99; ET: *Community and Abbot* (Kalamazoo, MI: Cistercian, 1979 [I] and 1988 [II]). In RB 2, the additions either replace the omissions or precede them, which is more natural there. But Benedict cannot omit the finale of the common text here, since Prol 46–49 fits grammatically. Therefore, he removes a passage before the addition.

11 There are fifty-two words in the omission of Prol 33 and sixty-one in the addition of Prol 46–49. Note that Prol 50 again has three fewer words than Ths 50.

12 Perhaps Benedict better preserved it in some cases. Thus Prol 6–7 is more accurate than Ths 3–4, where *non* and *nec ut* are missing; Prol 12 (*Et quid dicit*) coincides better with Augustine than with Ths 8 (*Quid*); Prol 21 (*uocauit in regnum suum*) conforms more to 1 Thes 2:12 than to Ths 17 (*in regnum suum uocauit*). See, however, Adalbert de Vogüé, *La Règle de Saint Benoît*, Sources Chrétiennes 181–186 (Paris: Cerf, 1972), I.418, n. 21. Henceforth, this entire six-volume work will be referenced as *La Règle* plus volume (I–VI) and page number.

13 *Obsculta* (Pr 1 and 8); *o* (1); *praeceptorum* (10); *cordis tui* (8); *admonemus* and *admonet* (16). If it is true that, at least in part, *pii Patris* designates God (cf. also Thp 11: *hanc piam uocem*), one could also connect *pii* with *pietas* (Pr 7). *Efficaciter conple* is equivalent to *factis adinple* (Pr 21–22).

14 RB 2.24 (= RM 2.24). Cf. RB 63.13.

15 This is all the more significant in that, in RM, the call to action only appears from the third paragraph forward and is clearly formulated only in the last two. However, there is a reference to "actions" in Prol 3.

16 See especially Cyprian, *Ep.* 65.6; Augustine, *Ciu.* 11.28.

17 Th 18 (*quae abrenuntiauimus*) and 21 (*renuntiemus*).

18 *Ad te ergo nunc mihi sermo dirigitur.* Cf. Jerome, *Ep.* 22.15: *Nunc ad te mihi omnis dirigitur oratio; Ep.* 128.3: *Ad utrumque ... noster sermo dirigitur; Ep.*130.7: *Omnis mihi sermo ad uirginem dirigatur*; Ps.-Ambrose, *De lapsu uirg.* 5: *Ad te ergo nunc mihi sermo sit*; Leander, *Ad Flor.* 13: *Dum ergo ad te meus ... sermo dirigitur.* See also A. Mundo, "L'authenticité de la Regula Sancti Benedicti,"*Commentationes in Regulam S. Benedicti cura B. Steidle* (Rome, 1957), 118, n. 34.

19 Ths 40 (= Prol 40): *oboedientiae militanda.* Cf. Prol 3: *militaturus oboedientiae.* In this last case, however, the two words are not linked by any grammatical tie.

20 See RB 58.10: *lex sub qua militare uis* and especially 61.10: *uni Domino seruitur, un regi militatur.* Cf. 58.7 and 17: *oboedientia.*

21 RM 50.20: *ut antequam incoent laborare orent*; 50.47–50: *laborem ... cum incoant oratione praecedente incipiant.*

22 RM 3.48 (omitted by RB 4).

23 Thp 71: *incessabiliter est praecandum ad Dominum*; Thp 79: *rogantes incessabiliter Dominum.* Note that these passages are in "we," while Benedict remains faithful to "you" (second-person singular).

24 Ths 1: *finita ad Dominum oratione ... agamus nunc....* This use of *agamus* ("let us treat") is quite different than that of the Benedictine *agendum.*

25 Th 14. The connection of the "weapons" with the "yoke" is not my own. One finds it in Ps.-Basil, *Admon.* 1.

26 PL 103.683–700. A critical text has been edited by Paul Lehmann, *Die Admonitio S. Basilii ad Filium spiritale* (Munich: Verl. der Bayerischen Akad. der Wiss., 1955), 3–63. See also E. Manning, "L'*Admonitio S. Basilii ad filium spiritualem* et la Règle de Saint Benoît," *Revue d'Ascétique et de Mystique (RAM)* 42 (1966): 475–479. These two authors suppose that it is an authentic Basilian work, probably translated by Rufinus. I side with J. Gribomont, *In tom. 31* PG, p. 13, in thinking that it is not from Basil.

27 In the following sentence, the variations are equivalent: 10–10–16 (Basil) and 13–14–13–19 (Benedict).

28 This pair (*fili/patris*) is found in Proverbs 1:8; 4:1; 6:20.

29 The expression *aurem cordis* is common in earlier literature. For example, see Augustine, *Serm.* 132.1; *Conf.* 1.5; 4.11.16; 4.15.27, etc.; Leo, Serm. 29.1; Juvencus, *Ev.* II.814; III.147.

Chapter 2: The Prologue of Benedict

30 This was also a common expression. See *Sacram. Veron.* 182, Mohlberg, p. 23.21–22; Arnobius, *Ad. Gregor.* 10; *Passio Sebastiani* 26. Cf. Jerome, *Adu. Jouin.* I.35 (*uero imperatore Christo*); *Ep.* 60.10 (*suo regi*).

31 Ps.-Basil, *Admon.* 11. The generality of the precept (*quodcumque opus*) reminds one of the *quidquid agendum* of RB.

32 RB 58.8: *omnia dura et aspera per quae itur ad Deum.*

33 RB 35.13; 38.10.

34 See Adalbert de Vogüé, "Alimentation et travail," *La Règle* VI.1191–1194.

35 RB 40.2, where *a nobis ... constitutur* is comparable to *nos constituturos* (Prol 46).

36 At least this is what *et si* ("even if") seems to imply, although one can interpret it otherwise by linking *et* with *sed*.

37 RB 2.40 (= RM 2.40): *a uitiis emendatus*; RB 7.70 (= RM 10.91): *mundum a uitiis et peccatis*.

38 Cf. Cassian, *Conl.* 15.2: charity, another name for *actualis scientia*, belongs to those who have been made "perfect," *uitiorum omnium expulsione et morum emendatione*. The expression *emendatio uitiorum* is found in *Inst.* 9.9 and *Conl.* 18.1. Its equivalent *emundatio uitiorum*: *Inst.* 5.34.

39 RB 64.19. It is a matter of ascesis (*opera secundum Deum*) and of manual labor (*opera secundum saeculum*). Cf. 48.24: *nec uiolentia laboris ... effugentur*).

40 Pr 14. This shared trait of the "narrow way" links even the final addition of Benedict with the Prologue of the Master.

41 In fact, in Matthew 7:14, *arcta via* corresponds with *angusta porta*. As compared with the Vulgate, Benedict seems to have assigned the attributive adjective of the "gate" (*angusta*) to the "way." But he undoubtedly read *angusta uia* in a pre-Vulgate text, as the identical behavior of the Master suggests (Pr 14). That the Master and Benedict would have known an early text of Matthew 7:14, where they read the words *angusta uia* (and not *arcta uia* as in the Vulgate) is confirmed by the edition of the first Gospel published by A. Juelicher, *Itala. Das neue Testament in altlateinischer Ueberlieferung, I. Matthäus-Evangelium* (Berlin: 1938), 37: *angusta uia est* is attested to by several manuscripts, whether from the *Itala* or the *Afra* (this latter adds *et arta* after *angusta*).

42 Hilary, *Tract. in Ps. 118*, Litt. IV.11–12; Ambrose: see following note.

43 Idea summarized by Ambrose, *In Ps. 118.32*: *Via sit angustior, cor latius, ut Patris et Filii et Spiritus Sancti sustineat mansionem*. The entire context confirms that Ambrose had read Hilary. The same is true for Augustine when he comments on this text (next note). Like Hilary, he recalls the divine indwelling announced by 2 Corinthians 6:16, as well as the *plateae* spoken of in Proverbs.

44 Augustine, *Enar. in Ps. 118, Serm.* 10.6: *ut in praeceptis eius non timore poenae angustemur, sed dilectione et delectatione iustitiae dilatemur*. See also *Serm.* 11.1: *illa dilatatio caritatem significat*.

45 Arnobius has nothing on this verse (PL 53.510c).

46 Cassiodorus, *Com. in Ps. 118.32*.

47 VP 5.3.16: *et postea inenarrabile gaudium* (cf. 1 Peter 1:8).

48 Macarius, *Hom.* 18 and 21, PG 34.633 and 656.
49 Gregory of Nyssa, *De Instituto christ.,* in particular, pp. 63, 72, 77, 85, 86 (grace and the Spirit) and p. 75 (agape). Elsewhere, Gregory depends on the *Great Letter* of Macarius.
50 Diadochus, Chapter 93.
51 Caesarius, *Serm.* 236.5.
52 Jerome, *Ep.* 22.40: *Nihil amantibus durum est;* Augustine, *Tract. in Joh.* 48.1: *Qui amat non laborat* (cf. *De bono uid.* 21).
53 RM 10.68 (= RB 7.68). Cf. Cassian, *Inst.* 4.39.3.
54 It seems that "faith" was almost synonymous with "religious life" (*conuersatio*). See Cassian, *Conl.* 11.1 and 6, where *post prima fidei rudimenta* is equivalent to *de Bethleemitici coenobii rudimentis;* RM 91.53: *domesticos fidei* (the brothers of the monastery. Cf. RB 53.2, where it is undoubtedly a matter of brothers in religious life). Understanding *fides* in the usual sense, one could no doubt attempt to link *conuersationis et fidei* with *fide uel obseruantia bonorum actuum* here (Ths 17 = Prol 21). But if it is normal that faith, taken in this sense, comes first, as is the case in Ths 17 ("faith and works"), it is more difficult to understand when it comes second, as is the case in Prol 49. See also *La Règle* I.425, n. 49.
55 This sequence is linked to Prol 4: the monk begins and God completes, providing that the monk implores God's assistance. Perhaps Benedict does not mention grace or prayer in this conclusion of the Prologue because he has previously spoken of it in the preamble. At the end of the chapter on humility, the two Rules add a reference to the Holy Spirit to the text of Cassian (RM 10.91 = RB 7.70).
56 The contrast is especially noticeable between the passages of Benedict and their immediate context in the Prologue of the Master. Certain parts of the *Thema,* especially the commentary on Psalm 33, are scarcely less enthusiastic and lively than the Benedictine additions.

Chapter Three

The Epilogue (RB 73)

The last chapter of RB is apparently unrelated to the very disjointed series of chapters that precedes it (RB 66–72). Dealing with the observance of the Rule and its connection with other more advanced works, this last chapter constitutes a true epilogue, intended to conclude the entire work, rather than simply complete what immediately precedes it.[1]

The Original Conclusion of RB

However, the conjunction *autem*, which is read at the beginning of the first sentence (*Regulam autem hanc descripsimus* ...), proves that Benedict did not always view this Epilogue as a distinct chapter. Originally, the passage must have been part of an earlier chapter. This leads us to search for a point of origin in the pages that precede it. There is in fact one that catches the eye at the end of the chapter on the porters. Benedict declares: *Hanc autem regulam saepius uolumus in congregatione legi, ne quis fratrum se de ignorantia excuset* (RB 66.8). This concluding phrase, enjoining the communal reading of the Rule, is clearly a fitting beginning for the reflection on the Rule that constitutes the Epilogue. Its first words even display a striking resemblance to the beginning of the latter: *Regulam autem hanc descripsimus.*[2]

Thus, from all appearances, the Epilogue of Benedict initially followed the chapter on the porters. This seems even more probable given that, as comparison with RM shows, *De ostiariis* (RB 66) was most probably originally the last chapter of the Rule.[3] Benedict would have written the appendix that comprises RB 67–72 later. In order to give the Epilogue its concluding place, he would have separated it from the chapter on the porters and inserted it after this appendix.

Public Reading of the Rule (RB 66.8)

Since we have found the probable beginning of our passage at the end of *De ostiariis* (RB 66), it seems right to begin our exploration of the Epilogue by examining this final sentence. If, at first glance, it has no parallel at the end of RM 95, it is clearly connected to another passage of the Master. When the latter discusses reading in the refectory, he prescribes that "this Rule," that is to say, his own work, be read each day.[4] Thus, "the entire community" will hear it and be able to observe it.[5] No brother will be able to claim ignorance and avoid correction.[6]

As we have seen, there is scarcely a single turn of phrase of Benedict that is not found in a parallel passage of RM. However, the latter is much longer because it abounds in repetitions and details. Among these latter, we will point out only those that pertain to place and time. The Master requires that his Rule be read in the refectory each day. Benedict presents neither of these specifications. As regards place, he is content to say: *in congregatione*. He is equally imprecise as regards frequency: *saepius*. Therefore, the summary that RB offers here is vague and very brief.

This difference between the two Rules is not explained simply by Benedict's usual propensity to abbreviate. It is also due to the move that the prescription has undergone. For the Master, it is a matter of regulating all the particulars of the duties of the weekly reader. The comments on the reading of the Rule become part of this regulation, for which they espouse the minutiae. In contrast, Benedict is solely concerned to conclude his Rule with a prescription for its public reading.

Moreover, the brevity of RB virtually necessitates the abandonment of *cottidie*. Three times shorter than RM, it could hardly be read each day from one end of the meal to the other as the Master required. One would hear it too often. Benedict comes up with another frequency that leaves the determination to the superiors. It could be that the exclusive role that RM gives to the Rule by designating it as the only common reading is no longer fitting in a milieu where, as the Epilogue will show, one seeks to supplement this basic document with a group of advanced readings.

If one can easily explain why the Rule is not read "each day," it must be acknowledged that the vagueness of *saepius* contrasts with the precision of all the earlier monastic Rules that discuss this point. The daily reading of the Master is previously found in the *Rule of the Four Fathers*.[7] Augustine[8] and the *Tarnatensis*[9] speak of "once a week." Aurelian[10] and Ferreolus[11] require that one reread the Rule "every thirty days, that is to say, at the beginning of the month." It is only in Donatus, who uses RB rather slavishly, that one finds its characteristic imprecision.[12] Another disciple of Benedict, Waldebertus, will demonstrate the need to return to a certain precision: at the discretion of the abbess, a chapter or more of the Rule is to be read before each meal.[13]

Taking into account some certain or probable[14] descendants, the history of the reading of the Rule can be summarized in the two following tables:

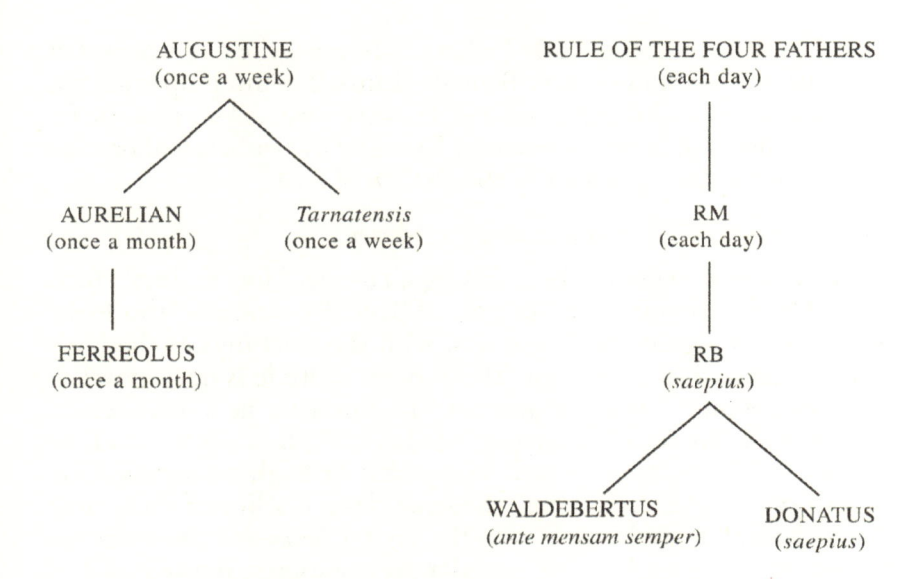

Chapter 3: The Epilogue (RB 73)

```
      AUGUSTINE                    RULE OF THE FOUR FATHERS
     (once a week)                         (each day)
      /        \                              |
AURELIAN     Tarnatensis                     RM
(once a month) (once a week)              (each day)
    |                                        |
FERREOLUS                                   RB
(once a month)                           (saepius)
                                          /      \
                                   WALDEBERTUS   DONATUS
                                 (ante mensam semper) (saepius)
```

However, the frequency of the reading is not the only point on which these various documents agree or disagree. While the Augustinian tradition unanimously places the prescription at the end of the Rule, the other family presents some variations. In the *Rule of the Four Fathers*, the requirement to "read these precepts" is found at the end of the third discourse. Considering this discourse in and of itself, one might again speak of a final position. But in relationship to the work as a whole, the prescription is found at the midpoint of the text. As we have seen, it is the same for RM. It seems that Benedict originally intended to close the Rule with this prescription, in the style of Augustine.[15] But he undoubtedly drafted the Epilogue even before adding Chapters 67–72. In any case, neither Donatus nor Waldebertus will be concerned about placing the prescription at the end: the first will insert it in his Prologue, the second in a chapter on silence and table reading, therefore, in the same context as RM 24.

These remarks suffice to place Benedict in the tradition. If he depends on the Master for the tone of his prescription, he follows Augustine in initially granting it the final position. However, one cannot go so far as to claim that Augustine directly influenced him in this regard, since it is quite natural to conclude a Rule, or portion of a Rule, with a comment of this type, as evidenced by the example from the *Rule of the Four Fathers*. Moreover, it could be that the *Explicit* at the end of RM[16] contributed to the formation of the texts that were originally read at the end of RB. This *Explicit regula sanctorum Patrum* speaks of both the "Rule" and the "Holy Fathers." These are the two words that the Epilogue meditates upon, Benedict himself coming up with the prescription to "read this Rule often." However, we will see that the tie that Benedict establishes between the Rule and the Fathers is altogether different from that indicated by the *Explicit* of RM.

The Epilogue (RB 73): Benedict and the Master

The Master actually attributes his *regula* to the "Holy Fathers" themselves. On the contrary, the Epilogue of Benedict contrasts "this Rule," considered as a guide for beginners, with the teachings of the Holy Fathers that lead to perfection. This modest attitude is quite novel. It contrasts not only with the *Explicit* of RM, but with the Master's claim that the Rule has been "dictated by the Lord."[17] This calls to mind the Prologue of the Master in which he says that through his mouth, God himself calls out to the listener. The same claim is affirmed every time that a chapter of RM opens with the saying *Respondit Dominus per magistrum*. It is true that this oracular presentation is not opposed to recognizing the superior value of other writings. In fact, the Master continually cites Holy Scripture and happily refers to the authority of the Fathers.[18] But one searches in vain for a formal declaration of the insufficiency of his work. Rather, inspired by God, corroborated by Scripture and tradition, he presents his *regula* as an integral whole, capable of leading the disciple to perfection.[19] Starting with truth, it leads to justice[20] and seemingly lacks nothing.

It is precisely from this self-sufficiency that the Epilogue of Benedict diverges. One recalls that previously the Prologue eschewed any direct affirmation of the divine origin of the Rule. This idea appears nowhere in RB. While the Rule is holy (RB 65.18), Benedict never says that it has been dictated by the Lord or that the Lord speaks through his mouth. To these silences, he now adds a long declaration on the shortcomings of his work. Although it is probably a later addition, the title of this chapter clearly expresses this modest intent straightaway. "The Rule leads to justice," said the Master. "All justice is not contained in this Rule," corrects Benedict. The first two sentences of the chapter develop the same idea by contrasting the "beginning" of religious life with its "perfection" or "summit," the first taught by the Rule, the second by the writings of the Fathers.

At the other end of the text, Benedict will again contrast "monks who live and obey well" with the "lax monks that we are, living badly and negligently" (RB 73.6–7). These are strong expressions, which reflect on the Rule itself. Although the latter is not named, one cannot say that it does not share in the blame. The authentic monks whom we have just spoken of are those inspired by Cassian, the *Lives of the Fathers*, and the Rule of Basil. The parallelism suggests placing opposite these excellent documents "this Rule" that we observe. Our faults that cause us to blush do not come only or even primarily from poorly observing the Rule. They come, above all, from the very imperfection of this norm. Benedict makes no secret of it: his weekly Psalter is good for those who are lukewarm and his hemina of wine is not suitable for real monks.[21] The weakness of contemporary monasticism requires this diminishment of the ideal of the Fathers. The Rule is the fruit of an era of decadence and has no room to be proud of itself.

The last phrase of the Epilogue almost literally repeats the first. The Rule is described as "minimal" and "introductory," while the writings of the Fathers appear as "summits of doctrine and virtue." Besides the comments on the necessity of grace, the only slightly new element is the express command that in order to set out for these heights, one must first fulfill the Rule. Although he disparages his legislation, Benedict does not intend to exempt the reader from it. In spite of its mediocrity, or rather because of it, the Rule is the required point of departure for those who strive for perfection today.

Therefore, there is a very striking difference in attitude between the Master and Benedict. Of monumental proportions, RM presents itself as a complete whole. Making itself only one-third as long as RM, RB abandons these claims to be a magnum opus. The Rule seems small compared with the doctrinal "peaks" that loom over it.

This contrast between the Master and Benedict originates in their differing assessment of their situation in relationship to the "Fathers." Each time the Master speaks of the latter, it is simply to prescribe that one conform to their teachings and examples.[22] He is convinced that his Rule can and must use them as its norms and models. In contrast, Benedict speaks of the "Fathers" only to juxtapose their matchless perfection with the degenerate lifestyle of the "monks of our time."[23] Instead of reproducing their norms, the legislator must reduce or set them aside. The Master thinks that he is on the same level as the Fathers; Benedict sees himself as far below.

The Theme of Modesty in the Sixth and Seventh Centuries

This pessimistic judgment and somewhat defeatist and discouraged attitude are far from unique to RB. Already Cassian is fond of comparing the fervor of the monks of Egypt or the East with the laxity of the monks of Gaul,[24] in part due to the difference in climate. He acknowledges the evident and inescapable fact that, as compared with its origins, even Egyptian monasticism has experienced a certain decline.[25] In his wake, the anonymous author of the *Life of the Fathers of Jura* recognizes a similar decline in his contemporaries (*Vita Patr. Jur.* 2.15). In particular, he believes that he must explain why he and his confreres follow a Rule very different from the teachings of Basil, the Fathers of Lérins, Pachomius, and Cassian. It is not that they disregard these "eastern" documents. On the contrary, they read them each day. But climate and work require that they adopt easier norms, conforming more to "Gallic weakness" (*Vita Patr. Jur.* 3.23).

With the *Regula Pauli et Stephani*, we come to a text that is strikingly similar to the Epilogue of Benedict. In their second-to-last chapter, the authors of this Rule recommended the diligent reading of the *Vitae Patrum* as a means to drive away tepidity. Certainly, the present Rule does not wish to slight these holy Fathers and their venerable writings! This would be presumption, reckless impudence:

> We have only wished to take some particular points from their constitutions and put them in writing for you. Every day when we read the Rules of these holy Fathers, who have received from divine grace the merit of an exemplary life and teaching authority, we are presented with religious life in its fullness and the perfect teaching of the spiritual life (*Reg. Pauli et Steph.* 41).

This key text presents the modern rule as a simple "excerpt" from the early Rules. The same idea appears in Isidore. In writing his Rule, he claims only to summarize and clarify the precepts of the early Fathers that are scattered in many different works and often transmitted by their successors in a vague and obscure form. This synopsis in popular style will facilitate understanding of the traditional monastic teaching (Isidore, *Reg. Praef.* 1). Of course, the generous reader will go beyond this and embrace the rigorous discipline of the ancients, as much as he is able. But if one cannot climb so high, then one has at least the present Rule. This is a minimum that is proposed, beneath which there is no monastic life worthy of its name. The ancient precepts make the monk perfect. Those of the Rule rank him last among monks; they are suitable for those who are turning away from their sins (Isidore, *Reg. Praef.* 2). Moreover, Isidore does not intend that the Rules of the Fathers cease to be read in community.[26] As he will say again in his conclusion, "we wish that by following this Rule, you will be led to observe more lofty norms" (*Reg.* 24.3).

Chapter 3: The Epilogue (RB 73)

Thus, the anonymous Jurasian, *Regula Pauli et Stephani*, and Isidore have similar attitudes toward the great classics of monasticism. To these three texts, so close to the Epilogue, we must add some very brief and scattered texts from Caesarius that reveal the same attitude. He too refrains from any "presumption." What he writes does not come from himself but from the superabundant source of Scripture and the Fathers (*Reg. virg.* 63). These references to the "Early Fathers" and the "Holy Fathers" return several times in his Rule (*Reg. virg.* 1 and 65). Like the *Regula Pauli et Stephani* and the Rule of Isidore, that for the nuns of Arles will be a simple "selection" of traditional prescriptions, especially adapted for feminine life.[27]

Both intimidated by their predecessors, Caesarius and Benedict will in turn become intimidating to their successors. Donatus of Bensacon will be content to combine their Rules with that of Columban. Again, he fears that he will be reproached for having dared to take excerpts from their works and to change some of their institutes. He also thinks it necessary to present an apology before beginning. He has only ventured to write in response to the entreaties of the nuns, since the masculine Rules of Benedict and Columban need to be adapted for women, and that of Caesarius, although written for women, is not directly applicable due to varying circumstances. But he also will only "make selections" from among the numerous prescriptions of these venerable works.[28]

The case of Donatus illustrates well the law of intimidation that is constantly at work in the monastic tradition. Even if one takes into account a certain laziness that encourages reusing earlier works rather than composing new, it is impossible not to give some credence to these constantly repeated declarations of humility. The prestige of earlier works is so imposing that one must apologize for anything that one adds. In truth, the new work will be less an addition to the already existing literature than a series of choice passages from them. Moreover, this manual so compiled does not excuse monks from returning to its sources. It is from these that they must seek a more complete teaching once they have accomplished the rudiments of the new Rule. Members of community will listen to the reading of these earlier Rules and each strive, as much as their generosity enables, to put their sublime prescriptions into practice.

Benedict is therefore in good company when he develops the idea that "the observation of all justice is not prescribed in this Rule." However, it must be noted that none of his colleagues express it with so much severity toward themselves and their readers. If all bow before the superior authority of the Fathers, some, such as Caesarius and Donatus, have no lower opinion of themselves than does the Master: their "excerpts" differ from the originals less by quality than by quantity. Others, like the anonymous author of Jura, acknowledge the inferiority of their institutes, but justify it in virtue of their different locale. The *Regula Pauli et Stephani* and *Regula Isidori*, while recognizing the distance that separates them from the Fathers, still claim to follow them, acknowledging that they take excerpts from them.

None of these correctives tempers the humility of Benedict. Neglecting to clearly state that his Rule draws its substance from the Fathers,[29] he notes only its inferiority in comparison with them. And he does not offer local demands as an excuse for this inferiority. Therefore, no one has gone further in his expression of abjection. Likewise, the digression "We weak and negligent monks, living badly, blush with embarrassment!" goes further than any other judgment of contemporary monasticism. One senses an unusual vehemence, tied to nostalgia for an over-idealized past. Perhaps Benedict has taken certain edifying tall tales of the *Vitae Patrum*, such as the story of the Psalter recited in a single day,[30] too seriously. Maybe he also seeks to bring about a collective *metanoia*, to enflame the ardor of his monks by a sense of shame.[31] Finally, he may be conscious of having witnessed and consented to certain concessions. Many facts suggest this, as will become particularly apparent in his treatises on the Office and fasting.

Allusions to the Rule of the Master?

If one relies on this last explanation, the disparagement of the Rule derives less from the idealization of a distant past than from a sense of having recently abandoned certain observances. We are thus brought back to the immediate source of RB, that is to say, to the work of the Master. It would not be surprising to find some allusion to it in this Epilogue. Should we see one in the two instances in which Benedict uses the verb *describere* at the beginning and the end of the chapter? *Regulam autem hanc descripsimus ... hanc minimam inchoationis regulam descriptam?* One of the meanings of *describere* is "to transcribe," and it is one that could seem plausible here.[32] Thus, Benedict would very discreetly acknowledge the derivative character of his work. Even if he did not overtly claim, as do so many others, to use "selected passages" from the Fathers, he would nevertheless recognize his dependence on an unnamed source.

Following this hypothesis, one is led to search for a motive for such discretion. Could it be that the source that Benedict draws from is well known to all? Or, on the contrary, that its author does not possess sufficient authority? These two reasons are not necessarily mutually exclusive: the same author could be well known in the limited circle of the first readers, while lacking sufficient renown to be designated by name to a more extended public.

However, it may also be that RM is implicitly contained in the *doctrinae sanctorum Patrum* to which Benedict next refers. Perhaps its appendage to the *Rule of the Four Fathers* and the *Explicit* that names it *regula sanctorum Patrum* previously existed in the manuscript that Benedict used, assuming that he himself was not the creator. Thus, after having noted the "transcription," Benedict would have referenced his source, just as *Regula Pauli et Stephani* and *Regula Isidori* announced that they had made a "selection" and then referenced the texts of the Fathers.

These allusions of the Epilogue could be compared to that made by the Prologue, when it gives to the ensuing work the name of *praecepta magistri*.[33] At the beginning and end of his work, Benedict would have referenced RM in veiled terms, the first time as the "precepts of the Master," the second as the source of his "transcription" and, perhaps, as the "teachings of the holy Fathers." However, it cannot be denied that both of these allusions are very tentative.

The Recommended Books and Their Public Reading

We have not yet considered the core of the passage, that is to say, the list of higher authorities recommended to readers and the various expressions of the ideal toward which they are invited to strive. After the *doctrinae sanctorum Patrum*, Benedict lists the Old and New Testaments, Holy Catholic Fathers, Conferences, Institutes, Lives of the Fathers, and the Rule of our Holy Father Basil. The order and descriptions are not perfectly clear. Given that the actual monastic Fathers mentioned last are scarcely distinguishable from the "Catholic" or ecclesiastical writings listed first, what does *doctrinae sanctorum Patrum* at the beginning refer to? Probably to the whole of the writings of the Fathers, ecclesial as well as monastic. This general reference at the beginning of the passage would be easily understood if it was not immediately followed by a reference to Holy Scripture, which seems to separate it from the two specific references. Of course, it is not impossible that Scripture itself is contained in the rubric "teachings of the holy Fathers." The saints of the Old and New Testaments could have been designated as such at that time.[34] However, the expression *sermo diuinae auctoritatis* sets Scripture apart, as does the absence of any reference to *Patres* in the same sentence. Therefore, in spite of the conjunctions *enim* and *aut* that tie it to its two neighbors, this phrase on Scripture interrupts the development on the writings of the Fathers. Like the other authors we have examined, the original intent of Benedict was simply to recommend patristic literature. But when explaining this, he wished to pay homage to the Book par excellence, the source of all those that he would name.

In fact, the works of the Fathers are scarcely more than commentaries on the Bible. Benedict himself notes this relationship in prescribing the readings for Vigils: along with "the books of divine authority, the Old Testament as well as the New," one will read "expositions written by renowned and orthodox Catholic Fathers."[35] Clearly parallel, this passage from the liturgical section not only sheds light on the sequence that we seek to explain, but also suggests that Benedict has the practices of reading in common and reading at Office in mind while writing the Epilogue. Likewise, the next sentence of the Epilogue echoes the prescriptions for reading at Compline, where among other things, "the Conferences and the Lives of the Fathers" are to be read.[36] Thus, the three categories of works listed here have been mentioned previously in the Rule in the same order. These references concerned public reading. Therefore, as we saw with the penultimate chapter of *Regula Pauli et Stephani*, it would seem that the Epilogue wishes to recommend chiefly patristic works for common reading. Although this conclusion is correct, the title of the Epilogue is more connected to the prescription for the reading of the Rule (RB 66.8). While explicit in this last passage, the clause *in congregatione* also, at least implicitly, applies to the readings recommended in the Epilogue, without excluding private use. Just as the Rule is read "in community," — perhaps during the meal — so Scripture, the Fathers, and monastic authors are read at the liturgical gatherings of Vigils and Compline, as well as during the hours of *lectio diuina*.

The Ends to Attain and the Influence of Cassian

Each time Benedict suggests a reading, he assigns it a specific role. The Rule leads to "a certain moral decency and a beginning of religious life," the teachings of the Fathers to the perfection of this same life or "the heights of perfection." Scripture is a very sound norm for human life, the books of the Catholic Fathers lead us straight to our Creator, and the monastic works inspire the virtues of true monks. Finally, the last sentence speaks of both the Rule and the "summits of doctrine and virtues,"[37] two stages of the journey "toward the heavenly homeland."

Thus, it is only in the concluding phrase that the eschatological end clearly appears. Before this it is only suggested by "to reach our Creator,"[38] a vague expression that could perhaps be extended to the encounter with God here below. Everywhere else the goal proposed is merely earthly. It is a matter of reaching the perfection of religious life, indeed, perfection itself, or, in its absence, a beginning of *conuersatio*. Before, and if one dares to say so, more than the afterlife, the Epilogue is concerned with the spiritual ideal realized here below.

This perspective of perfection calls to mind the theory of spiritual ascent discussed by Pinufius-Cassian and reproduced with varying degrees of fidelity by RM and RB in their chapters on humility.[39] As we will see, while the Master radically transforms this ascending scheme and places its end in heaven, Benedict will remain closer to Cassian and, at least in the conclusion of his chapter, not go beyond the earthly goal of "perfect charity." Similarly, right before the eschatological conclusion of the Prologue, we saw Benedict introduce a passage promising his disciple that joyous progress would follow the stark narrow passage at the beginning (Prol 46–49). By what it omits and adds in the treatise on humility and the Prologue, RB abandons the almost exclusive emphasis placed on the eschatological goal by the Master and focuses on the development of the spiritual life here on earth.

This attitude of Benedict is reminiscent of Cassian. The similarity is in no way coincidental, as everything indicates that the Epilogue was written by an assiduous reader of the *Institutes* and *Conferences*. They are not only the most highly recommended of the monastic works; they also suggest the majority of the expressions in this chapter that specify the ideal to be attained. The editions of Butler and Montserrat have already demonstrated in their *Fontes* that the Epilogue is permeated with Cassian. We, for our part, have found some additional parallels.[40] One of the most significant facts is that the expression *ad perfectionem festinare* is previously found in the *Conferences*.[41] After reproducing it at the beginning of his Epilogue (*ad perfectionem conuersationis qui festinat*), Benedict modifies it in the last phrase to make it *Quisquis ad patriam caelestem festinas* (73.8). One sees that he receives from Cassian his impetus toward "perfection" and extends it *in extremis* in a race toward the "heavenly homeland."

Conclusion: The Epilogue and the Prologue

Having examined how the Epilogue and the Prologue are connected by the theme of spiritual progress, we now take a broader look at the relationship between these two passages. First, note the similarity of the second sentence of the Prologue (*Ad te ergo ... quisquis ...*) with the last sentence of the Epilogue (*Quisquis ergo ...*). In both, Benedict uses the same enthusiastic words and tone to summon his reader. In the first, the disciple is represented as a soldier taking up arms, in the second, as a traveler rushing toward his homeland.[42] This second image resembles that of the "return" described in the first sentence of the Prologue.[43] It is also noteworthy that the "you" singular, characteristic of the additions of the Prologue, reappears at the end of the Epilogue.[44]

The Epilogue demonstrates a particular continuity with the final addition of the Prologue. Both texts speak of the "beginning" of "religious life" and "running."[45] Both characterize monastic life as a progression in two stages: an unimpressive *initium* and a prestigious *cursus*. However, the two passages each present this shared sequence of "beginning" and "running" very differently. According to the Prologue, the humility of the beginning is due to the sense of constriction that the novice experiences from the fact that the way is new to him and contrary to his bad habits. As he advances, the expansion of heart, owed to love, replaces this feeling of "narrowness." Therefore, the change occurs in the subjective domain. In contrast, the Epilogue is situated in the objective realm. Beginning and running are defined in relationship to adopted norms: the first, the very small Rule that teaches decency of morals, the second, the writings of the Fathers that lead to perfection. One moves from an unimpressive program to a more perfect observance.

In spite of this difference, there is a real similarity between the two schemas. In fact, the Prologue describes the *angustum initium* of the "way of salvation" traced by the Rule, and the *initium conuersationis* of the Epilogue is none other than the observance of this same Rule in monasteries. In both cases, it is the same consistent norm that is involved. One recalls that, in the first passage, Benedict declared his intention "to establish nothing hard or oppressive" (Prol 46). If the Rule seems disconcerting at first, it is only because of the weakness of those involved. Objectively, Benedict wishes it to be and judges it easy. Consequently, one understands the other judgment that he brings to bear on it in the Epilogue. By the very fact that the Rule is "easy," it is a "minimum," a less-advanced norm, good for beginners. One sees how the two passages are connected and complete one another: the Prologue indicates that the Rule is actually not difficult to observe and encourages the postulant to bear with initial small hardships; at the end of the work, the Epilogue again states and almost accentuates the Rule's easy character by suggesting that the reader go further.

These two symmetrical passages offer a reflection on the Rule. Whether the perspective is that of subjective expansion or objective transcendence, it is always a question of observing the present Rule. The manner in which this discourse on the Rule emphasizes ease, excuses hardships, and gives itself a very modest place in the ascetic literature is a profoundly new approach in comparison with RM. The Master was content to tranquilly propose his own work, call it the word of God, and place it in the succession of the writings of the Fathers, beyond and above all challenge.[46] Benedict is less sure of himself. He feels the need to explain, excuse, and contextualize. He is as concerned with what the postulant will think of him as he is with the impression that he creates toward Scripture and the Fathers. These two very human concerns stem from a profound knowledge of the weakness of his contemporaries, which implies his own inadequacy. He must reassure the reader frightened by the Rule and, at the same time, warn against the illusion of finding perfection there. The degeneracy of the times is such that those seeking to be monks may still shy away from even such a modest Rule.

Certainly, the Master did not ignore this human weakness. In fact, no one has recognized it so candidly (RM 92.47). But different from Benedict, he seems to have come to terms with it and does not register it as a present concern. It is simply the human condition. In contrast, Benedict seems to suffer from what he considers a disgraceful and irreparable decadence. He must settle for an undemanding Rule for the majority of the "monks of our times." Only some generous individuals can be encouraged to surpass it. If religious life has two eras, that has been the history of institutions, from the Fathers down to us. The task of contemporary monks is to climb the slope from which monasticism has descended.

Therefore, the Prologue and Epilogue reveal what can be called a two-staged mental structure. This is one of the distinctive traits of Benedict as compared with the Master. It gives RB a dynamism that is lacking in the other text. The Rule is no longer a self-contained whole, but an initiation into more advanced teachings. The concern of the Master was to root the Rule in Scripture and the monastic vocation in the call to Baptism. The intent of Benedict is to point to other heights beyond the Rule, those of Scripture and the Fathers.[47] Monks are called to run generously across the endless expanse that extends from the beginning of monastic life to its perfection.

Endnotes

1. It is true that the last sentence of RB 72 sounds like a conclusion and foreshadows the Epilogue. But, as we will see, this sequence of chapters 72 and 73 is probably the result of a later arrangement.
2. RB 73.1. The repetition may seem awkward, but one finds similar examples in the rest of the chapter and throughout the Rule (cf. RB 22.6–8, etc.).
3. See RM 95. These different factors have already been pointed out by G. Penco, "Ricerche sui capitolo finale della Regola di S. Benedetto," *Benedictina* 8 (1954): 25–42.
4. RM 24.15: *legat namque cottidie regulam hanc.*
5. RM 24.26: *Ideo ... debet regula legi quia tunc omnis congregatio in unum redacta....*
6. RM 24.31: *Ideo ... diximus regulam ... legi ... ut nullus fratrum excuset se ignorantia faciente non emendare.*
7. *RIVP* 3.31: *custodienda sunt haec praecepta et per singulos dies in aures fratrum recitanda.* Recension P specifies *omnibus fratribus simul audientibus recitanda,* which calls to mind RM 24.26 (see n. 5).
8. Augustine, *Reg* 16.207–209: *Vt autem in hoc libello tanquam in speculo possitis inspicere, ne per obliuionem aliquid neglegatis, semel in septimana uobis legatur,* etc.
9. *Reg. Tarn.* 23 (reproduces Augustine).
10. Aurelian, *Reg. mon.* 55 (thirty days); *Reg. uirg.* 40 (one month). Aurelian depends on Augustine, from whom he repeats the words *ne per obliuionem aliquid neglegatis.*
11. Ferreolus, *Reg.* 39. Ferreolus depends on Augustine, as evidenced by his paraphrase of words stemming from Augustine (*ne aliquid ... per obliuionem sitis negligentes*), along with the fact that, like Aurelian, he moves from a week to a month.
12. Donatus, *Reg.,* Prologue (*saepius*).
13. Waldebertus, *Reg.* 9. This method of reading a chapter each day will spread. See *Ordo Reg.* 2, *CCM* I.101.8; *Memor. Qualiter* 6, *CCM* I.235.3; *Suppl. libel.* 1, *CCM* I.321.12–13; *Legisl. Aquisgr.* (817) 36, *CCM* I.480.1–2. One will note that with its 73 chapters, RB could be read around five times each year.
14. The *RIVP*/RM connection is probable; all the others are certain.
15. He also has a second directory for the abbot (RB 64), which corresponds to that of Augustine, *Reg.* 15. See A. de Vogüé, *La Communauté et l'Abbé* (Brussels: Desclée des Brouwer, 1961), 369, n. 1; ET: *Community and Abbot* (Kalamazoo, MI: Cistercian, 1979 [I] and 1988 [II]).
16. Although attested to by the two manuscripts, it does not appear that this *Explicit* can be traced to the author himself. See n. 17 in Chapter One. However, it may be that Benedict had it in front of him.
17. RM 11.T; 13.65; 22.12.
18. See n. 22 below.

Chapter 3: The Epilogue (RB 73)

19 See the concordance in Jean-Marie Clément, Jean Neufville, Daniel Demeslay, *La Règle du Maître* III, SC 107 (Paris: Cerf 1964–65) on the words *perfecte, perfectio,* and *perfectus.*

20 Pr 24 (cf. Pr 26). See the concordance (cited in previous note) on the word *iustitia*. See also RM 11.1 and 62.10–12.

21 RB 18.25; 40.6 (cf. 49.1–2).

22 RM 26.12; 34.2; 63.3; 90.92; 92.57. Cf. 11.31, 33 and 95.15 (Saint Eugenia); 28.43 (Saint Sylvester); 72.8 (the Apostles John and Andrew).

23 RB 40.6; Cf. 18.25; 73.1–9.

24 Or their incompetence. See Cassian, *Inst., Praef.* 8–9; 2.2–3; 4.10–11 and 15, etc. Sulpicius Severus, *Dialogues* 1–3, has the same inferiority complex but reacts vehemently against it.

25 Cassian, *Inst.* 2.5; *Conl.* 7.23; 18.7; 19.5, etc.

26 Isidore, *Reg.* 7.2: This reading could replace the talk of the superior at the three weekly conferences. Cf. Fructuosus *Reg.* I.20.

27 Caesarius, *Reg. virg.* 2: *elegimus pauca de pluribus* (cf. Isidore, *Reg. Praef.* 1: *haec pauca uobis eligere ausi sumus*). In fact, Caesarius uses the Augustinian and Lerinian Rules.

28 Donatus, *Reg.*, Prologue. Among others, he borrows the formula *elegi pauca e plurimis* from Caesarius.

29 Except perhaps the very discrete reference to the "transcription," that we will speak of later.

30 See RB 18.25 and my commentary in Adalbert de Vogüé, *La Règle de Saint Benoît,* Sources Chrétiennes 181–186 (Paris: Cerf, 1972) V.554, nn. 30–32. Henceforth, this entire six-volume work will be referenced as *La Règle* plus volume (I–VI) and page number. Cf. my article "Origine et structure de l'office bénédictine" in *Coll. Cist.* 29 (1967): 197–198.

31 Compare the treatment of the shamed individual in RB 43.7 (cf. RM 23.56; 53.9–10; 53.33, 53–55).

32 At least if one recalls that RB 73 originally followed RB 66, that is to say, the last chapter where Benedict is bound by the subject order of RM. However, one can hardly say that even these first sixty-six chapters of RB are presented as a simple "copy" of RM. Possibly valid for the Prologue and RB 1–7, such a description seems mistaken when applied to RB 8–66. This objection can only be avoided if one discovers some texts where *describere* means "to copy," not in the narrow and usual sense of transcribing a text word for word (cf. Fulgentius, *Ep.* 5.12), but in the broader sense of imitating or being inspired by that does not exclude the personal intervention of the "scribe." Among the examples furnished by the *Thesaurus Linguae Latinae (TLL)*, only that of Horace (*Sat.* 2.3.24) seems capable of being understood thus. Otherwise, *describere* usually means "to write, to put into writing," and it is not surprising that the *TLL* ranks RB 73.1, 8 among the witnesses of this interpretation. The first phrase of Benedict is similar to Dionysius, *Vita Pach.* 54: *Haec igitur nos ex multis descripsimus pauca … ut* (G² 90: *gegraphèkamen*). Cf. *Vita Pach.* 28: *descripsit eis regulas* (G² 28: *grapsas*).

33   Prol 1. See p. 49 above. Cf. A. Genestout, "La Règle du Maître et la Règle de S.Benoît," *Revue d'Ascétique et de Mystique (RAM)* 21 (1940): 91.

34   The biblical characters are thus the "saints" par excellence (cf. RB 64.18). Gregory, *Hom. Ez.* 3.4, also calls them "fathers" (cf. *Hom. Eu.* 17.8–10; 22.9). See also A. Blaise, *Dictionnaire Latin-Française de auteurs chrétiens* (Strasbourg, 1954), s.v. *Pater* §2.

35   RB 9.8. Note the insistence on the equality of the Old Testament with the New and on the mark of orthodoxy for the Fathers.

36   RB 42.3. Are the *instituta* that Benedict adds here different from the *Conferences* themselves? Cf. Cassian, *Conl.* 1.Praef., end, where *collationes eorum et instituta* designates the first ten *Conferences*. Of course, Benedict may be thinking of the *Institutes*, like Ferrandus, *Vita Fulgentii* 23: *Aegyptorum monachorum Vitas admirabiles legens, Institutionum atque Collationum spiritali meditatione successus,* a text exactly parallel to RB 73.5, but better ordered (cf. *Vita Fulgentii* 24: *de Institutionibus et Collationibus*).

37   RB 73.9: *maiora quae supra commemorauimus doctrinae uirtutumque culmina*. It appears that it is both a matter of the aforementioned works and of the state to which they lead the reader.

38   RB 73.4. Cf. Prol 2 (*ut ad eum... redeas*) and similar expressions in the introductions of the Master.

39   Cassian, *Inst.* 4.39; RM 10 and RB 7. See our commentary on humility in Chapter Seven.

40   Compare RB 73.2 and Cassian, *Conl.* 20.3 (*celsitudine,* equivalent to *culmen*). For the expression *culmen* (or *culmina*) *perfectionis,* add *Inst.* 5.28; 7.13; *Conl.*1, *Praef.*; 2.4; 3.22; 21.33.1. The last sentence (RB 73.8–9) curiously resembles the penultimate of the Preface of *Conl.* 1 (*si quis... festinet prius... et tunc demum ea quae supra...*), although the corresponding words have a different significance. Cf. also *Conl.* 9.16: *ad illa sublimiora quae praediximus... peruenire.*

41   Cassian, *Conl.* 21.5. The word *perfectio* is one of twenty-one *hapax legomena* in RB 73 highlighted by E. Manning in "Le chapitre 73 de la Règle bénédictine est-il de S. Benoît?" in *Archivum Latinitatis Medii Aevi* 30 (1960): 129–141. The influence of Cassian, which is one of operative words, suffices to account for the use of *perfectio* in the Epilogue, without needing to raise the question posed by E. Manning. The three interrogative constructions of RB 73.3–6 are adequately explained by the particular character of the Epilogue: in this instance Benedict uses eloquence.

42   Cf. Augustine, *Serm.* 351.3: *Quis ergo festinat... ad patriam remeare, nisi quem peregrinationis suae paenitiuerit?*

43   Prol 2: *ut ad eum... redeas,* phrase that also has parallels in Cyprian and Augustine (see n. 16 in Chapter Two).

Chapter 3: The Epilogue (RB 73)

44 Apart from the second (*qui festinat ... hominem*) and last (second-person singular) phrases, the Epilogue is written in first-person plural.

45 Compare Prol 48 and 73.1 (*initium*); Prol 49 and 73.1–2 (*conuersationis*); Prol 49 and 73.4 (*cursu*; cf. 73.1 and 8: *festinas*).

46 This attitude is similar to that of the first legislators (Pachomius, Basil, Augustine), except that they did not refer to the early "Fathers," and for good reason. It is even closer to that of *RIVP*, whose presentation is impacted by the desire to be under the patronage of the Ancients. The connecting of RM with *RIVP* proceeds from this same concern. References to the Fathers are found in *Tarnatensis* 11 (Evagrius) and 13 (Cyprian). There is no reference of this type in Ferreolus or Aurelian.

47 See Adalbert de Vogüé, "La Règle de S. Benoît et la vie contemplative," *Coll. Cist.* 27 (1965): 99–100 (to clarify n. 34: while certain texts of Cassian speak of "summits," and obviously consider unceasing prayer or contemplation, others, like *Inst.* 4.8 and 23; 5.28, are aimed at cenobitic obedience); ET: "The Rule of Saint Benedict and the Contemplative Life," *Cistercian Studies Quarterly*, 1, no. 1 (1966): 54–73.

Part Two
The Spiritual Art

Chapter Four

The Treatise of the Master (RM 3–6)

I. The Group and Its Connections

The Master develops the metaphor of the *ars sancta* in four chapters. After describing the art itself and its reward (RM 3), he examines the instruments to be used (RM 4) and the impurities that must be removed (RM 5), before concluding with the workshop and the means for using the instruments (RM 6).

The Original Version of the Treatise

When one examines this vast group closely, it is readily apparent that it was not written in one fell swoop.[1] It seems that the original core contained only the *ars sancta* (3.1–78), the *ferramenta spiritalia* (4.1–10), and the *officina* (6.1–2), and that these three passages formed a single continuous development. The eschatological *merces* (3.79–95) and the list of *uitia* (5.1–11) seem to have been added later.[2] The same must be said for the chapter titles. Those of Chapters Three, Four, and Six are clearly artificial.[3] The title of Chapter Five serves to connect a list of vices that makes no use of the art metaphor to the *Ars Sancta*.

The Witness of E

Given the information provided by the complete manuscripts, we will see what we learn from the witness of Florilegium E*. The following table shows what it has kept and omitted:

	P* and A*	E*
Conclusion of *De abbate*	2.39–40	2.39–40 (no. 28)
The Council	2.41–50	
The Abbot, Master of the Art	2.51	2.51 (no. 28)
The art taught in the workshop of the monastery and practiced with spiritual tools	2.52	

	P* and A*	E*
The art taught by the abbot in the monastery	3.T	[*Qualis debeat esse praepositus*] (no. 29)
List of the art	3.1–77	[*Regula Pachomii* 159 (no. 29)]
Conclusion: the art and the spiritual tools	3.78	
Heavenly reward for the art	3.79–94	
Return from the path toward heaven	3.95	
The spiritual tools	4.T–10	
The vices to eliminate	5.T–11	5.T–11 (no. 20)
The workshop and the use of the tools	6.T–2	
Beginning of *De oboedientia*	7.T–15	7.T–15 (no. 21)

Three important facts appear in this summary. First, the Pachomian directory for the *praepositus* (*Reg. Pach.* 159) is substituted for the *Ars Sancta* of the Master (RM 3.T–77). We definitely say substituted, as it is clear[4] that the compiler of the florilegium read this passage of the Master in the *Ars Sancta* and chose to replace it with a passage of the same style, also addressed to a monastic superior. The fact that the Pachomian directory is supplemented with seven additional precepts in E*, several of which are clearly reminiscent of the *Ars Sancta*, suffices to remove any remaining doubt in this regard. Thus, in spite of the absence of RM 3, the florilegium certainly attests to the presence of the *Ars Sancta* after RM 2 in the text of the Master that it utilized.

Only the first of the two transitions that link the *Ars Sancta* to the treatise on the abbot (RM 2.51 and 52) is present in E*. It is clearly in context, since it presents the *Ars* solely as a program for the personal conduct of the superior,[5] which is exactly what the Pachomian directory for the *praepositus* is. In contrast, the second transition, which makes the *Ars* the subject of a teaching for disciples, does not correspond to the character of the Pachomian text that is substituted for the *Ars*. Was this second transition intentionally omitted by the editor of E* or was it missing in the edition of RM that he used? It is difficult to decide. If the second connection seems unnecessary after the first, one cannot refrain from pointing out that the double task they impose on the abbot is exactly the same as what is prescribed in *De abbate*: the abbot must first fulfill the divine precepts and then teach them verbally.[6] If the texts of *De abbate* in question were not missing in E*, this similarity of content with the abbatial directory would be a serious argument in favor of both the congruity of RM 2.51–52 and of the presence of the second transition in the original redaction.

These observations lead us to the second fact that must be highlighted in regard to E*: not only does the florilegium not possess RM 4 and 6, but it makes no reference to the *ferramenta* and the *officina*. In fact, these are introduced in RM 2.52.[7] Therefore, the absence of the second transition means that there is no trace of them in E*. Here again, one may be tempted to think that E* simply reflects an original version of RM, where the *ferramenta* and *officina* had not yet been added to the *Ars Sancta*. But, conversely, if one supposes that the second transition (RM 2.52) was part of the original redaction and was intentionally omitted from the florilegium, one must say that RM 4 and 6 also existed in the model of E* and were likewise omitted.

The third significant fact to note in E* is that RM 5 is reproduced *in extenso*, not following the treatise on the abbot and the Pachomian directory that corresponds to the *Ars Sancta* (nn. 28–29), but earlier in the florilegium (no. 20), immediately before RM 7 (no. 21), the treatise on obedience. This complex occurrence enables us to make two conclusions of varying probability. First, if one recalls that RM 5 is viewed as a later addition, the presence of this passage in E* seems to prove that the redactor of the florilegium read the *Ars Sancta* in its finished state, including the last of the additions.[8] Next, one can ask whether the position of RM 5 directly before RM 7 is the result of a revision made by the compiler of the florilegium or if it instead reflects the actual state in which it was originally found in the text of RM. In favor of this last hypothesis, one will note that it is quite conceivable that a supplementary passage such as RM 5 could have originally been placed following the series that it must have completed. The eschatological conclusion that ends the chapter (RM 5.11) corresponds well to this final position. From here, the chapter would have been transferred and placed within the treatise proper on account of its evident affinity with RM 4.

The Ars Sancta *and the Treatises That Follow*

Thus, the testimony of E* draws our attention to the relationship between the *Ars Sancta* and the treatises that follow. In fact, whether the compiler of the florilegium found RM 5 before RM 7 or made this connection himself, there is no doubt that the two chapters are to some extent related. The list of vices begins with *primo superbia deinde inoboedientia multiloquium* (RM 5.2), which corresponds to the *humilitas oboedientia taciturnitas* sequence (RM 4.3) from the list of virtues. These three virtues are precisely those that are examined in the three treatises that follow: *De oboedientia* (RM 7), *De taciturnitate* (RM 8–9), *De humilitate* (RM 10), although the order is not exactly the same.[9] Therefore, it seems that the list of RM 4 and, more clearly still, that of RM 5,[10] is intended to introduce the long treatises of RM 7–10 and attach them to the *Ars Sancta*. Moreover, a long section of the *Ars* itself unmistakably parallels the first step of humility (cf. RM 3.50–67; 10.10–51). The latter simply develops in a continuous discourse the ideas that the *Ars* delivered in separate points. Thus, in essence, RM 3 already contains the doctrine of humility toward God that will be the most original and completely developed aspect of RM 10.

The Ars Sancta *as Bridge*

Therefore, the *Ars Sancta* serves as a bridge between the treatise on the abbot and those on the three great virtues. One will recall that the beginning of the *Ars* is attached to the double transition of RM 2.51–52 that depicts RM 3 as a norm, first for the personal conduct of the abbot,[11] then for his teaching. However, by the end of the chapter, it is no longer a question of the abbot. "We" seems to designate the entire gathered community (RM 3.78–82). The same "we" dominates RM 4–5. Thus, one moves imperceptibly from the abbatial directory to the catechesis addressed to all the brothers. The shift is accomplished very naturally. *Ars doceri et disci debet* (RM 2.52): what the abbot must fulfill and teach is the same as what the brothers must learn and put into practice. Thus, Master and disciples are united at the end of the *Ars Sancta*. It will be different in the treatises on obedience, silence, and humility that are intended particularly for the brothers. There, the abbot no longer appears as the exemplar of good works, but as the superior to whom one submits. Superior and subjects quit mixing, each rank demanding a different role. From this point forward, it will be the role of the subjects that is the particular, although not exclusive,[12] focus of the legislator.

Thus, the *Ars Sancta* serves as a transition between the counsels reserved for the abbot and those meant for the brothers. The didactic theme that commands the *Ars* assures the congruence of the former with the latter. According to RM 4, humility, obedience, and silence are three of these "spiritual instruments" that the abbot, thanks to the experience that he has gained in practicing them himself, teaches his disciples to use.[13] The description of these virtues in RM 7–10 will show that they are not only learned from the abbot, but also practiced in relationship to him. The abbot alone facing the brothers, the abbot and the brothers united, the brothers alone facing the abbot: this then is the path that leads from *De abbate* to *De oboedientia* via the *Ars Sancta*.

A superficial glance gives the impression that the appendix on the council forestalls the intermediary role of the *Ars* (RM 2.40–50). However, while the instructions regarding the council concern the brothers as well as the abbot, the superior and subjects are instructed of their duties separately, a practice that emphasizes their distinct roles. Therefore, one must wait until the *Ars Sancta* to find the abbot and brothers perfectly united in a common effort, the fulfillment of God's commandments. It is only here that they together, as master and apprentices, devote themselves to the same "art."

The Ars Sancta *as a Handbook of Christian Morality*

Therefore, the *Ars Sancta* serves as a bridge between Chapters 1–2 and 7–10. But this function does not fall to it merely in virtue of some artificially imposed transitions. Rightly seen, the bond that connects it to *De abbate* appears intrinsic and indispensable. The abbatial directory requires this addition. As the mission of the abbot consists essentially of teaching and enforcing the divine precepts (RM 2.4–6, 11–12), it is necessary to present them in the form of very striking and easily remembered maxims. Thus, the *Ars Sancta* is intended to serve as a handbook of Christian morality for use by professor and students.

It is clearly a matter of Christian morality rather than monastic ascesis. The latter will only be dealt with in RM 7–10, where, in the final analysis, the Master takes the obedience-humility-silence trilogy from the *Institutes* of Cassian and adds several modifications that tend to accentuate the cenobitic characteristics of these virtues. In contrast, characteristics of this sort are almost completely absent from the *Ars Sancta*. The abbot and the obedience owed him are mentioned only once (RM 3.67). No other function, institution, or practice proper to monasticism is readily apparent. The teaching rests on Scripture and is of value for all Christians.

This very general thrust, which the alterations of Benedict will hardly modify, has been so well understood by readers that several have been unafraid to reproduce it almost unchanged in instructions addressed to the faithful. Thus one finds all or nearly all of RB 4 in the *Instrumentum Magnum* of the priest Agimund,[14] the *Scarapsus* of Pirmin,[15] the Capitulary of Theodulf of Orléans,[16] and a false decree of Isidore Mercator,[17] not to mention fragments reproduced in various works.[18]

The Ars *and the* Thema

Thus, the *Ars Sancta* constitutes a sort of general introduction to the special treatises of RM 7–10. Before developing the particular duties of the cenobite, the Master summarizes the universal duties all Christians. This introductory role is reminiscent of that played by the *Thema* and its appendices at the beginning of the Rule. Before treating the "life of monks in monasteries" (RM 1.T), the Master presents at length the conversion and baptism of the unbeliever, the Lord's Prayer, and the teaching of the Psalms. As a whole, this great baptismal catechesis is no more monastic in content than the *Ars Sancta*. While the monastery is mentioned, it is only at the end, just as it appears only in the last lines of the *Ars Sancta*. These two passages of very general Christian doctrine end on the same monastic note: "to persevere in the monastery until death" (Ths 46) and "to labor with perseverance in the workshop of the monastery."[19]

If one considers the intent and style of the *Ars*, it also proves particularly similar to the commentary on the psalms (Ths). In citing and commenting on Psalms 33 and 14, the *Thema* seeks to present a rudimentary program of good works to attain "life" and the "tent." The *Ars Sancta* has the same goal. Undoubtedly, RM 3 is noticeably more developed than the *Thema*, whether it is a question of the list of good works or the evocation of paradise. Its method is also clearly different: in the the *Thema*, the Master follows the texts of the psalms step by step, sometimes commenting briefly; in the *Ars Sancta* he brings together at his own discretion various New Testament and non-scriptural precepts. But in both cases, it is clearly the same sort of elementary moral catechesis from Scripture. One can even detect some parallels between the two lists of precepts. While some are questionable and seem coincidental,[20] others may indicate that the redactor of the *Ars* has the psalm texts from the *Thema* in mind.[21] Even if it is only a coincidence, they emphasize the connection of the two passages. The guidelines for conduct, drawn up for neophytes by the Lord himself in the *Thema*, have become the *Ars* that the abbot must practice and teach to his disciples in the monastery.

Beyond these general similarities, the *Ars* and the *Thema* present several parallel details. First, the Gospel's Golden Rule appears both in the fifth petition of the *Pater* (Thp 59) and among the first maxims of the *Ars Sancta* (RM 3.9). The commentary on the fourth petition consists of a promise of reward very similar to that which concludes the *Ars*.[22] Moreover, the metaphor of the "worker" used in Thp 56 and Ths 10 heralds that of the "artisan" that is fundamental to the *Ars*. The word *optare*, in the sense of prayer, appears only three times in RM: twice in the commentary on the *Pater* (Thp 16 and 20) and once in the *Ars Sancta*.[23] The same doctrine of grace appears both in the commentary on the Psalms (Ths 25–28) and in RM 3.46. The similarity is evident even in the very particular play of the prepositions *in* and *ab*.[24] In both the commentary on the *Pater* (Thp 36) and RM 3.53–54, the expectation of death is connected with vigilance in the "deeds of life." One searches the rest of the Rule in vain for the expression *actus uitae* that is employed in these two passages. Finally, the commentary on the psalms makes reference in passing to the allegory of the "infants dashed against the rock" (Ps 136:9), and this image reappears in an article of the *Ars*, also in regard to evil thoughts.[25]

The Ars *and the Beginning of* De Taciturnitate

It is true that this allegory does not characterize only the *Ars* and the *Thema* since it is also found in RM 8.22–23. But the beginning of *De taciturnitate* (8.1–25), like the *Thema* and *Ars*, with which it presents several points of agreement,[26] is a passage of very general teaching and lacks any strictly monastic elements.[27] Consequently, far from weakening the relationship of the *Ars* with the *Thema*, the return to the allegorical exegesis of Psalm 136:9 in RM 8.22–23 only corroborates it. It seems that in these three cases, we are dealing with some texts of ecclesiastical rather than monastic origin, which the Master has redrafted to serve as introductions to various sections of his Rule.[28]

A Preexisting Document?

This means that, at least in part, the list of RM 3 could have been borrowed from a preexisting document. There is no shortage of similar lists of precepts in the early literature. While Butler has clearly shown that none of those that have come down to us is the source of the RB/RM,[29] the existence of a source of this type remains plausible. As A. Wilmart[30] wrote: "the least that we can say is that if Saint Benedict (or, we add, the Master) composed this list of maxims himself—and did not simply modify a traditional series to some extent—even in that he followed the example of his predecessors. In any case, the *Instrumenta* belongs to another time." This judicious remark is confirmed by our observations: the *Ars* evidences a connection with two other passages of the Rule that clearly stem—especially the *Thema*—from texts written for non-monastics. Therefore, it is probable that RM 3 is based on a document of this same genre. Although the Master certainly revises and completes this list, he does not invent the whole of it.[31]

One indicator pointing in this direction is that RM 3 and RB 4 begin with the double commandment of love, followed by some items from the Ten Commandments and the Golden Rule. This same series is previously presented, with a reversal of the second and third elements, at the beginning of the ancient Latin version of the *Diadache* (*Duae Vitae*).[32] In their turn, the *Syntagma* and the *Pistis* from the Council of 362, two Alexandrian documents undoubtedly influenced by the *Didache*, begin with two commandments and several articles from the Ten Commandments.[33] Certainly, the articles from the Ten Commandments that one finds in RB and RM are drawn directly from the Gospel. But Butler, who brought this fact to light, concluded a bit too quickly that there was no connection between RB and these other works. In fact, the Gospels contain no passages in which the two great commandments are combined with the Ten Commandments or the Golden Rule. This characteristic series links the *Duae Viae* with both its derivatives and RM/RB. While it may have shaped both independently, it nonetheless remains very likely that the Master received it from a tradition to which the texts in question witness.

The Ars *and the* Passio Juliani

Thus, several facts lead us to believe that the *Ars* is not purely the creation of the Master. Naturally, this conclusion prompts us to consider its connections with the *Passio Juliani*. It contains a discourse in which the martyr reveals to his judge the "magic formula" that permits him to work miracles.[34] This magical *carmen*, also called the *Ars*, contains some twenty maxims of which almost half agree, literally or very closely, with those of RM and RB. Consequently, there are three possibilities: (1) the *Passio* is their source; (2) the *Passio* depends on them; and (3) the Rules and the *Passio* depend on a common source.

At first glance, the last of these three hypotheses is tempting, given that we have just established that the *Ars* of the Master probably depends on a preexisting document. Could not the *carmen* of the *Passio* depend on the same document? However, a fact must be taken into account that renders this explanation unlikely. The parallels between RM and the *Passio* are not limited to these brief passages of the *Ars* and the *carmen*. One finds them in many other passages of the two works.[35] The whole of the facts demands a broader explanation than appealing to the particular source of the *Ars*. Either the entire *Passio* depends on RM or vice versa.

Solving the problem will be difficult as long as no one has uncovered the literary history of the *Passio*. While it is commonly accepted that the Latin text, preserved in numerous manuscripts, is a translation from a Greek original,[36] this is only an opinion, plausible *a priori*, but one that needs to be verified. My investigation of the text has not furnished definite confirmation. At the most, one could point out that the use of the word *papas* to designate a simple priest (*Pass. Jul.* 53) is perhaps better understood in Greek than in Latin. While, in fact, the East seems to constantly have given this title to priests,[37] the West has reserved it for bishops, and especially for the Roman pontiff. To my knowledge, the only case of a priest being called *papas* in a Latin text is that of the hero of the *Passio Mammarii*.[38] This short African *Passio* presents other unquestionable parallels with the *Passio Juliani*,[39] such that one can affirm that one depends on the other. Would not the *Passio Juliani*, translated from Greek to Latin, have transmitted this use of *papas* to the *Passio Mammarii*? This hypothesis is clearly in accord with the suggestion that Roman Africa was the intermediary by which the *Passio Juliani*, originating in Egypt, would have spread to Spain and Gaul.[40] In its passage to Africa, it could have also influenced the redaction of the *Passio Mammarii*.

One would like to know—and this is tied to the previous question—where and when the Latin text appeared. It definitely existed in the seventh century since it appears in a Passionary from this period[41] as well as in the celebrated *Lectionary of Luxeuil*.[42] Can one go back a century earlier, relying on a verse of Fortunatus that mentions Basilissa, the companion of Julian?[43]

Whatever the problems concerning the Greek and Latin origin of the text, one can highlight some traits in it that seem very ancient. First, there is something unusual and archaic in a certain formula used to designate Christ that cannot avoid at least the appearance of Modalism.[44] Next, the *Passio* mentions a *cursus* of prayer containing only six Offices per day: *tertia, sexta, nona, uespertina uel nocturna et matutina* (*Pass. Jul.* 19).[45] This list, which does not achieve even the classic *septies in die* and, in particular, omits Prime and Compline, is more conceivable in the fourth or fifth century than in the sixth.

Therefore, there exist some reasons, apart from the hypothesized Greek original, to place the *Passio* before RM and RB. A priori, given that the Master definitely uses other Passions, there would be nothing surprising about him borrowing from the *Passio Juliani*. So it would seem that the *carmen* of Julian can be considered a secondary source of the *Ars Sancta*, along with the principal source, of ecclesiastical origin, whose existence we previously established. One will note that the Master not only borrows around ten maxims from the *Passio*, but also and especially the title of *Ars* that he gives to the entire list. On the lips of Julian, *ars* is synonymous with *carmen* and means "magical spell." As written by the Master, *ars* is no longer a magical process but a trade that one practices in a workshop with some tools.[46] The image has changed, but the word remains the same.

Before leaving the *Passio Juliani*, we must mention a final difficulty presented by this text. We have seen that RM has many parallels with it beyond the *Ars*. The same cannot be said for RB. One would be right to conclude that it is RM rather than RB that depends directly on the *Passio*. Yet, there is one maxim from RB 4 that is more closely related to the *carmen* than the corresponding maxim from RM 3:

RM 3.68	*Passio Juliani* 46	RB 4.62
(a) Non *cupire* dici *se* sanctum antequam sit,	Qui non *uult* dici sanctus[47] antequam sit,	Non *uelle* dici sanctum antequam sit,
(b) sed prius esse quod uerius dicatur,	sed ut sit quod uerius de illo dicatur.[48]	sed prius esse quod uerius dicatur.
(c) et sic dici debere.		

Here, the variants of phrase (a) and the addition of phrase (c) distance RM from the *Passio*. This phenomenon, contrary to those we have just referenced, suggests that, in this instance, the manuscripts of RM transmit a more evolved text than that of RB. As we will see, this is not the only passage of the *Ars Sancta* that seems later than the corresponding text of RB.

The Organization of the Ars Sancta

Now that we have indicated two probable sources of the *Ars Sancta* (one lost, the other preserved in the *Passio Juliani*), we must attempt to understand its organization. One is right in thinking that this is no easy matter because, in principle, no order is required for a group of maxims in which each stands on its own.[49] However, truly isolated maxims are very rare,[50] and it is obvious that most of them are linked in small groups, some more clearly structured than others. Moreover, the constitutive link of each group differs from case to case. Sometimes it is a similar ideological theme,[51] sometimes a similar literary form,[52] and sometimes a similar inspiration from Scripture.[53] Sometimes content, form, and source converge to knit a sequence together (RM 3.3–7). The successive or simultaneous intervention of these three elements throughout creates multiple and changing relationships between maxims and groups of maxims.

II. The Details of the *Ars Sancta* (RM 3)

The Beginning (RM 3:1–21)

After the Trinitarian confession, which, as we will see, is probably an addition, the list begins with the two great commandments followed by six articles from the Ten Commandments and the Golden Rule. This first sequence attests to the intent to give a Christian stamp to the series. Purely scriptural, it perfectly fulfills the mission given to the abbot: to teach nothing outside of the precepts of the Lord (RM 2.4). The rest of the text will not consistently maintain this level of pure and simple biblicism. But scriptural or not, all will be ordered by this solemn beginning, which ties the entire passage to the revealed will of God.

Up to and including *Honorare patrem et matrem* (RM 3.8), the Master filters and groups Old Testament precepts according to the Gospels. The Golden Rule (RM 3.9) is also proper to both Testaments. In contrast, the precept of renunciation specifically introduces Christ by name and refers solely to the New Law (3.10). This transition to the New Testament is confirmed when immediately afterwards one hears the *Corpus castigare* of Saint Paul (RM 3.11). And when, by means of mental associations taken from the *Passio Juliani*, RM passes from renunciation of self to charity toward others, this program of good works is again inspired by some words from Christ the Judge (Mt 25:36).[54] Just as the Pauline *Corpus castigare* is explained by two non-scriptural articles,[55] the first three forms of charity drawn from Matthew 25 are continued with five good works that are similar but extraneous to the list from the Gospel.

Thus, these first twenty maxims are primarily punctuated by contrasts between the Old and New Laws, renunciation and charity, and the word of God and human commentary. There is a clear progression from the crimes condemned by the Ten Commandments to the acts of renunciation and charity commanded by the Gospel. Henceforth, one will constantly adhere to the same properly Christian and Gospel-based plan.

The Introductions Drawn from the Passio *(RM 3.10 and 22–23)*

The two maxims that open the next section (3.22–23) closely resemble the opening maxim of RM 3.10 that was also binary. Both require two steps, one negative, the other positive, the first that of renunciation, the second, dedication to Christ:

3.10: *Abnegare semetipsum ut sequatur Christum.*	3.22: *Saeculi actibus se facere alienum.*
	3.23: *Nihil amori Christi praeponere.*

The first simply cites the Gospel;[56] the second utilizes non-scriptural formulas.[57] But this contrast is diminished by the fact that both texts stem from the *Passio Juliani*, which interweaves them:[58]

Ut se ab omnibus actionibus[a] saeculi[b] faciat alienum,
ut[c] solam uocem Domini audiat imperantis et dicentis:
Si quis uult post me uenire, abneget semetipsum[d] et tollat
crucem suam et sequatur me.[e] Nihil[f] amori[g] Dei[h] praeponat.

Such is the beginning of the *carmen* of Julian. It successively contains:

1. Renunciation of worldly deeds
2. Obedience to the call of Christ: to renounce oneself, take up the cross, and follow him
3. To prefer nothing to the love of Christ

First, the Master removes the scriptural portion (2) and uses it to introduce one of his sections (RM 3.10). Then he combines the two adjacent elements (1 and 3) and uses them to create the introduction of the following section (RM 3.22–23). Therefore, it is he who has constructed the two symmetrical pairs[59] and featured them at the beginning of two successive sections. Thus, the double law of renunciation and love heads both detailed lists of Christian duties. In the first case, one renounces negotiating one's own life in order to care for that of others; in the second, one abstains from evil actions that would offend against charity toward Christ and neighbor.[60] In the first, renunciation curbs concupiscence and love finds expression in good deeds; in the second, irascibility is mortified and love becomes patient.

Chapter 4: The Treatise of the Master (RM 3–6)

Development of the Ars *from the* Passio

Not only is the beginning of the *carmen* of Julian divided to create two parallel section heads, but the material presented in the rest of the *carmen* is also divided between the two sections of the *Ars*. The following table shows this division:[61]

RM 3	***Passio Juliani* 46**
13–14	Nihil[a] aliud desideret, nisi quod ipse Dominus promittit. Non consideret[b] patrem aut[c] matrem, non[d] filos et[e] cetera quae[f] nouerunt intelligentes inpedimenta animae.[g] Ante omnia[h] qui[i] curam pauperum[j] sollicite egerint;[k] qui contenti[l] sunt esurire, ut alios refocillent.[m] Satis Deo acceptum est munus,
14–15	quo indigens saturatur, quo nudus uestitur,[n]
24	quo ira non perficitur,
34	quo malum pro malo non redditur,[o]
25	quo iracundiae tempus non reseruatur,
(35)	quo inpatientia[p] per patientiam superatur.

Thus, the Master finds the constitutive elements of his two successive sections in the *Passio*. Without modifying the order in which they are presented, he separates these elements by placing them respectively under one of two introductions provided by the beginning of the *carmen*. He also considerably develops this core derived from the *Passio*. Moreover, it is quite significant that his personal contribution always follows some borrowed maxims. After *nudum uestire*, with which the *Passio* concludes, he adds six other good works; after *iracundiae tempus non reseruare*, he adds eight other recommendations along the same lines; after *malum pro malo non reddere* and the maxim on patience, he adds three similar articles to close the section. We observed the same phenomenon after RM 3.10: the Master expanded upon the beginning of this introduction taken from the *Passio* with some original maxims. Throughout, the Master seems to depend on and develop the brief instructions of the *Passio*. In the first section he begins by having recourse to Scripture,[62] then uses his own imagination. We will see that his process in the second section is different, but no less methodical.

Modification of Irascibility and Patient Charity (RM 3.24–38)

The section that we now embark upon (RM 3.24–38) will be noticeably longer than the preceding. While the former called to mind the positive aspect of the scene of the Judgment (Mt 25:36), the framework now becomes the part of the Sermon on the Mount (Mt 5:20–48) that systematically contrasts the newness of Christ with the imperfect precepts of the ancient law.[63] It is possible that the last of the "charitable works" brought to the author's mind this passage from the Gospel.[64] In any case, he draws inspiration from it on several occasions in the new series that he begins, as demonstrated by the following table:

Matthew 5	RM 3
[22]Omnis qui irascitur fratri …	[24]Iram non perficere [25]Iracundiae tempus non reseruare
[33]Non periurabis … [34] … non iurare omnino ([37]Sit autem sermo uester est est, non non)	[32]non amare iurare, ne forte periuret ([33]Veritatem ex corde et ore proferre)
[39]Non resistere malo …	[34]Malum pro malo non reddere [35]Iniurias … factas patienter sufferre
[44]Diligite inimicos uestros … Benedicite maledicentibus uobis	[36]Inimicos plus quam amicos diligere [37]Maledicentes se … benedicere

The parallel progression of the two texts seems to indicate that the sequence of the *Ars* is drawn from the Gospel of Matthew. The two initial maxims on anger (RM 3.24–25) are undoubtedly taken from the *Passio Juliani*, but they remind the author of the condemnation leveled by Christ against this vice. Is anger not the first of the faults denounced by Christ in Matthew 5:22? Understandably, the second and third concepts of concupiscence and divorce (Mt 5:27–32) do not figure in the *Ars*, but the following three elements (swearing, vengeance, and hate) appear there in order.

In the space between anger and swearing, left vacant by the omission of sexual faults (RM 3.26–31), the *Ars* inserts a series of six maxims all concerning charity toward one's neighbor. More specifically, they aim at breaches of charity through lack of loyalty. The maxims on anger have suggested to the author other difficulties that exist in the area of fraternal relations. Moreover, while forbidding delayed anger, *iracundiae tempus non reseruare* already attacked a sort of prolonged grievance very close to "deceit" and "false peace." Therefore, there is close continuity between the maxims on anger, inspired by the Gospel via the *Passio*,

Chapter 4: The Treatise of the Master (RM 3–6)

and the six maxims on the charity of loyalty that the *Ars* adds to them. The two following maxims on taking oaths and speaking the truth (3.32–33), the first of which clearly calls to mind Matthew 5:34, are easily attached to these six added maxims: in both cases, it is a matter of loyalty. Thus, the *Ars* glides smoothly from "anger" to "taking oaths," that is to say, from the first to the fourth of the faults reproved by Christ in Matthew 5, before sequentially and uninterruptedly presenting the last two sections of the same passage.

Only the second of these sections is actually represented accurately by *inimicos diligere* (RM 3.36 = Mt 5:44). One finds only an echo of *non resistere malo* (Mt 5:39) in *Malum pro malo non reddere*, a maxim that reproduces 1 Peter 3:9 literally. This interruption of the Sermon on the Mount, which provides the general inspiration, and provision of an exact formula from another source is reminiscent of the case of *Iram non perficere* encountered above. The rest of the verse from 1 Peter will later be combined (RM 3.37) with the exhortation from the Sermon on the Mount to "bless those who curse you."[65] Thus, the Epistle of Peter twice supersedes the Gospel text. The first time it is substituted for it; the second time it completes it:

Matthew 5 (Luke 6)	RM 3	1 Peter 3
([39]Non resistere malo)	[34]Malum pro malo non reddere	[9a]Non reddentes malum pro malo
[44]Diligite inimicos uestros	[36]Inimicos … diligere	
Benedicite maledicentibus uobis	[37]Maledicentes se … non remaledicere, sed magis benedicere	[9b]nec maledictum pro maledicto, sed e contrario benedicentes

But in the second case, a new interruption occurs because "to bless those who curse" is reminiscent of a phrase from Saint Paul, which will supply the next maxim of the *Ars*.[66]

Matthew 5 (Luke 6)	RM 3	1 Corinthians 4
[44]Benedicite maledicentibus uobis	[37]Maledicentes se … benedicere	[12]Maledicimur et benedicimus
	[38]Persecutionem pro iustitia sustinere	persecutionem patimur et sustinemus

When one notices that through its Pauline verse this last maxim of the *Ars* incorporates a reminiscence of Matthew 5:10,[67] a flood of examples enables one to immediately grasp the process of the Master. From one recollection to the next, he spontaneously links or blends different *testimonia* on bearing with and loving one's enemies. It is striking that the last word in this group belongs to the Sermon on the Mount. Through the text of Paul the series returns to and concludes with Matthew 5: this final characteristic confirms the unity of the long series inaugurated by *Iram non perficere* (RM 3.24–38).

Thus far our analysis has focused solely on the scriptural sources of this section. But its results acquire their full meaning only when connected with some previous observations from the *Passio*. One will remember that it provides the *Ars* with its two initial maxims on anger (RM 3.24–25), the maxim *Malum pro malo non reddere* (RM 3.34), and perhaps the idea for the next. But these four articles are consecutive and in a different order in the *Passio*. It is the Master who joins the two maxims on anger and connects *Malum pro malo non reddere* with the maxim on patience, these last two being separated from the first two by a long series of additions. It is also he whose construction of the entire section is inspired by the Sermon on the Mount. While the maxims of the *Passio* on anger provide a beginning that corresponds with Matthew 5:22, the maxims on bearing wrongs occur later, in conjunction with Matthew 5:39. Thus, the original core of the *Passio* is divided into two passages, each connected to a paragraph from Matthew 5. Scripture replaces the *carmen* as the organizing principle of the text.

Before leaving this series, it is significant to note that two restrictive qualifications are imposed on the sublime doctrine of the Sermon on the Mount. First, the maxims on anger (3.24–25) only forbid acting under its impulse (*perficere*) or anticipating a time to express it (*tempus reservare*). They do not condemn irritation that seethes in the soul but is not outwardly expressed. To appreciate the significance of this nuance, we must compare the Master's maxims with those of Jerome that probably inspired them. Jerome expressed this idea at least twice, and by means of the same formula: anger is inevitable, but the Christian can master it and put a stop to it:

Irasci hominis est, et iram non perficere christiani.[68]
Irasci hominis est, et finem iracundiae imponere christiani.[69]

Neither the *Ars* nor the *Passio* has retained this first part of the sentences of Jerome. However, it is this beginning that gives the second part its true importance. Jerome implicitly recognized that the condemnation

Christ leveled against all anger[70] required a distinction: given that anger is a natural emotion, it is only its outward manifestation and prolongation that are forbidden. It seems that the *Passio* and the *Ars* have appropriated this moderate doctrine, each specifying the two faults that are to be avoided in terms that are particularly reminiscent of those of Jerome.[71]

Still, this first qualification does not go as far as the second. This latter aims to prohibit taking oaths. In Matthew 5:34, Christ declares, "*Ego dico uobis non jurare omnino.*" In the *Ars,* the prohibition loses its absolute character: "*Non amare iurare, ne forte periuret.*" While the Master cannot claim to follow the *Passio Juliani* this time, it is not on his own authority that he mitigates the Gospel rule by glossing *amare*. Previously, Ambrose and Augustine had explained that the intention of Christ was only to forbid the frequent or habitual swearing of oaths by which one inevitably falls into perjury.[72] Based on the example of Saint Paul, whose letters contain several oaths, Augustine wrote: *intelligendum est illud quod positum est omnino ad hoc positum ut quantum in te est non affectes, non ames, non quasi pro bono cum aliqua delectatione appetas iusiurandum* (*De mendacio* 28). One will recognize the *non amare* of the Master in this exegesis. Consequently, this restrictive qualification contains nothing surprising. The maxim of the *Ars* conforms wholly with the teaching of the two great Latin Doctors.

Six Faults to Avoid (RM 3.39–44)

The *Ars* reaches its midpoint at the conclusion of the section on which we have just commented. Throughout the entire first half, it has been easy to distinguish the Master's central theme. The Gospel, alone or with the *Passio Juliani*, has constantly served as our guide. Because of this, a certain continuity is observed from one section to the next. In contrast, the small section that we now begin (RM 3.39–44) presents us with a blatant interruption. These six brief negative maxims, at first glance new and uniform, have no apparent connection to what precedes or follows them.

However, they share a common structural trait with the sequences that we have just analyzed. Here as before, the first maxims of the series come from a specific passage of the New Testament, while those that follow are inspired by various scriptural texts or the imagination of the author. The key passage of Scripture is Titus 1:7, which *non esse superbum* and *nonuinolentum* are drawn from. Moreover, it is significant that, in the text of Paul, these two faults to be avoided are separated by *non iracundum*. The fact that the *Ars* omits anger here is probably explained by the condemnation already leveled against this vice in the previous section. It would suggest that when the Master writes RM 3.39–44, he is cognizant of the first half of the *Ars* and avoids repeating it.[73]

The Pauline list from Titus 1:7 contains five faults to avoid. The *Ars* retains only the first and the third faults, but adds four others, such that the new list is slightly longer. *Non multum edacem*, the first fault added, clearly completes *non uinolentum*. From food, one then passes to sleep, by virtue of a connection well known to the Master.[74] In its turn, sleep calls to mind idleness (cf. RM 1.62–65; 69.7), and perhaps it is not unrelated to the murmuring that closes the series (cf. RM 57.14–16). These four additional vices pertain more specifically to the readers of the Master than do the impulse to strike a neighbor (*non percussorem*) and the love of money (*non turpis lucri cupidum*) that Paul prohibits to the bishop. The author of the *Ars* lets himself be carried away by a spontaneous play of associations evoked by the Pauline *non uinolentum* that brings to mind some well-known faults of cenobites.

Five Theological Maxims (RM 3.45–49)

The short series of faults to be avoided constitutes a sort of erratic block between the first and second parts of the *Ars*. All things considered, the biblical character of its beginning situates it with the first part. The second part, which we now begin, does not retain this structural trait that has thus far been constant. Henceforth, biblical passages will be rarer and more oblique. Most importantly, they will no longer control and structure the sequences. This is noticeable as soon as one approaches the first group of this second part: neither *Spem suam Deo conmittere*[75] nor the maxims that follow have specific scriptural origins. Thoughts and formulas will consequently take a more personal and reflective turn.

The five maxims in this first group are distinguished by their loftiness and doctrinal implications. The attitude of humble dependence on God that they attempt to describe rests on a simple but profound theology. The very fact that God is named four times here is itself worth mentioning. We must go back to the beginning of the *Ars* or, if one desires, to two symmetrical references to Christ (RM 3.10, 23), to be explicitly in the presence of God. The first part of the *Ars* is much more interested in one's manner of relating with others than in one's attitude toward the Lord. At present, and for a long time, the situation is completely reversed: the question of the neighbor does not return until the last ten maxims of the *Ars*;[76] until then, one remains in constant dialogue with the Creator.

Hope is the first movement required toward God.[77] *Spem suam Deo conmittere.... Substantiam suam a Deo sperare.* The inclusion is perfect, clearly indicating the predominant tone of the group. It is a matter of placing one's confidence in God rather than oneself. This theological hope is alternately affirmed in the spiritual and temporal domains. While 3.46–47 clearly aims at the first, and 3.49 at the second, it is difficult to say which 3.45 and 3.48 pertain to, as their very general formulas seem to include both. In fact, hope can have eternal rewards,[78] temporal goods (RM 3.49; 11.99), or even grace (RM 14.57 and 66; 15.45) as its object in RM. "Desires" can likewise be related to what is passing[79] or lasts eternally,[80] and while *desiderium* is never paired with grace, the expression *a Deo perfici* is reminiscent of the *uelle adiacet nobis, perficere autem tuum est* that the penitential rite, paraphrasing Romans 7:18, puts on the lips of the repentant excommunicant (RM 14.55). Is this contrast between *uelle* and *perficere* not similar to that established here between *desideria* and *perfici*? Does it not invite us to recognize in this last the interaction of human freedom with divine grace? One could offer prayer[81] here to obtain the assistance of grace, as one does in other passages of the Rule.[82] Thus, like the two that precede it, this maxim is actually situated in the spiritual domain, from which it draws a practical conclusion before shifting to material realities in the following maxim.

If this interpretation of 3.48 can be regarded as probable, it remains difficult to specify the thrust of 3.45. Moreover, it would be a mistake to overemphasize the contrast between temporal and eternal hope since the Master himself is careful to unite them: Does he not say that by providing the necessary things for the present life, Providence grants a "pledge of future promises?"[83] There is an obvious link between hope in grace and eschatological hope. Thus the three forms of hope are closely joined. Those who have put themselves at the service of God simultaneously anticipate earthly food, the assistance of grace, and eternal life from him. Eternal life is the supreme good, prefigured by temporal goods and obtainable with the help of grace.

Thus, understood in its broad sense, the maxim on hope fittingly opens the entire group. On the other hand, it may also link it with the six faults to be avoided found at the end of the preceding group, which is to say to the maxims on constancy in persecution (RM 3.37–38). In fact, the fourth degree of humility will link "the hope assured from divine recompense" with the Pauline attitude toward persecutors and those who curse.[84] It is possible that this very natural tie led the author of the *Ars* to proceed from the maxims on patience to one on hope. The group of faults to be avoided is so poorly situated in its context that it would not be surprising if it was interpolated and broke up an original sequence.[85] However, adopting this hypothesis requires that one interprets *spem suam Deo conmittere* in the same way as *securi de spe retributionis diuinae* (RM 10.56), that is to say, understanding it principally, if not exclusively, as eschatological hope.

This is not the place to go into depth on the doctrine of the two correlative maxims on the good and evil that one sees in oneself (RM 3.46–47). Some categorical remarks that will enable us to contextualize them will have to suffice. We have already mentioned the quadruple repetition of the word *Deo* (God) in the five maxims. We note now that, in three of four instances, it is more precisely *a Deo* that is used: *a Deo factum, a Deo perfici, a Deo sperare*. In each, divine intervention is juxtaposed with human action, whether it is a matter of previously accomplished works, desires for perfection, or work to earn a living. Considering these shared traits, one is tempted to regard the maxim *Bonorum ... extimet* as the true beginning of the group, of which *Spem suam Deo conmittere* would be only the introduction, forming a link with what precedes it.[86] However, the maxims *Bonorum ... extimet* and *Malum ... inputare* are clearly separated from the others by the fact that they consider the past, not the future, while *Spem suam Deo conmittere* is, in this regard, fully consonant with *Desideria sua a Deo perfici optare* and *Substantiam suam ... a Deo sperare*. In sum, the guiding principle of this group seems to be the recognition of the place due to God in all dimensions of human destiny: moral and material life, time and eternity, the past and future.[87] It is only evil actions that can in no way be attributed to God.

The Last Things and Reformed Conduct (RM 3.50–67)

The following section (RM 3.50–67) ties in easily with what we have just examined. The theme of hope, at least under the general form that it assumes in 3.45, necessarily evokes consideration of the last things. The examination of our good and evil deeds (3.46–47) anticipates the "day of judgment." Even if the "desires" of 3.48 have as their immediate end a faithful life here below, they naturally lead to "eternal life."

But this general and obvious relationship becomes much clearer if one considers the last of the five theological maxims (RM 3.49). It asks one to depend as much or more on God for one's livelihood as on the work of one's hands. This idea returns frequently in RM and each time it is closely associated with concern for the kingdom of God and the last things. If the brothers must rely on the Lord to sustain them, it is because earthly cares and manual labor must never prevent them from thinking about the afterlife. In contrast with seculars, who are totally occupied with work in order to obtain food, clothing, and footwear, the servants of God are to be less concerned with things here below

Chapter 4: The Treatise of the Master (RM 3–6)

than with things eternal, that is to say with the rewards of eternal life and the punishments of hell (RM 82.4–10). "Therefore, in this life, our minds are unceasingly occupied with these heavenly concerns, with the desire for these goods, and the fear of these evils, as if we were already there below" (RM 82.11). Nothing prevents us from attending to these thoughts since the Lord provides all that is necessary (RM 82.16. Cf. 16.1–26). This double attitude of eschatological attentiveness and abandonment to Providence prohibits the use of brothers to work the farms (RM 86.3–16) and requires that the manual labor of the deans be reduced.[88] "Relying on *hope*, we believe that when *our own hands* have not managed to provide for all of our needs, the Lord *God* will do so."[89]

One will recognize in this phrase all the elements of the maxim from 3.49. Consequently, its goal becomes obvious: by encouraging reliance on Providence more than manual labor, the Master intends to bring about *Sursum corda* (cf. RM 86.15). Souls must be free from temporal concerns in order to attend solely to the kingdom of God and his justice, in other words, to eschatological consequences and the accomplishment of the will of God here below. This, in fact, will be the object of the two series of precepts that immediately follow: first, the consideration of the last things (3.50–53), then, under the gaze of God, vigilance in the actions of this present life (3.54–60).

The group of "theological maxims" is therefore closely tied to the group that follows, especially by its last maxim. Hope in God and awareness of his interior action already prepares us to begin correcting our conduct in light of eternity. Confidence in the temporal assistance of Providence removes the last obstacle that could prevent us from focusing on this one necessity.

Noting this intimate connection between the two groups, one may be tempted to place only a secondary caesura between them. Nevertheless, the second is clearly detached from the first, both by its characteristics of content and form and by its parallelism with the first three degrees of humility (RM 10.10–51). This parallelism will be studied in detail in our commentary on RM 10. For the moment, it suffices to say that, in virtue of this fact, RM 3.50–67 appears to be a clearly separate whole from both the group that precedes it and that which follows.

The Four Maxims on Reading and Prayer (RM 3.61–64)

Moreover, comparison with *De humilitate* shows that RM 3.50–67 is not perfectly uniform, but contains an interpolation: the set of maxims on reading, prayer, confession of sins, and amendment (RM 3.61–64). Not only are these four maxims absent from the first degree of humility, their positive form also contrasts with the negative series of maxims that they interrupt. It is clear that *desideria carnis non perficere* (3.65) is in the same vein as *Risum multum aut excussum non amare* and the two preceding maxims (3.58–60). Both warn against evil instincts or actions. In contrast, the four interpolated maxims recommend laudable practices. The aim here is completely different, even if two of these practices, confession and amendment, can be linked with the evil actions and desires condemned in the surrounding text.

To say that these four maxims are interpolated is simply to acknowledge that they break a certain sequence, without going so far as to claim that they are from a different author. Perhaps the reason for their insertion in such a context is to be sought in the role played by reading as an antidote to unprofitable speech. The Master wishes that reading take place as often as possible during work, "so that by closing the mouth to evil words, and listening to and speaking good words, we may never sin" (RM 50.28–33). The fact that RM 3.61 recommends *listening* to reading, not doing it oneself, agrees with the hypothesis that we propose. The maxim is addressed[90] in particular to brothers who have to listen to one of their own read while they work.[91] Let them listen gladly!

If such is perhaps the relationship that joins the maxim on reading to those on speech and laughter, it must be recognized that *Orationi frequenter incumbere* suggests something else. In fact, the Master never alludes to prayer frequently interrupting reading or manual labor.[92] On the other hand, the *lectio-oratio* pair is standard in early Christian literature, and the two maxims of RM 3.61–62 present a striking similarity with certain formulas of Jerome.[93] Therefore, it seems that the *Ars* reproduces some traditional recommendations here, of which at least the second has no specific application in the observance regulated by the Master.

While *Orationi frequenter incumbere* is not connected with the legislative part of the Rule, the idea of frequent and even "constant" prayer is not completely absent from RM. The commentary on the last two petitions of the *Pater* speaks of the *crebris gemitibus*, with which one must entreat the Lord (Thp 69), and goes so far as to command: *incessanter est praecandum ad Dominum* (Thp 71), *rogantes incessanter Dominum* (Thp 79). This connection between *Ars* and *Thema* is confirmed in the following maxim (3.63), where it is a matter of "groans", as in the commentary on the sixth petition,[94] while the "daily confession of faults in prayer" undoubtedly calls to mind the fifth petition.[95] These parallels are not surprising, given that the relationship between the *Ars* and the *Thema* is also an established fact.[96] But it is quite significant that this relationship is affirmed here in a little group of maxims that are certainly

Chapter 4: The Treatise of the Master (RM 3–6)

out of context. In fact, the *Thema* itself is unquestionably a borrowed passage. The maxims that we are studying could originate from the same source, and this outside origin would explain their artificial insertion in the series that parallels the degrees of humility, which seem to be, at least in part, the composition of the Master.[97]

We will conclude by noting some traits that link the last two maxims with the ritual of reconciliation. The confession of faults "with tears" is prescribed for repentant excommunicants, and they must also promise to improve in the future.[98] In this last case, the similarity of expression with our maxims is particularly striking. It is also important to note that the penitential ritual is probably also inspired by an ecclesiastical source.[99] Thus the similarities in form that we observe between the prescriptions of RM 14 and the maxims could be explained by the fact that both belong to the same stratum of texts of non-monastic origin, the latter being also the source of the *Thema*.[100]

The Last Maxims (RM 3.68–77)

The conclusion of the *Ars Sancta* holds several surprises for us. First, one unexpectedly finds the *Passio Juliani*. Abandoned since 3.34–35, this source resumes here at the same point where it left off. However, the maxim of 3.68, which is distinguished from the rest by its length,[101] reproduces only the beginning of a considerably longer development in the *Passio*. Although one cannot find the next maxim (3.69) in and of itself in the source, it seems to have been at least inspired by it.[102] In the *Passio* it is a matter of the "masters" of the perfect life, who must do what they say.[103] In the *Ars*, the formula calls to mind the treatise on the abbot.[104] It would be natural for the "masters" of the *Passio* to remind the Master of the monastic "master," the abbot.

The two maxims from 3.68–69 are not sequential in the *Passio*. Brought together, they both insist on authentic conduct, which they contrast with a premature reputation or words unaccompanied by deeds. If it is really the abbot who is aimed at in the second case, it may be that these maxims are juxtaposed with what immediately precedes them: *Oboedientiam ad monitionem abbatis parare* (3.67) is addressed to inferiors; immediately afterwards, one turns to the abbot to remind him of his own duties. But it is also possible that the author continues to think of the inferiors. It is all religious that are addressed in the only passage of RM that picks up on the thought of 3.68.[105] The words *praecepta factis implere* from 3.69 are found very frequently in the Rule, and notably in the conclusion of the *Ars* (RM 3.83) that concerns all members of the community.

Should the seven precepts that follow (3.70–76) be considered as a series of *praecepta Dei* intended to illustrate 3.69? In fact, several of them have a rather clear scriptural parallel. This return to Scripture following the return to the *Passio* merits our attention. It confirms that, in this finale, the *Ars* rediscovers the characteristics of its first part. The return to the former becomes even more apparent if one considers the principal theme of these last *praecepta*. Apart from *Castitatem amare*, which has the appearance of an erratic block,[106] they all concern fraternal relations, and more specifically the sins of the irascible: hatred, jealousy, envy, disputes, dissension, and insubordination.[107] This theme hardly differs from that developed by maxims 3.24–38. Its very form links *Inuidiam non exercere* (3.73) with *Iram non perficere* (3.24). This last group appears to be a supplement to the first part, obtained through recourse to new scriptural sources.

Following this passage dedicated to fraternal relations, the last maxim (3.77) returns to hope in God. Such a conclusion establishes a link not only with the five maxims that occupy the middle of the *Ars*,[108] but also with the entire first maxim on faith and the love of God (3.1). The *Ars Sancta* begins and ends with actions relating to God. Certainly, it is natural that the "first commandment" opens such a list. On the other hand, the idea of ending on a note of theological hope seems rather subjective. One will notice that the prayer of the excommunicated ends in the same manner: *quod in nobis desperatio inpossibile putat, tua gratia possibile indicat*.[109] In light of this parallel, it seems that the last maxim of the *Ars* points especially to the assistance of grace.

Overview: Themes and Sources

Having come to the end of the *Ars*, we can now take a look at it as a whole. In examining its themes, the agenda can be divided quite easily into duties toward God, neighbor, and self. Those toward God appear only at the beginning, middle, and end,[110] where, in very general terms, one is encouraged to believe, love and especially to trust him (3.45–49 and 77). Duties toward neighbor occupy almost the entire first part (3.2–38) but only a few maxims toward the end of the second (3.71–76). Duties toward self are almost all grouped around some central maxims on hope[111] at the end of the first part (3.39–44) and the beginning of the second (3.50–69), of which they fill the largest part. Thus, fraternal relations dominate the first half and personal ascesis the second. Duties toward others and self often depend on the opening precepts relating to God or Christ. This progression is particularly clear in the second part where it recommends hope in divine assistance (3.45–49) before requiring ascetic effort (3.50–67).

Chapter 4: The Treatise of the Master (RM 3–6)

As regards sources, the *Ars* takes Scripture as its point of departure (3.1–9). The Golden Rule of the Gospels, introduced by an *Et* of conclusion,[112] closes this first purely biblical section. After Scripture, the Master's greatest inspiration comes from the *Passio*, but he supplements its propositions: first with maxims taken directly from Scripture, then with some more or less original directives. Recall that Matthew 25 and Matthew 5 alternate as the basis of the series on fraternal charity (3.10–38). This method of development from Scripture also shapes the list of faults to be avoided (3.39–44). In contrast, the second part follows a more logical order in which biblical allusions are less numerous and, in particular, less determinant in the composition of the sequences (3.50–67). However, the *Passio* and Scripture regain their significance toward the end of the *Ars* (3.68–76).

The List Related to the Thema *and the* Passio *of Julian*

The question of sources is relatively simple if one limits oneself to Scripture and the *Passio*. It is especially complex if one takes into account the data suggesting that the author uses a list similar to the *Thema* and other passages of non-monastic origin that contain the Golden Rule. It will be helpful to present this data here in a table:

3.1–8	the Two Commandments and the Ten Commandments (cf. Athanasius)
3.9	the Golden Rule (cf. Thp 59)
3.30	not to deceive (cf. Ths 29)
3.33	to speak the truth from one's heart (cf. Ths 22)
3.46	God accomplishes the good in us (cf. Ths 25–26; 2.51)
3.48	*optare*, to pray (cf. Thp 16 and 20)
3.48	God "perfects" our desires (cf. 14.53)
3.53–54	anticipation of death and vigilance in life's actions (cf. Thp 36)
3.56	exegesis of Psalm 136:9 (cf. Ths 24; 8.23)
3.62	prayer with tears (cf. 14.2)
3.62–63	frequent prayer and confession with groans (cf. Thp 57–79)
3.63	amendment of evil deeds (cf. Ths 36; 14.24–25)
3.77	not to lose hope in God (cf. 14.66)
3.79–82	reward for accomplishment of the divine will (cf. Thp 55–56)

It is clear that almost all of the parts of the *Ars* present some parallel with the *Thema*. Therefore, the list similar to the *Thema* seems to have been used from beginning to end of RM 3, while the areas influenced by the *Passio* are more limited.

The Original List in the Second Part

It is interesting to compare this hypothesis of a preexisting list with the facts demonstrated by our study of the second part. One recalls that the long pericope corresponding to *De humilitate* (3.50–67) contains four maxims that are clearly "interpolated" (3.61–64). Yet, this interpolation is no less rich in parallels with the *Thema* than the surrounding pericope. From this point of view, the "interpolation" appears at first glance consistent with its context. However, one will note that the last parallel of the surrounding pericope with the *Thema* appears in 3.56, that is to say, in the maxim prescribing the dashing of evil thoughts against Christ. The subsequent maxims, which treat speech (3.57–60) and the desires of the flesh and self-will (3.65–66), show no indications of belonging to the original list. Yet it is precisely these that make up the very conspicuous negative series that the "interpolation" clearly interrupts.

One sees here how the analysis of sources, without contradicting that of form, requires adding to and nuancing the results. When one considers only the text of the Master, section 3.50–67, by virtue of its parallelism with *De humilitate*, appears as a uniform whole that a group from an extraneous source (3.61–64) divided. But the hypothesis of a source of the *Ars* similar to the *Thema* leads one to link this group (3.61–64) with the first part of the section (3.50–56), while its second part (3.57–60 and 65–67) proves different from both. By combining the results of these two inquiries, the structure of this part can be represented as follows:

Original List	Additions
3.45–49: hope in divine assistance	
3.50–56: consideration of the last things and vigilance in thought and deed	
	3.57–60: vigilance in speech;[113] condemnation of chattering and laughter
3.61–64: reading, prayer, confession of faults, amendment	
	3.65–67: condemnation of desires of the flesh and self-will; obedience to the abbot

The insertion of maxims on speech after one on thoughts is self-evident, the thoughts-speech sequence being common in RM.[114] On the other hand, one cannot immediately see why the maxims on desires and the will would not have been put after those on speech and laughter, rather than later. Perhaps we are dealing with an unconscious phenomenon of compilation: the addition, first written in the margin, would have been inserted into the text in two separate sections, following the place it occupied alongside the text.[115] As we have seen,[116] it could also be that the connection between reading and silence suggested joining 3.61–64 with 3.57–60.

The Conclusion of the Ars *(RM 3.78–83)*

The transition from the *Ars Sancta* to the eschatological reward is made by means of a surprisingly awkward and redundant phrase. The words *ars ... cum fuerit a nobis ... Domino Deo ... in die iudicii* are repeated with rare clumsiness, while a play of adverbial and participial assonances reinforces the impression of delay.

Although acknowledging these weaknesses, one must not exaggerate the flaws of construction. The verb *adsignauerit* (3.80), which one is tempted to take as a simple active equivalent of *fuerit reconsignata* (3.81),[117] probably means something else. One must think back to the beginning of the *Ars* (2.51) to understand it. It says there that the abbot must "attribute to the Lord (*adsignans Domino*) the ministry of the art," since "all we accomplish that is holy is achieved by the grace of the Lord." It seems that the same idea inspires the phrase *cum unusquisque in die iudicii Domino Deo factorum suorum operam adsignauerit* (3.80). On the day of judgment, not only the abbot, but also each of us ought to be able to attribute to the Lord the actions that he (the Lord) will have accomplished. One recognizes a concept of judgment here that is introduced elsewhere in the Rule (RM 1.91–92): God the judge recognizes as his own and rewards the works that he himself accomplishes, whether by commanding them or giving the strength to accomplish them. Thus, those who have continually exercised the art day and night (3.79) will proclaim on the last day that all their deeds proceed from and belong to the Lord (3.80).

This first clause is not simply identical to the following, where the images and idea are somewhat modified: there the *ars* appears as a command issued by God, which the individual carries out in full and offers to God without fault. The two presentations complement one another: all of the individual's acts must be in accord with God; all divine commands must be accomplished by the individual.

A Critical Study of the Rule of Benedict: Volume 2

The Description of Paradise (RM 3.84–94)

The eschatological finale of the chapter, inspired by the *Visio Pauli*, is closely related to a passage from the homily addressed to the postulant at the end of the Rule (RM 90.19–27). The two passages are in particular accord in how they utilize a phrase from the *Passio Sebastiani* cited in the eschatological description that ends RM 10.[118] In addition, immediately after this, RM 3, by itself this time, borrows from RM 10 another phrase from the same *Passio* (cf. RM 3.90 and 10.106). The following table indicates these parallels:

RM 3	RM 90	RM 10 (*Pass. Seb.* 13)
84	20	
85	19	
86	22	
87	23	
88	24	
89	25	112–114
90		106
92	17	
(94)	(27)	

Few indicators lead one to believe that the redaction of RM 90 is earlier than that of RM 3.[119] It seems that the latter is only indirectly dependent on RM 10.112–114. However, it is certain that it depends directly on RM 10.106.

These two particular excerpts are of less importance for us than the general similarity of RM 3 with RM 10. In both, the moral program concludes with a picturesque view of eternal life. The *Ars Sancta*, like the ladder of humility, leads straight to heaven. The length of each finale corresponds to that of the body of the treatise: shorter in RM 3, longer in RM 10. Whether or not it depends on RM 90, the description of RM 3 is, in any event, more original than that of RM 10, which is copied almost entirely from the *Passio Sebastiani*. The personal mark of the Master is recognized in the effort to organize the scene. Instead of piling up little juxtaposed positive and negative comments haphazardly, as does the *Passio Sebastiani*, the Master proceeds with a certain method: resplendent earth, rivers, banks of the river planted with trees, the fruits of these trees, organs set on the banks, voices that join with the organs, and finally the resplendence of the city where the Alleluia resounds, all linked rather closely with the help of a great many repeated words and connecting relative pronouns. Thus, one passes from one source to another without warning: *Visio Pauli, Passio Sebastiani,* Revelation of Saint John, and the Book of Tobit. The paradise that rewards the *Ars* is as eclectic as the *Ars* itself.

III. The Additions (RM 4–6)

The List of Virtues (RM 4)

The last chapters of the *Ars* have already been briefly considered in relationship to the origin of the treatise and the witness of E*.[120] We will now examine them more closely.

The first striking fact is that just as RM 3 began with a series of commandments from the Gospels, RM 4 begins with a series of New Testament virtues. Both combine elements taken from various lists: in the first, the two great commandments are followed by excerpts from the Ten Commandments and the Golden Rule; in the latter, the three theological virtues are linked with the fruits of the Spirit.

However, RM 4 presents a unique phenomenon. The list of the fruits of the Spirit does not unfold all in one piece, but is interrupted.[121] Three virtues appear after *mansuetudo* (4.2) that one searches in vain to find in Galatians 5:22–23, but that make up the great trilogy familiar to every reader of RB and RM: humility, obedience, and silence. The comment *prae omnibus* that follows these virtues should probably be referred back to them.[122] It seems that the words *humilitas oboedientia taciturnitas prae omnibus* are a marginal gloss inserted into the text. Finding a list of scriptural virtues in which the trilogy of monastic virtues was lacking, the editor saw fit to add them, with the comment *prae omnibus* to highlight their importance.[123] It may also be that the first monastic virtue was brought to mind by the fourth fruit of the Spirit: *humilitas* and *mansuetudo* follow one another in another passage of Saint Paul.[124]

While it is quite easy to discern the meaning of the first *prae omnibus* (4.4), at first glance it is difficult to see what the second refers to (4.7). The virtues that precede it and that it seems to emphasize are not highlighted at all in the rest of the Rule. Perhaps it is a matter of a simple duplicate of the first *prae omnibus*. If these words were first written in the margin, after *humilitas oboedientia taciturnitas*, they could have then been inserted into the text twice: correctly the first time (4.4) and erroneously the second (4.7).[125] However, *misericordia* is a virtue of such importance in the Bible that one could understand why an editor would have endowed it with this comment. Moreover, one will note that *misericordia* comes immediately after the last fruits of the Spirit, at the beginning of a series of eleven virtues that do not seem to be drawn from any scriptural list. Perhaps the words *prae omnibus* are meant to insist on the primacy of mercy in this series.

Perseuerantia usque ad finem occupies a very natural place at the other end. This last *ferramentum* is reminiscent of the end of the commentary on the Psalms: *usque ad mortem ... perseuerantes* (Ths 46). It also announces the last prescription of the entire treatise: *perseuerando* (RM 6.2). Thus, perseverance is presented first as a "spiritual tool," then as the "means of employing the spiritual tools."[126] The second image harmonizes poorly with the first, but the repetition clearly marks the insistence of the redactor on this major point: it is the one who perseveres to the end that will be saved (Mt 10:22. Cf. RM 10.53).

The List of Vices (RM 5)

While RM 3 and 4 each begin with a scriptural series, RM 5 opens with three vices that are contrary to the "monastic virtues": *primo superbia, deinde inoboedientia, multiloquium.* Therefore, more clearly than the preceding chapters, it foreshadows the three great treatises that will fill chapters seven to ten. Moreover, it then uses the same scriptural source as RM 4: the passage of Galatians where, with the fruits of the spirit, Paul lists the "works of the flesh" (Gal 5:19–21).

E* puts this little chapter before RM 7, and it may well have originally occupied this intermediary place between the *Ars* and the three great treatises.[127] Consequently, according to E*, it possessed a title that granted it autonomy, while tying it to the artistic metaphor. In contrast, chapters four and six originally formed a single continuous development after RM 3. It is probably the insertion of chapter 5 in its current place that led to the establishment of RM 4 and 6 as distinct chapters and the insertion of their titles. In fact, the presence of a finalized chapter with a title between the list of "tools" and the definition of the "workshop" suggested giving the same chapter form to these two passages, especially the second.[128] In creating the two new titles, the editor also made use of the isolated expression *ars diuina*, as opposed to *ars sancta*, which was his usual expression until now. This detail clearly separates the secondary titles (4.T and 6.T) from the earliest layer of the *Ars*.

Although RM 5 was introduced into the *Ars* later, the hand that wrote its introduction and conclusion seems to be the same as the one responsible for the notes on grace in RM 3. The expression *in nobis* (5.1) calls to mind 2.51 and 3.46.[129] The last phrase repeats the teachings and terminology of 3.46–47: the vices are not from God but are the work of the devil. These connections seem to indicate that in content, RM 5 belongs to the earliest layer, what we have called the "original list."

On the other hand, one will notice that the final evocation of the "day of judgment" and "hell of eternal fire" is clearly in the style of the conclusion of the first chapter (1.91–92), whose positive elements are reminiscent of the finale of the *Ars*.[130] The expression *lima iustitiae* in the title probably stems from the *Passio Juliani*.[131] Finally, one of the vices listed here is the *risus multus uel excussus* already condemned by the *Ars Sancta* in one of its seemingly later articles (RM 3.60. Cf. 92.24). Such indicators suggests that, like RM 3 and 4, RM 5 is not homogenous but a work that was gradually added to.

The Workshop and Instructions for Using the Tools (RM 6)

As brief as it is, the last chapter of our treatise contains two parts. Following the title, it first describes the workshop, then the work, or, we could say, the instructions for using the spiritual tools. The single sentence of the chapter is actually divided into two clauses. The main clause, very clear, declares that the workshop is the monastery, while a rather awkward relative seems intended to define the *operatio* referenced in the title.

This second clause is not only grammatically obscure and difficult to interpret, but it also contains the expression *diuinae artis* that, as we have seen, characterizes the titles added to chapters four and six. Moreover, the tools are not called *ferramenta spiritalia*, as everywhere else,[132] but *ferramenta cordis*, evidently to introduce the additional indication *in corporis clusura reposita*. The latter, which calls to mind both RM 8.22 and RM 17.1–4, disrupts the phrase by introducing a second "place": after *in qua (officina)*, one now has *in corporis clusura*. The workshop that is the monastery is paired with a closed chamber that is the body. The two images fit together very poorly. The second has the effect of a superfluous detail or clumsy embellishment.[133]

Therefore, it seems that certain elements of RM 6.2 do not belong to the original redaction. The revision in which they are inserted is perhaps responsible for the anacoluthon that rends the phrase almost unintelligible. What then was the original content of this clause?[134] It is difficult to say. In any event, it must have been a simple appendix containing a definition of the workshop, not a second definition related to a distinct object, as the title would like to make one believe. Clearly an addition, this presentation fits poorly with the subordinate function of the clause, even in the current redaction. One will also note that there is no question of the *operatio ferramentorum* (6.T) in the announcement of 2.52. There, the little chapter is simply represented with the words *in monasterii officina*.[135] Thus, there is every reason to think that the division of RM 6 indicated by the title is a later creation. From a phrase that was originally limited to defining the workshop, the editor tried to develop a second definition containing "instructions for use" of the tools, consisting of the "practice of diligent vigilance" and "perseverance."

IV. The Geneses of the Treatise and the *Ars*

We will now attempt to bring together our results from this analysis of the *Ars Sancta*. They are of two sorts. First, the testimony of E* and internal criticism enabled us to reconstruct the genesis of the treatise as a whole. Then, the detailed study of the *Ars* proper (RM 3.1–77) revealed various series of maxims stemming from separate sources: an original list of non-monastic origin and the *Passio Juliani*, combined and added to by the redactor.

Is it possible to synthesize these two types of results into a general view that considers both the framework and the internal structure of RM 3.1–77? In other words, how are the different series of maxims situated in comparison with the developmental phases of the treatise?

We take up each of the terms to be compared. First, if one trusts the testimony of E*, it seems that the *Ars* is originally a simple continuation of *De abbate*. The transition of 2.51 introduces a series of directives for the personal conduct of the abbot. Unfortunately, these directives are not reproduced in E*, but replaced by a directory for the dean borrowed from Pachomius. However, five of the seven precepts added by E* from the Pachomian text echo, more or less clearly, maxims from the *Ars*. These are: *Nulli detrahat* (cf. 3.29), *Nulli malum pro malo reddat* (3.34), *Non murmuret* (3.44), *Non desinat orare* (3.52), and *Neminem oderit* (3.71).[136] After this series of maxims for the abbot, which serves as a conclusion to *De abbate*, it seems that the text that E* follows proceeds immediately to a separate chapter on vices to be avoided. This small chapter that will later become RM 5 is addressed to all of the brothers,[137] announces the three great treatises on humility, obedience and, silence,[138] and is immediately followed by *De oboedientia*. By virtue of its content, it is intended to introduce the following treatises, that is to say, the directory for the brothers. Nonetheless, it is given a title that connects it with the *Ars* and, thus, with *De abbate*.

Such is the earliest version that we can reconstruct. Later, the maxims for the personal conduct of the abbot are changed into a program for the entire community: therefore, the abbot must teach the *Ars* to

Chapter 4: The Treatise of the Master (RM 3–6)

the brothers (2.52). Next, it becomes a separate chapter from *De abbate* (3.T) and "we" appears in a sentence of the conclusion (3.78). Moreover, the *Ars* is now completed with two connected metaphors: the tools and the workshop. The list of the first and the definition of the second follow immediately after the *Ars Sancta* and form with it a single chapter.

The following stage is characterized by the insertion of two new elements: the eschatological reward, introduced by a long unwieldy sentence (3.79–95), and the list of vices (5.T–11). The latter, which previously existed outside of the *Ars*, is now incorporated into it. It follows very naturally after the list of tools, before the definition of the workshop. This image divides these two passages into distinct chapters.[139] In the small final chapter, the directive for how to use the tools is added to the definition of the workshop: with diligent vigilance and perseverance (6.T–2).

Thus, one can distinguish three stages in the development of the treatise: in its initial state, attested to by E*, the list of the *Ars* is a simple appendix to *De abbate*, preceding a chapter on the vices. Next, it becomes a separate chapter, where the *ferramenta* and *officina* are inserted into the conclusion. Finally, it is expanded with the *merces* and the chapter on the vices, while the *ferramenta* and the *officina* become separate chapters.

Alongside these stages, we place the different layers of the texts of the *Ars*. First, we distinguish a list of precepts of non-monastic origin, related to the *Thema*, consisting of 3.1–9, 45–57 and 61–64, then those drawn from the *Passio Juliani* (3.10, 22–25, 34–35, 68–69). The editor has made numerous additions to these two series, in particular 3.58–60, 65–67.

Certain elements from this third layer do not correspond to the initial state of the *Ars*. Thus, maxim 3.67 (*Oboedientiam ad monitionem abbatis parare*) is obviously addressed not to the abbot but to his subjects. Yet this maxim is joined to 3.58–60, 65–66. Thus, one can reasonably exclude this entire group from the initial stage. In fact, none of the five maxims reproduced more or less faithfully by E* belong to this little group.

To what layer of text should one attribute these five maxims attested to by E*? One of them belongs to the original list (3.62), another to the *Passio* (3.34). The last three are placed either in the section influenced by the *Passio* (3.29 and 71) or in the middle section of faults to be avoided (3.44). They may all three be the work of the editor, although one is not able to prove anything.[140] In any case, it seems certain that the initial version of the *Ars* contained the maxims that stem from the *Passio*. This conclusion is confirmed by 5.T, a text represented in E*, where *lima iustitiae*, the expression from the *Passio*, appears.

Therefore, in addition to the elements drawn from the original list, one can suggest that, from the beginning, the *Ars* contained items stemming from the *Passio* and, very probably, also a good number of maxims added by the editor. Perhaps the whole does not differ much from what we know from the complete manuscripts of RM and RB. The time has come to turn our focus toward this latter.

Chapter 4: The Treatise of the Master (RM 3–6)

Endnotes

1   See Adalbert de Vogüé, *La Règle du Maître*, Sources Chrétiennes 105–107 (Paris: Cerf, 1964–65), I.182.

2   The *uitia* are not mentioned in 2.52, 3.78, or 6.T–2. The announcement of the *ferramenta* from RB 4 in 3.78 and the backtracking of 3.95 suggest that the entire passage in between (3.79–94) is interpolated. Admittedly, we will see that the introductory phrase of this passage (3.79–84) is similar to the *Thema*, and seems by virtue of this fact to belong to the original list. For another explanation of the relationship of 3.79–84 to the *Thema*, see n. 22 below.

3   See *La Règle du Maître*, I.157, nn. 3 and 158.

4   For all this, see A. de Vogüé, "Nouveaux aperçus sur un Règle monastique du VIe s.," *Revue d'Ascétique et de Mystique (RAM)* 41(1965): 29, 36–40.

5   In 2.51, it is not necessary to suppose a transfer of responsibility, which would make the abbot the master of the works accomplished by his disciples (to correct the note *in loco*). The abbot is considered master here simply by virtue of his responsibility for his own conduct.

6   Cf. RM 2.11–15 and 26–29. See also 92.26–32, of which at least one phrase deserves to be cited: the future abbot will be the one who has perfectly carried out the teaching of his predecessor, *artem dominicam, quam ipse iam perfecte adinplet, Christi discipulis monstraturus* (92.27). See n. 13 below.

7   The *ferramenta* are also mentioned in 3.78.

8   Admittedly, the position that RM 5 occupies in E* could suggest that the redactor found this chapter somewhere else than in the *Ars Sancta*, but the title of the chapter, reproduced by E*, seems to clearly indicate that a relationship existed at that time between this list of vices and the *ars* metaphor.

9   On this difference of order, see Adalbert de Vogüé, *La Communauté et l'Abbé* (Brussels: Desclée des Brouwer, 1961), 213–214; ET: *Community and Abbot* (Kalamazoo, MI: Cistercian, 1979 [I] and 1988 [II]). If RM 4–5 reflects the original order of the three treatises here, it seems that the RM 5 + 7 sequence, given by E*, was already later. In fact, it supposes that *De humilitate* was placed after the other two treatises.

10 In RM 4.3, the three monastic virtues come only after a series of six scriptural virtues. In contrast, the three corresponding vices of RM 5.2 are at the top of the list, and the two first are emphasized with *primo … deinde*.

11 RM 3.67 (*Oboedientiam ad monitionem abbatis parare*) is the only item that is addressed to the disciples to the exclusion of the abbot.

12 *De oboedientia* contains some directives for the abbot: how many times to repeat orders and questions (RM 7.16–21).

13 Cf. RM 92.27–32. See n. 6 above.

14 See L. Traube, *Textgeschichte der Regula Sancti Benedicti* (Munich: 1898), 38, 93–94, 106–107.

15   PL 89.1047–1049. Although the text that Pirmin cites is that of Benedict, it oddly begins with the confession of Trinitarian faith from RM 3.1 (col. 1047a). On this subject, see Adalbert de Vogüé, "Scholies sur la Règle du Maître," *Revue d'Ascétique et de Mystique* 44 (1968): 149–150.

16   *Cap.* XXI, PL 105.197–198.

17   *Ep. Clem. I ad Jacob.*, PL 130.35–36. According to C. Butler, "The Instruments of Good Works," *Journal of Theological Studies (JTS)* 12 (1911): 265, Isidore would have found and reproduced a text of RB 4 separate from the rest of the Rule, like the *Instrumentum* of Agimund. That is not the case. Isidore borrowed directly from the Rule, as evidenced by the echoes of RB 5 and the Prologue that one finds a little later (PL 130.36d).

18   Ps.-Ambr., *Serm.* 24.11, PL 17.654b (RB 4.9, 15–16, 22–23, 25, 27, 41); Martin of Braga, *Op.* V.6, PL 72.42a (RB 4.42). See Butler (article cited in n. 17) 266–267. One finds RB 4.11–21 cited and commented upon on an isolated page of manuscript *Paris, BN n. acq. lat. 2389* (f° 17). See K. Hallinger, "Das Kommentarfragment zu Regula Benedicti IV aus der ersten Hälfte des 8. Jahrhunderts," *Wiener Studien* 82 (1969): 211–232.

19   RM 6.1–2. Cf. 4.10: *perseuerantia usque in finem*.

20   Compare Ths 13.22 and 3.26 (*dolum*); Ths 13 and 3.27 (*pacem*).

21   Compare Ths 22 and 3.33 (*ueritatem ... corde*); Ths 29 and 3.30 (*et non decipere*). In this last case, *qui iurat proximo suo* (Ps. 14:4) has been replaced by *promissum complere*, perhaps because of *Non amare iurare* (3.32).

22   Thp 55–56 and 3.79–82 (see n. 2 above). Note in both passages: *uoluntas, cum fuerit a nobis adimpleta, inculpabiliter, merces*. In the first case, the reward for work is daily bread, in the second, eternal happiness. However, one must take the concluding phrase of 90.55 into account. The latter, which clearly has a "monastic" character, strongly resembles Thp 55–56, but presents no particular parallels with 3.79–82. Thus the phrase of the *Thema* is independently related to each. It may be that it served as the common model, and that 3.79–82, like 90.55–56, was a compilation created by the Master himself, rather than a text that was borrowed from a preexisting document.

23   RM 3.48. We read *optare* (A*) rather than *adoptare* (P*), which does not give this sense (cf. n. 81 below).

24   Compare *ipsa in se bona non a se posse sed a Domino fieri existimantes, operantem in se magis Dominum magnificent* (Ths 25–26) and *Bonum aliquid in se cum uiderit, a Deo factum magis quam a se extimet* (3.46). The comparison suggests that it is good *deeds* that are referenced in the first part of 3.46 (*Bonum aliquid in se cum uiderit*), in spite of *in se*, which makes one think of good qualities. This is also demonstrated by 2.51, where the same play of prepositions is found: *cuius in nobis gratia fabricatur, quidquid a nobis sancte perficitur*. See n. 129 below.

25   Ths 24 and 3.56. See the following connections described in nn. 94–95 (Thp 57–59 and 3.62–63) and n. 100 (Ths 35 and 3.64).

26   See Chapter Six, n. 4 regarding the connections between RM 8 and the *Thema*. Regarding the relationship of RM 8 to the *Ars*, compare 2.51 with 8.6 (*ministerio*) and 21 (*fabricasse*); 6.2 with 8.6 and 23 (*corporis clusura*).

Chapter 4: The Treatise of the Master (RM 3–6)

27 See my commentary on RB 6 in Chapter Six, nn. 2–3.

28 RM 14 undoubtedly also belongs to the same layer of borrowed texts. See nn. 98 and 99 below.

29 C. Butler, "S. Benedict and the *Duae Viae*," *JTS* 11 (1910): 283–288; "The Instruments of Good Works," *JTS* 12 (1911): 261–268.

30 A. Wilmart, "Le discours de S. Basile sur l'ascèse en latin," *Rev. Bén.* 27 (1910): 233, n. 1.

31 Maxim 3.67, which advocates obedience to the abbot, is definitely one of these monastic revisions. One will see later that 3.57–60 and 65–66 are probably of the same origin.

32 See J. Schlecht, *Doctrina XII Apostolorum* (Fribourg: 1900), 7. The *Didache* inserts a long interpolation between the Golden Rule and the Ten Commandments (1.3–2.1).

33 *Syntagma doctrinae* 1, PG 28.836a; *Pistis*, PG 28.1639c. On these two texts and their Coptic parallels, see H. Leclercq, art. "Alexandrie (Archéologie)" in *Dictionnaire d'archéologie chrétienne et de liturgie (DACL)* (Paris: Letouzey et Ané, 1907) IV.1163–1166; C. Butler, *JTS* 12 (1911): 261–264 (cited in n. 29). One detail confirms this relationship of RM 3 with the *Syntagma* and the *Pistis*. These documents prescribe that one should love God "with all one's heart and all one's soul." These are also the two faculties that RM 3.1 mentions, neglecting the "mind" and "strength" spoken of in the Gospel texts. Like the *Duae Vitae*, *Syntagma*, and *Pistis*, RB 4.2 omits *diligere* in the second commandment that is joined with the first, while RM 3.2 repeats this verb. But these variants go back to the Synoptics themselves (cf. Mt 22:39 and Mk 12:31 that repeat *diliges* while Lk 10:27 omits it). For *in secundis* (RM), cf. Mt, Mk, and the *Duae Viae* (*secundo*).

34 *Passio Juliani* 46. See *Acta Sanctorum (AS), Jan.* I.584; P. Salmon, *Le Lectionnaire de Luxeuil* (Rome: 1944), 49. Unless otherwise indicated, we will cite the *Acta Sanctorum*, while indicating the variants from the *Lectionnaire* (L) and the Greek (G). As well as the texts of the *Passio Juliani* that appear in the *Acta Sanctorum* (AS) and the Lectionary of Luxeuil (L), see what A. Fábrega Grau, *Passionario Hispanico*, II (Madrid-Barcelona: 1955), has published in *Monumenta Hispaniae Sacra*, Liturgical Series, VI, based on a tenth-century manuscript of Saint Peter of Cardeña (today in *London, British Museum Add. 25, 600*). The *carmen* of Julian (*Passio Juliani* 46) is found there in No. 47, 137–138. We designate this new witness with the initial P. In the majority of cases, P agrees with AS against L.

35 In addition to those that have been highlighted in *La Règle du Maître* II.503 (cited in n. 1), one can also note: *Passio* 3 = RM 91.48 (*audite ... salubre ... consilium*); *Passio* 4 = RM 3.70 (*his qui castitatem diligunt*); *Passio* 7 = RM 86.23 (*inpedimenta animae*); *Passio* 14 = RM 5.T (*lima iustitiae*); *Passio* 49 = RM 3.1 (*Deum credas ... qui est unus in Trinitate et Trinitas in unitate ... trina maiestas et una deitas*). As regards this latter passage, see n. 44 below and Chapter Five, n. 21. The preceding passages are discussed in some detail in my *Scholies* (cited in n. 15), 261–292. The expression *lima iustitiae* (RM 5.T), present in *Pass. Jul.* 14 according to AS, not present according to L, is read in P (No. 16, p. 125).

36 A. Wilmart, "Les lectures non bibliques du Lectionnaire de Luxeuil," *Rev. Bén.* 28 (1911): 232; P. Salmon (cited in n. 34) LXXIV–LXXVI; B. de Gaiffier, "Source d'un texte relatif au mariage dans la Vie de S. Alexis," *Analecta Bollandiana (AB)* 63 (1945): 53 and n. 2, where the three known manuscripts of the Greek text are indicated (BHG 970). Thanks to the helpfulness of P. de Gaiffier, we have been able to consult photos of MS *Vat. graec.* 1667, fol. 180–208ᵛ. The passage that we are concerned with (*Passio* 46) appears there in folio 201, which is, unfortunately, seriously damaged.

37 See G. W. H. Lampe, *A Patristic Greek Lexicon*, s. u. Particularly interesting is the witness of Cyril of Scythopolis, *Vita Sabae* 54 and 85 (see the notes of A. J. Festugière, *Les Moines d'Orient* III/2 (Paris: 1963), 75, n. 146; 121, n. 286.

38 *Passio Mammarii* 2, in *AS, Jun,* II.265. The text of the *Acta Sanctorum* contains *pater noster*, but that of Mabillon, *Analecta* IV.94, contains *papa noster*. Already Du Cange connected the two Passions: *Glossarium*, s. u. *Papa*.

39 The two Passions repeat ad infinitum the accusation of "magical spells" (*artes, maleficia*) leveled by the pagan judge against the Christian wonderworker. See *Pass. Jul.* 20–21, 23–26, 31, 36–37, 43, 53, 57; *Pass. Mam.* 5, 7, 8, 10. Compare the resurrection of a dead person at the request of the judge in *Pass. Jul.* 39 and *Pass. Mam.* 8, the psalmody of the saints in the midst of the fire in *Pass. Jul.* 45 and *Pass. Mam.* 7–8.

40 Cf. P. Salmon (cited in n. 34), LXXVI.

41 MS *Clm 3514* of Munich, previously used by the Bollandists. See P. Salmon (cited in n. 34), LXXV; B. de Gaiffier (cited in n. 36), 49.

42 Its editor dates it at the end of the seventh century.

43 Fortunatus, *Lib. de Virg.* 8, carm. 6, PL 89.267a.

44 *Pass. Jul.* 49: *Ipse est Christus Deus aeternus, Pater in Filio est et Spiritus Sanctus.* G and L omit *est²*. G (203.9–10) omits *aeternus* and reads *Spiritu Sancto*. One reads *Pater in Filio Sanctus Spiritus* in the *Vat. Lat. 5771* manuscript, where a later hand added *in utroque* above the line. See also Chapter Five, n. 21. The same passage from the *Passio* contains two other Trinitarian formulas that we have already cited (see n. 35 above). One of them poses a problem because it agrees with the beginning of the *Quicumque* Creed: *unus in Trinitate et trinus* (*Trinitas* GL) *in unitate*. Yet, according to J. N. D. Kelly, *The Athanasian Creed* (London: 1964), 119–124, the Creed comes from the circle of Caesarius of Arles. Therefore, if the *Passio* depends on the Creed, it must be considered a rather late Latin text, which can hardly be prior to RM. But is the *unus in Trinitate et Trinitas* formula characteristic enough to prove this dependence? Although Kelly (24–34) does not provide specific testimony before Caesarius of Arles, did it not exist prior to the *Quicumque*? One can point to a formula in Paulinus of Nola, *Ep.* 37.5 that is quite close: *unitatem Trinitatis sine confusione iungens et Trinitatem ipsius unitatis sine separatione distinguens*. The formula *Ipse et Christus Deus aeternus, Pater in Filio est et Spiritus Sanctus* (*Pass. Jul.* 49) becomes in P: *Ipse est Chritus Deus aeternus, Pater in Filio et Spiritu Sancto* (No. 51, p. 139).

45 The six offices listed by *Pass. Jul.* 19 are reduced to five in P (No. 21, p. 128) by the omission of *matutina*.

46 In RM 93.19–22, *artes* has yet another meaning: medicine, remedies.

47 *Qui (quo* L) *non dicitur sanctus* GL. At the beginning of the cited phrase (Pass. Jul. 46), P concurs with L and G against AS in writing *Quo non dicitur sancto* (No. 47, p. 138).

48 AS replaces this phrase (b) that we give according to L with *hic placet Deo*. G follows L, but omits *sed ut sit* and *de illo*.

49 The commentators have tended to seek a very strict sequence. See I. Herwegen, *Sinn un Geist* (Einsiedeln: 1944), 88–106; C. Hartmann, "S. Benedikts Ordnungen der geistlichen Werke," *Benedictus Der Vater Des Abendlandes 547–1947*, ed. H.S. Brechter (Munich: 1947), 233–240. The commentary of P. Delatte, *Commentaire sur la Régle de saint Benoît* (Paris: 1913), 69–93; ET: *The Rule of Saint Benedict: A Commentary* (London: Burns, Oates, and Washbourne, Ltd., 1950) is more flexible and often more judicious.

50 The clearest case is that of *Castitatem amare* (3.70). See n. 106 below.

51 Cf. RM 3.45–49 (hope in God).

52 RM 3.39–44 (*non* + adjective).

53 RM 3.1–10 (the Gospel).

54 Matthew enumerates six works: to give food, give drink, offer hospitality, clothe the naked, visit the sick, and visit the prisoner. *Pauperes recreare* (RM 3.14) undoubtedly represents the first two (note the plural) in accordance with the sense of *recreare* in Th 13 (drink) and 1.58, etc. (meal). The third good work is omitted, which one can attribute to the severe attitude of the Rule toward guests. One proceeds directly to the fourth: *nudum uestire* (3.15) and fifth: *infirmum uisitare* (3.16). The last good work is also omitted, perhaps both because visiting prisoners is scarcely possible in the monastery and because the excommunicated must not be drawn out of their seclusion (RM 13.44–49 and 54–59). The *Passio* speaks only of feeding and clothing. It seems to be the source of the reference to *pauperes* in RM 3.14.

55 It is possible that *Corpus castigare* (3.11) and *Delicias fugire* (3.12) already aim specifically at the dietary restrictions that *Jeiunium amare* (3.13) speaks explicitly of. *Deliciae* designates food in RM 53.24 and 90.21. The ancients usually understood *corpus castigare* as the fast. Cf. Cassian, *Conl.* 1.10 and 21.15.

56 Contrary to the *Passio* (at least according to AS), the Master omits *et tollat crucem suam* as in the two other passages where he will cite Matthew 16:24 (RM 7.52; 90.10). On the other hand, the context of the *Ars* seems to give this maxim the same significance that it has in the *Passio*: it is not a matter of renunciation of self-will and obedience as in RM 7.52 and 90.10 but of bodily mortification and the practice of charity.

57 Note, however, that *Saeculi actibus se facere alienum* probably alludes to 2 Timothy 2:4 (cf. Dionysius, *Vita Pachomii* 46, PL 73.264c: *Nimis anima illa probatur infelix ... quae saeculo renuntians, iterum saeculi actibus implicatur*; Isidore, *Reg.* 5, PL 103.560d: *liberi ab actibus saeculi esse debemus, ut Christo placeamus*, following the Pauline citation). See also n. 60 below. The maxim *Nihil amori Christi praeponere* implicitly refers to the Gospel (Mt 10:37), as is particularly evident in *Pass. Jul.* 32: *paternum nomen et maternum Christi nomini non praepono*; Dionysius, *Vita Pachomii* 31 (251c): *parentes non debeo diuinae praeponere charitati*, following Matthew 10:37. Cf. *Vita Pachomii* 29 (249d): *nihil horum quae sunt in hoc saeculo amori tuo praepono*.

58 a) om. L; b) *delectationibus* add. L; c) *et* L; d) *sibi* add. L; e) *et tollat ... me* om. L; f) *et nihil* L; g) om. G; h) *Christi* GL. There is no testimony from G for abc.

59 The first pair is obtained from Matthew 16:24 by the omission of one of the three phrases (see n. 55 above). The second is created from two disparate elements in the *Passio*.

60 In fact, it seems that the *actus saeculi* in the *Ars* are the evil actions that are listed next (3.24–27, etc.). In contrast, when the *Passio* or patristic texts use the expression *actus saeculi*, it instead designates the "affairs of the world" (cf. 2 Tim 2:4). One can add Cassian, *Inst.* 12.25 to the texts cited above (n. 57): *cum renuntiatio nihil aliud sit nisi mortificationis et crucis indicium ... ut se non solum actibus huius mundi spiritaliter nouerit interemptum, uerum etiam corporaliter cotidie credat esse moriturum.*

61 a) *nihilque* GL; b) *Non consideret: Et non consideret* G *Et non considerans nec* L; c) *et* G *nec* L; d) *et* G *neque* L; e) om. GL; f) om. G *quae optime* L; g) *inpedimenta animae* om. GL; h) *uere* add. GL; i) *ut* L; j) *curas* GL; k) *sollicite gerant: recipit* G *sollicite egerint* L; l) *contempti* L; m) *alii reficiantur* L; n) *quo ... uestitur* om. G; o) *reddetur;* p) *inpatiens* GL.

62 RM 3.11: *corpus castigare* = 1 Corinthians 9:27; RM 3.16: *infirmum uisitare* = Matthew 25:36.

63 RM 3.38 (*persecutionem pro iustitia sustinere*) will use an earlier portion of the same chapter (Mt 5:10).

64 RM 3.20 (*mutuum dare*) and 21 (*indigenti donare*) probably allude to Matthew 5:42; Luke 6:30 and 35 (cf. RM 16.36).

65 Matthew 5:44 = Luke 6:28. The phrase is only authentic in Luke, but it has entered into many of the witnesses of Matthew.

66 Cf. RM 10.60 where 1 Corinthians 4:12 will take over Matthew 5:39–41 in the same way; see n. 85 below.

67 *Beati qui persecutionem patiuntur propter iustitiam* (Mt 5:10). Perhaps 1 Peter 3:14 (*si quid patimini propter iustitiam beati*) also influenced it. This text is very similar to 1 Peter 3:9 (cited by RM 3.34–37).

68 Jerome, *Ep.* 79.9 (based on Ps 4:5 and James 1:20).

69 Jerome, *Ep.* 130.13 (based on Ps 4:5 and Eph 4:26).

70 Matthew 5:22: *omnis qui irascitur fratri suo*. Cassian adds that even internal anger is appalling (*Conl.* 5.11).

71 Only in the case of RM 3.24 can one speak of a real similarity. In that of RM 3.25, one is not required to "put an end" (to the feeling), but to not await an opportunity to act on it. The expression of the *Passio* and RM calls to mind Cassian, *Inst.* 8.11: *rancorem animi reseruantes*; 8.14: *indignationis amaritudinem reseruemus*. According to Cassian, *Inst.* 8.11, it is forbidden to hold onto suppressed anger for several days.

72 Ambrose, *De uirg.* III.28, PL 16.228b (cf. *Exh. uirg.* 74, PL 16.358b, which draws the same teaching from Eccl 23:9); Augustine, *De mendacio* 28, PL 40.507; *Ep.* 157.40, PL 33.693; *Serm.* 307.4, PL 38.1407. Cf. RM 11.66–67. See Chapter 5, n. 33. It is not necessary to suppose that Ambrose, Augustine, and the Master read a particular Gospel text. It is a matter of exegesis, not of the reading of the sacred text (to correct the note on RM 3.32).

Chapter 4: The Treatise of the Master (RM 3–6)

73 One cannot say that *Non multum edacem* (3.41) repeats *Jeiunium amare* (3.13), although the subject is similar.

74 Cf. RM 16–28 (food) and 29–32 (sleep).

75 Cf. Psalm 77:7: *ut ponant in Deo spem suam*, etc.

76 In this regard, section 3.39–44 prepared the second part, since the neighbor is not named in this list of personal faults.

77 Faith and charity toward God figured previously in RM 3.1.

78 RM 10.56; 53.53; 86.13; 90.35; 92.46–47.

79 Th 25; 92.51, 57, 69.

80 RM 82.11–13; 86.5, 13; 90.35; 91.28, 58.

81 While reading *optare* (see n. 23 above).

82 Thp 69–79; Ths 41; 1.79; 14.57–58. All of these passages belong to what we have called the "ecclesiastic" or "non-monastic" layer of texts.

83 RM 16.6: *quasi pignus futurae repromissionis*.

84 RM 10.56 and 60 (cf. n. 66).

85 On the other hand, *Non murmuriosum* (3.44) calls to mind difficult situations (cf. 3.37–38) where hope flourishes. Cf. RB 68.5: *confidens de adiutorio Dei oboediat*.

86 However, it is possible that *spem suam* from 3.45 is contrasted with *Deo*: individuals must not rely on themselves, but on God.

87 Only the future is called to mind as concerns the material life (3.49), without any appeal to past experience. In RM 16.23–24, the reminder of the past is only a scriptural argument (Ps 36:25–26), not an appeal to personal experience.

88 RM 11.94–106. Here the motive is not strictly heaven, but the "kingdom of God and his justice," "the cause of God," and "the cause of the Spirit."

89 RM 11.99. The last word (*perficere*) calls to mind 3.48.

90 Without excluding, however, the brothers who do *lectio* during the three prescribed hours, as this reading is done in groups of ten, therefore, also listened to by most. Cf. RM 50.11.

91 In contrast, the counsels of Jerome (*Ep.* 58.6 and 130.15) presuppose personal reading.

92 See Adalbert de Vogüé, "Le sens de l'office divin," *RAM* 42 (1966): 400–401.

93 See n. 91 above. Cf. Adalbert de Vogüé, "Orationi frequenter incumbere," *RAM* 42 (1966): 469, n. 9.

94 Thp 69. RM does not speak of "groans" elsewhere. The expression *cum lacrimis uel gemitu* (RM 3.63) is found in the same context in Pseudo-Ambrose, *Exhort. ad. uirg. laps.* 43, PL 16.381a: the culprit will repeat Psalm 50 each day *cum lacrimis gemituque*.

95 Thp 57–66. It is true that the commentary only develops the theme of pardon, without touching on that of confession. In the fifth degree of humility (10.61), the Master inserts an expression reminiscent of 3.63 into the text of Cassian: *mala*

... *per... confessionem*. The same phrase from the fifth degree greatly resembles 3.56 (*cogitationes malas cordi suo aduenientes*).

96   See nn. 19–25 above.

97   See nn. 113–116 below.

98   *Cum lacrimis*: RM 14.2, 33, 67; *de cetero emendare*: RM 14.24–25 (cf. 13.61 that belongs to a passage clearly different than the text that precedes it). Other parallels between RM 3 and 14 are indicated below in n. 109.

99   See *Scholies*, 273–275 (cited n. 15).

100 Compare Ths 36: *propter emendationem malorum*; 3.64: *de ipsis malis ... emendare*; 14.41: *malis nostris ad emendationem ... uitam ... largiris*.

101 See nn. 47 and 48 above.

102 Cf. *Pass. Jul.* 46: *se primum lucrantes, deinde proximos, facientes quae dicunt, ut non solum doctores sint, sed ueredici factores (ut ... factores* om. AS). Who is this tirade aimed at? The masters of pagan wisdom?

103 Cf. RB 4.61, citing Matthew 23:3: *quae dicunt ... quae autem faciunt....*

104 RM 2.12: *factis suis diuina praecepta monstrare*.

105 RM 95.20: *cum forte sancti putemur esse quod non sumus*. The members of the community are called saints in RM 13.4; 14.5; 90.78, 92; 91.52. *Abbas sanctissimus* is an isolated term (94.6).

106 See n. 50 above. Cf. *Pass. Jul.* 4: *his qui castitatem diligunt*. In addition, *Castitatem amare* is reminiscent of *Jeiuniam amare* (3.13), added by the Master in developing the *Passio*. Cf. *non amare* in 3.29, 32, 58, 60, 74, *odire* in 3.66. All of these maxims seem to be the work of the Master. However, see n. 140 below.

107 The last two maxims (3.75–76) are positive, but suppose difficulties to be surmounted (cf. Eph. 4:26, source of 3.75).

108 RM 3.45–49. Here the form is negative (*nunquam desperare*). Compare 3.71 (*nullum odire*) that recasts 3.2 (*diligere proximum*) in a negative form.

109 RM 14.66. See n. 98 above.

110 Add 3.55, 63, 69 and the references to Christ (3.10, 23, 56). In sum, twelve maxims, or less than one-sixth of the *Ars*.

111 RM 3.45–49. There are also some maxims of personal ascesis such as RM 3.10–13 and 22–23, but, as we have seen, both are oriented toward fraternal charity.

112 RM 3.9. It is the only case besides RM 3.77.

113 But maxim 3.57 undoubtedly still belongs to the original list. In fact, it is in positive form like those that precede it and calls to mind 3.54 (*custodire*). Moreover, the thoughts-speech pair appears in the "non-monastic" passage of 8.1–25. Finally, the seventeen syllables of 3.57 connect this maxim to 3.50–51, 52, 53, and 55. See nn. 32–34 in Chapter Seven.

114 RM 8.26–37; 10.14–22. However, taking into account the previous note, it may be that the intervention of the Master here is limited to adding 3.58–59.

Chapter 4: The Treatise of the Master (RM 3–6)

115 Cf. the case of RM 12.5–6 analyzed in my commentary on the penitential code, Adalbert de Vogüé, *La Règle de Saint Benoît,* Sources Chrétiennes 181–186 (Paris: Cerf, 1972) V.727, n. 12. Henceforth, this entire six-volume work will be referenced as *La Règle* plus volume (I–VI) and page number. See also n. 125 below.

116 See RM 50.28–33 and nn. 89–90 above. It may be that this reading-silence relationship already existed in the original list (see n. 112 above).

117 Thus we hear it translated by the same word: "hand over ... we hand over."

118 RM 10.112–114. One will note that 10.114 and 90.25 concur in writing *hoc unicuique,* while 3.89 contains *unicuique hoc.* This is an additional indicator of the dependence of RM 3 on RM 90 (see notes of the edition on 3.84–87).

119 See n. 118.

120 See nn. 1–3 and 7–8 above.

121 It is difficult to specify where it resumes because we are not sure what version of Galatians 5:22–23 the Master read. One perhaps reads *castitas* (RM 4.4) and *abstinentia puritas* (RM 4.5) there, certainly *benignitas bonitas* (4.6). On the other hand, *conscientia simplex* (4.4) and *simplicitas* (4.5) do not correspond to any of the nine virtues of the Greek text or twelve virtues of the Latin Vulgate.

122 Contrary to what our punctuation and translation of the text indicate. One can scarcely invoke Caesarius, *Serm.* 86.5 (*castitatem ante omnia ... custodite*) in favor of it, as the similarity appears coincidental.

123 This best explains the fact, surprising at first glance, that *prae omnibus* is presented in the text and not at the head of the list.

124 Ephesians 4:2: *cum omni humilitate et mansuetudine.* Does this serve to explain why *humilitas* appears here as the first of the three virtues, contrary to the order of the treatises (RM 7–10)?

125 That is to say, next to the words from the text, close to where they were inscribed in the margin. Compare another case of a poorly inserted gloss (RM 12.5–7) in our commentary on the penal code, *La Règle* V.727, n. 12 (cited in n. 115 above).

126 RM 6.T: *operatio spiritalium ferramentorum.*

127 See p. 81 above.

128 In order to provide a title for the list of tools, it was necessary to insert the description of paradise (3.79–95) between the conclusion of the *Ars* (3.78) and it.

129 See n. 24 above. *In nobis* is less awkward here than in 3.46.

130 RM 3.79–82 (cf. 90.45). See also RM 1.91–92 and n. 22 above.

131 See n. 35 above.

132 RM 2.52; 3.78; 4.T; 6.T.

133 Perhaps the words *diligenti custodia* are connected with this excess. They seem to make *perseuerando* redundant, which calls to mind 4.10 (cf. RM 6.2, Mt 10:22, RM 10.53, and n. 125 above).

134 In any event, there must have been something there after the principal clause, which seems too short and uninteresting to have ever existed on its own, especially as a conclusion.

135 Cf. also 3.T: *in monasterio*.

136 See "Nouveaux aperçus," 37 (cited in n. 4).

137 Cf. 5.T–1: *nobis*.

138 *Primo superbia*, which I have tried to elucidate in *La Communauté et l'Abbé*, 213–214 (cited in n. 9) could, if necessary, be explained by the unparalleled seriousness of pride, universally considered as "the first" of all the vices. See n. 124 above.

139 The insertion of *merces* also contributed to this (see n. 128 above).

140 *Non amare detrahere* (3.29) is clearly in the style of the readactor (see n. 105 above), but the scriptural origin of this maxim (Proverbs 20:13 VL) must be taken into account. *Non murmuriosum* (3.44) seems to be a monastic addition, incidentally a bit surprising if the list is addressed to the abbot. *Nullum odire* (3.71) stands a good chance of belonging to the original list. See our remarks in "Scholies," 8, n. 23 (cited in n. 15).

Chapter Five

The Treatise of Benedict (RB 4)

Overview

Our first task will be to situate the different parts of the text of Benedict in relationship to the passages attested to by the manuscripts of RM. To do this, it will suffice to add the data from RB to the table comparing P*A* and E*.[1]

	P* and A*	E*	RB
Conclusion of *De abbate*	2.39–40	2.39–40 (no. 28)	2.39–40
The Council	2.41–50		3.T–13
The Abbot, Master of the Art	2.51	2.51 (no. 28)	
The Art, the Workshop, the Tools	2.52		
Title …	3.T	[*Qualis debeat esse praepositus* (no. 29)]	4.T
List …	3.1–77	[*Regula Pachomii* 159 (no. 29)]	4.1–74
Conclusion …	3.78		4.75
Reward….	3.79–94		4.76–77
Return from the path …	3.95		
Tools …	4.T–10		
Vices …	5.T–11	5.T–11 (no. 20)	
Workshop …	6.T–2		4.78
De oboedientia …	7.T–9	7.T–9 (no. 21)	5.T–9

Looking at this schema, it would seem that Benedict has nothing that corresponds to RM 4. But one must take into account the fact that both the title (RB 4.T) and the conclusion (RB 4.75) of the Benedictine

123

list speak of *instrumenta*. These *instrumenta* clearly echo the *ferramenta* of the Master. Therefore, in a certain manner, Benedict does attest to the chapter of the Master on the tools (RM 4).

Consequently, the only passages of RM that are not represented at all in RB are the two transitions at the end of *De abbate* (RM 2.51–52) and the list of vices (RM 5). The absence of RM 5 is all the more surprising in that it is a chapter that is only linked with the *Ars* by its title and was seemingly a late insertion between the "tools" and the "workshop." Although we assume that Benedict knew of and intentionally omitted it, we cannot conceal that the facts would suggest a different hypothesis: RB would attest to a version of the text prior to the insertion of this chapter into the *Ars*, or even to its very composition. However, one notes that only a trace of RM 4 remains in RB: the word *instrumenta* in RB 4.T and 75. The body of this chapter of the Master, that is to say the list of virtues, has entirely disappeared from RB. Why would the list of vices not have suffered the same fate?

Another fact that provides food for thought is that Benedict does not separate the "workshop" from the "instruments," that is to say, from the "art" itself. There is nothing in RB that corresponds to the title of RM 6. All evidence suggests that this is a later title. Therefore, Benedict presents a text here that is seemingly less evolved than that of the Master. When the two authors write: *Officina uero*, this *uero* is normal in RB and unusual in RM. This fact seems to indicate that the RM read by Benedict did not contain a distinct chapter on the *officina* and that its definition was still part of the previous chapter.[2] Thus, RB would be linked with the second stage of the development of the *Ars* that preceded the insertion of the chapter on the vices between the *ferramenta* and the *officina*. However, one will note that RB possesses the description of the *merces* or reward (RB 4.76–77), characteristic of the last stage of the redaction. Therefore, the Benedictine redaction would be placed at the beginning of this last period. Although the *ferramenta* and *officina* were not yet separated by the list of vices, the *merces* was already found between the *ars* and *ferramenta*.[3]

This is where the most natural interpretation of *Officina uero* (RM 6.1; RB 4.78) leads. However, one cannot rule out another explanation. Benedict would have had the finished version of RM sitting before him, as presented in manuscripts P* and A*. Reducing the *ferramenta* to a simple trace — the word *instrumenta* applied to the *ars* itself — and totally removing the list of vices, he would have intended to preserve the *officina*,[4] but without dedicating a special chapter to it. The definition of the workshop, relieved of its title, would become again in RB

Chapter 5: The Treatise of Benedict (RB 4)

what it originally was in RM: a simple concluding phrase at the end of the chapter.

No matter how one attempts to explain these facts, one cannot ignore an overall finding: E* witnesses to RM 5 and has no trace of RM 4 and 6, while RB witnesses to RM 4 and 6 and has no trace of RM 5. One would be tempted to conclude that an original source consisting only in the *ars* itself (RM 3.1–77) was added separately in each instance, in the first case with a list of vices, and in the second with a list of "tools" and a "workshop," and that the merging of these two types of additions produced the treatise that we read in manuscripts P* and A*. This process, rather surprising in its complexity, could be visualized as follows:[5]

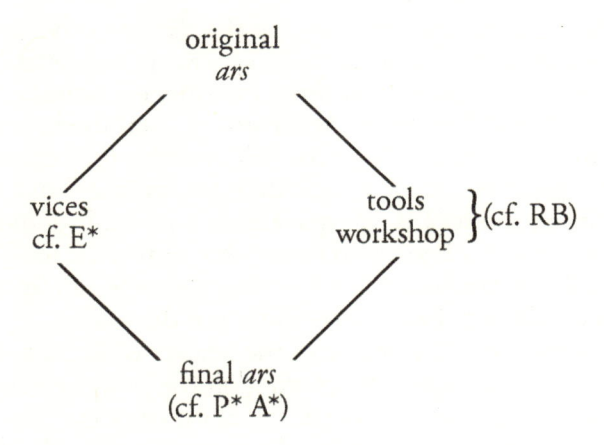

```
            original
              ars
           /        \
          /          \
       vices        tools      ⎫
       cf. E*      workshop    ⎬ (cf. RB)
                                ⎭
          \          /
           \        /
            final ars
           (cf. P* A*)
```

But enough of hypotheses! We have multiplied them only in order to be objective and demonstrate to the reader how difficult it is to take into account all of the facts without evading any. Perhaps detailed examination of the Benedictine text will shed more light on this very thorny question of the development of the treatise as a whole.

"Art" or "Instruments" (RB 4.T and 75–78)

The first peculiarity of RB 4 is that it does not call its list of maxims *ars*, but *instrumenta*. This word appears in both the title and conclusion of the chapter although the genitive that completes it is different in each case: *instrumenta bonorum operum* (4.T), *instrumenta artis spiritualis* (4.75). In the title, the genitive appears to be simply explanatory—the tools are nothing other than the good works. In contrast, in the conclusion, the genitive indicates purpose—the tools are the instruments with which one undertakes the spiritual art.

Instrumentum is equivalent to *ferramentum*, which is the term of the Master.[6] However, this latter is more concrete and colorful than *instrumentum*, whose metaphorical use is too old and ordinary to have retained all of its symbolic value.[7]

Moreover, Benedict does not seem in any hurry to develop the arts metaphor. After announcing in his title that the good works are "instruments," he waits until the end of the list to say how they play this instrumental role. Only then does the reader learn that "the instruments" are intended for a "spiritual art."

While this delay in introducing the theme of the chapter is surprising, the last lines of the chapter (4.76–78) are no less so. There Benedict explains that the previously listed instruments must be "accomplished" (*adimpleta*) and "executed" (*operemur*). Certainly these expressions are easily understood in light of the title, which posed the equation instruments = good works, but the title is far-removed and nothing in the immediate context calls the equivalence to mind. In addition, one cannot see why the salary is given to those who "return the tools" (*reconsignata*). Obviously, one earns a salary by using the tools, not by returning them. One must deliver the finished work, not the tools.

The corresponding phrase of the Master (RM 3.78–82) is more satisfactory in this regard. By playing on the two meanings of the word *ars*,[8] the Master can present the list of maxims as a work that one completes and delivers accomplished to earn the reward. The metaphor is coherently developed and effortlessly applied to the reality signified: the created object that is to be presented on the Day of Judgment is the "work of one's deeds."[9]

Therefore, one has the impression that the original text is found in RM rather than RB. The name *ars* better suits the list than does *instrumenta artis*. This latter term, which is that of Benedict, comes from a change in terminology. For the Master, the tools were not the maxims of RM 3, called *ars*, but the virtues of RM 4. It seems that Benedict intended to combine the two images of the Master into one. Removing the list of virtues, he transferred the title "tools" to the maxims. In concluding the *Ars*, the Master wrote: *Ecce haec est ars sancta, quam ferramentis debemus spiritalibus operari* (RM 3.78). In RB, this concluding phrase became: *Ecce haec sunt instrumenta artis spiritualis* (RB 4.75). It would have been logical to omit the reference to the tools here since they are not referenced in what follows. However, Benedict preferred to keep the word in the sentence by applying it to the previously stated maxims. Consequently, the chapter title itself was modified, but its last sentences did not reflect the change.

However, to some critics, the terminology of Benedict seems more satisfying than that of the Master. According to Capelle, Benedict would have followed his master Cassian in this respect.[10] The latter had already compared ascetical practices to the tools of a trade (*ferramenta cuiuslibet artis*) that one is not content to simply possess, but uses to practice the craft and achieve their end. In the spiritual order, the end consists of purity of heart or charity. Therefore, external practices are simply a means to attain the wholly interior goal of virtue.[11] In this sense, one can call them the "instruments of virtue"(*instrumenta uirtutum*).[12]

Such was the thought of Cassian and such would be that of Benedict. It is with this intent that RB would present the "good works" as "instruments." It would also indicate that the works are only a means to attain perfection, that is to say, charity.[13] This doctrine that Benedict would have drawn from Cassian would have been distorted by the Master. For this latter, virtues are instruments that one uses to accomplish works. The hierarchy of values is reversed; ends and means are inverted. Thus, Benedict follows Cassian, and the Master diverges. Capelle concludes from this that the three authors succeeded one another in the following order: Cassian, Benedict, and the Master.

These comments of Capelle are valuable in drawing our attention to antecedents of the artisan metaphor in the ascetic literature. Following information from Butler, Capelle turned toward Cassian. But, is it certain that RM and RB borrowed their images and their doctrine from the latter? The metaphor in question is not uncommon in the early texts. Without returning to *Passio Juliani* and its magical art, we note that already Evagrius advises the monk to take care of the "instruments of his art."[14] According to a saying of Abba Poemen, "These are the tools that the soul labors with: to throw oneself before God, not to boast, and to leave behind self-will."[15] Pelagius calls the Pauline pieces of armor (Eph 6:14–17) *instrumenta spiritualis pugnae*[16] and the anonymous author of the *Life of the Jura Fathers* speaks of the *curatio spiritalis artificii*.[17] Gregory of Nyssa and Hilary of Arles both depict the monastery as a "workshop of virtues."[18]

These few examples reveal how the words, *ars, artificium, instrumenta, ferramenta*, and *officina* are used to designate ascesis, its practices, and its cenobitic framework. To be able to affirm that Benedict depends on

Cassian here, both would have to present some distinctive terminology or clearly characterized teaching that united them and set them apart. The expression *instrumenta artis* is not particular to them: one finds it elsewhere, in Evagrius for example. We have encountered the idea that the works are instruments in the sayings of Poemen. Therefore, the expression and thought are too commonplace to create a dependent link between Cassian and Benedict.

This conclusion will appear all the more certain if one considers the profound difference of context in which the artisanal metaphor is developed in both. The purpose of Cassian is not to furnish a list of good works. He indicates only three or four by way of example.[19] What he wishes to convey is that every exterior work is only a means in service of a higher and more spiritual goal, "the kingdom of God within us," the possession of authentic sanctity here below.

In contrast, RM and RB set out to arrange a list of good works that they extend as far as possible. They do not consider subordinating these works to an interior end. Certainly, the proposed program tends toward a goal, but it is an eschatological reward rather than spiritual perfection reached here below. One fulfills the precepts of the art, uses its instruments, and by that very fact obtains a reward in heaven. No *scopos* or intermediate goal is placed between good works and the last end. The heavenly kingdom that rewards our deeds will begin "on the day of judgment." There is no question of possessing it "within us" in this life by the interior reign of charity. Consequently, there is no distinction between simple instruments of exterior practice and interior virtue in which perfection consists. This notion of virtue-perfection is not found in RB or RM. Undoubtedly, they both place perfect charity at the summit of the scale of humility, but this is only a passing reference from Cassian (*Inst.* 4.39), whom they heavily depend on in this treatise. Nothing indicates that Benedict and the Master have appropriated the theory of the primacy of charity, as expounded in *Conferences* One and Twenty-One, into their works.

Therefore, these *Conferences* are not the origin of what we read in RB 4 or RM 3–6. If the Master seems to diverge more than Benedict from Cassian when he calls virtues "tools," this digression only demonstrates with unusual clarity how both Rules are unfamiliar with the premises of the *Conferences*. The artisanal metaphor, common in ascetic literature, was used by the Master and Benedict without any reference to its particular use by Cassian.

Consequently, one cannot use the comparison between RM/RB and the *Conferences* to assert that the terminology of Benedict is more exact and traditional than that of the Master. Therefore, our earlier remarks maintain their original validity: the presentation of RM 3 seems earlier than that of RB 4. The true name of the list of maxims is not *instrumenta*, but *ars*.

The First Instruments (RB 4.1–9)

The series of Gospel commands contained at the beginning of the *Ars* in RB contains two important variants. First, one does not find the Trinitarian preamble of RM 3.1 in RB 4.1. Second, Benedict writes *Honorare omnes homines* (RB 4.8) in place of *Honorare patrem et matrem* (RM 3.8).

The first of these variants is not easy to interpret. At first glance, the Trinitarian preamble of the Master gives the impression of an addition. This profession of faith has nothing in common with the articles that follow. It differs both in its length and in its non-scriptural tone. Moreover, the transitional phrase *Ergo hunc*, which links it to the commandment to love God, is quite atypical for the *Ars*. It is as if the Master wanted to preserve the sacred numerical order of the "first commandment" when placing an added Trinitarian definition before it.

Consequently, it seems probable that Benedict presents the original text here that existed prior to the addition. Why would he who professes the same Trinitarian faith and prescribes that one stand at the "Glory be to the Father" that follows the response *ob honorem et reuerentiam sanctae Trinitatis* remove this confession of faith?[20]

The priority of the Benedictine text would thereby be entirely certain if one did not have to take into account an embarrassing fact: the Master seems to have drawn the confession of faith from the *Passio Juliani*, just like certain maxims of the *Ars*. In a passage that closely follows the *carmen* of Julian, the *Passio* successively proposes the two following formulas: *unum Dominum credas ... qui est unus in Trinitate et trinus in unitate* and *Credis unum et uerum Deum ... qui est trina maiestas et una deitas.*[21] These are the same words used by the Master. While the first formula is also found in the *Quicumque* Creed,[22] the same cannot be said for the second, which creates an undeniable link between RM and the *Passio*. In adopting for his own purposes the second formula of the *Passio*, the Master attaches it to the first with the words *... trinum in ... unum in ...* repeated in chiasmic form. Therefore, he has inverted the two words. Finally, he fleshes it out by introducing two new substantives: *substantia* and *potentia*:

Passio Juliani 49	RM 3.1
Unum in Trinitate	unum Deum in Trinitate
et trinus in unitate …	et trinum in unitate,
trina maiestas	trinum in una deitatis substantia
et una deitas	et unum in trina magestatis potentia

If RM depends, here as elsewhere, on the *Passio*, it seems that one is obliged to consider this confession of faith as part of the same layer of texts as *Iram non perficere, Iracundiae tempus non reseruare*, and the other maxims drawn from the *carmen* of Julian. Like these, the Master would have combined it with articles stemming from the original list, which certainly began with the first commandment. The same hand must have inserted all that comes from the *Passio*, the confession of faith as well as the maxims. However, it is not certain that the Master made these various insertions from the *Passio* at the same time, especially since the Trinitarian formulas do not belong to the *carmen* but appear slightly later. On the other hand, it would be surprising if Benedict himself had miraculously come up with the beginning of the original list. It is more likely that the confession of faith did not yet appear in the text of the *Ars* that he had at his disposal.

Therefore, one is correct in thinking that the Benedictine redaction stems from an intermediate state of the *Ars*: its sole author would have already plagiarized Chapter Forty-Six of the *Passio*, but not yet drawn upon Chapter Forty-Nine. For all that, we cannot deny the fragility of this hypothesis. Certain indications would suggest, instead, designating the *Quicumque* as the source of the Trinitarian confession of the *Ars*[23] and considering RM as the source of the *Passio*.

Whatever the immediate source of this Trinitarian passage — *Quicumque* or *Passio* — it was certainly added to the original redaction of the *Ars* that Benedict preserved or found. On the other hand, the latter seems to have altered a maxim whose original content is found in RM. *Honorare omnes homines* (RB 4.8) is clearly a correction of the article *honorare patrem et matrem* (RM 3.8) from the Ten Commandments. The correction is inspired by obvious monastic motives: this precept from the Ten Commandments is difficult to apply for those who have renounced family. Therefore, Benedict has replaced it with another precept of scriptural origin, which seems to be primarily a matter of hospitality for him.[24]

Chapter 5: The Treatise of Benedict (RB 4)

Renunciation and Charity (RB 4.10–40)

In these first maxims, Benedict and the Master seem to alternate in offering the original reading. This same interchange will be found in what follows. Thus, *Corpus castigare* (RB 4.11) stands a good chance of being the original text since it simply reproduces a Pauline formula, while *Corpus pro anima castigare* (RM 3.11) presents a glossed and probably later text.[25] On the other hand, it seems that "monastic" motives have caused Benedict to intentionally omit several articles that are missing next in RB. The first such case is *Mutuum dare. Indigenti donare* (RM 3.20–21). These maxims were probably part of the original list intended for the laity. Although retained by the Master, to Benedict they seemed incompatible with cenobitic disappropriation. The omission of *mutuum dare* can be placed alongside the energetic pronouncement of Benedict forbidding giving or receiving gifts that is found in a small chapter entirely his own.[26] Regarding *Indigenti donare*, the comments of Basil and the Master about almsgiving[27] suffice to show that accomplishing this good work posed some problems in communities. Both precepts are only admissible in the cenobitic milieu if addressed to the superiors responsible for the administration of the community, and it is undoubtedly in this sense that the Master first understood them. But one could understand them as invitations addressed to all monks, and this is what would have prompted Benedict to remove them.

A little later, the omission of *Fratri fidem seruare* (RM 3.28) and *Promissum conplere et non decipere* (RM 3.30) seems to follow a similar rationale. These maxims presuppose self-serving relationships that are hardly appropriate among members of a monastic community.[28] Therefore, Benedict would have removed from RM what was a remnant from a list for non-monastic readers.

It is also worth noting that oaths and loans are mentioned in two verses of Psalm 14 that the Master reproduces[29] but Benedict removes. The same "monastic" instinct dictates these parallel deletions by Benedict from the Prologue and RB 4.

Between *Fratri fidem seruare* and *Promissum conplere*, Benedict also omits *Non amare detrahere* (RM 3.29). However, a little later, he warns against this same vice under a different form: *Non detractorem* (RB 4.40). It is difficult to say where the original redaction is found because both have scriptural ties. The formula of the Master, which seems lax, stems from Proverbs 20:13 (LXX–VL).[30] On the other hand, the maxim of Benedict follows well from *Non murmuriosum* (RB 4.39). These two vices—murmuring and disparagement—follow each other in a similar manner in a text from the Book of Wisdom.[31] All things considered, the passage from *Non amare detrahere* to *Non detractorem* is perhaps more likely than the reverse. The first formula appears too lenient only if its scriptural origins are not attended to. "Not to love to disparage" allows one to suppose that disparagement is sometimes permitted. "Not to be disparaging" avoids this appearance of laxity.

Moreover, this is not the only case where Benedict presents a more abrupt formula, lacking the moderating *amare* of the Master. In RB *Non amare iurare* (RM 3.32) becomes *Non iurare* (RB 4.27). Here again, the Benedictine formula can claim to be representative of the very words of Christ,[32] and this reference to the Sermon on the Mount is even more pertinent as we have seen that the entire context depends on this very Gospel discourse. Would it not be the Master who introduces a concession contrary to the Gospel here, in order to show consideration for an inveterate habit of his contemporaries?

However, we have seen that the formula of the Master echoes the firm and explicit teaching of Ambrose and Augustine, who, relying on Sirach, ban only the habitual swearing of oaths or the inclination to take an oath lightly for the same reason invoked by the Master: "out of fear that one may commit perjury." Therefore, the maxim of the *Ars* agrees in all points with the teaching of the two great doctors, on which it definitely depends.[33] While *ne forte periuret* continues to witness to this connection and dependence, the deletion of *amare* weakens it. The first redaction here is undoubtedly that of the Master. Even more than in the previous case, it appears that Benedict does not appreciate the rationale and references for a doctrine that seems too lax to him. His redaction bears the mark of Gospel literalism and rigorism.

These objections that we have just raised must make us cautious regarding two other articles in RB that also have simpler content and conform more closely to Scripture than in RM. *Inimicos diligere* and *Maledicentes se non remaledicere sed magis benedicere* (RB 4.31–32) are closer than *Inimicos plus quam amicos diligere* and *Maledicentes se non solum non remaledicere sed magis benedicere* (RM 3.36–37), where the words *plus quam amicos* and *non solum* are additions as compared with the underlying scriptural texts. However, we note that this time the rigorism is on the part of the Master. The Gospel, followed by RB, requires only "to love one's enemies."[34] RM insists, "more than one's friends." But the important point is the conformity of the maxims to scriptural sources. Whether by excess or deficiency, it is always the Master who diverges from Scripture while Benedict is more faithful. At first glance, this fidelity argues in favor of the precedence of the Benedictine text. However, the argument of conformity to sources is never decisive when it is a matter of well-known scriptural sources whose exact content each author can call to mind.[35] In the present case, the argument would seem to be even more uncertain given that we have duly noted the tendency of Benedict to return to the sacred text. It is possible, even likely, that this tendency is at play again here. However, at present, we cannot provide patristic references like those that previously confirmed the antiquity of the formula of the Master. In the absence of such evidence, we cannot affirm that his formulas are earlier than those of Benedict.

The Theological Maxims (RB 4.41–43)

The group of maxims on hope (RM 3.45–49) presents the most differences in RB (RB 4.41–43). Only the first maxim is identical. The next two are quite different, and the last two maxims of the Master are absent from RB. The doctrinal importance of the two middle maxims, preserved by both, invites an attentive comparison of the two redactions:

RM 3.46–47	RB 4.42–43
a Bonum aliquid in se cum uiderit,	Bonum aliquid in se cum uiderit,
b a Deo factum magis quam a se extimet.	Deo *adplicet non sibi*.
c Malum a se factum iudicet	Malum *uero semper* a se factum *sciat*
d et sibi et diabolo inputare.	et sibi *reputet*.

The redaction of the Master draws a parallel between phrases *b* and *c* by the repetition of *factum a se* and by rhyme (*extimet ... iudicet*). On the other hand, in phrases *a* and *b*, it presents the play of expressions *in se ... a se*, which, as we have seen, is found in other passages dealing with grace, and in particular in the commentary on the Psalms in the *Thema*.[36] As this passage of the *Thema* is reproduced in RB Prol 29–30, it is presumable that, here also, *in se ... a se* was part of the initial content of RM and RB, and that the redaction of the Master provided the original content of this maxim.

In RB, it is not phrases *b* and *c* that correspond, but phrases *b* and *d*, owing to the repetition of *sibi* and the approximate correspondence of the verbs (*adplicet ... reputet*). This parallelism is less clear than that of phrases *b* and *c* in RM.

From a stylistic point of view, the most remarkable difference between the two Rules is observed in the last phrase. In RM, after three subjunctives, the infinitive in *et sibi et diabolo inputare* is shocking. Undoubtedly, *diabolo inputare* makes it a beautiful clause, but *diabolo inputet* would have also been effective.[37] If *inputare* is justified, it is owing to the context, where each maxim is concluded with an infinitive. In addition, *inputare* rhymes with the final infinitive of the two following maxims (*optare-sperare*). The attraction of these final syllables is probably what explains *inputare*. But since the two maxims in question are actually absent from RB, their affinity with *et diabolo inputare* would only be able to prove that this final syllable represents the original redaction.

In RB, the verb in the subjunctive gives a normal appearance to the phrase, but the phrase *et sibi reputet* is unusually brief: six syllables, only half of the previous.[38] This surprising brevity draws our attention to the absence of any reference to the devil in the Benedictine text. Not only does the harmony of the proportions suffer, but *et sibi reputet* simply repeats the previous phrase without conveying anything new. Therefore, both its meaning and form seem to call for the annotation *et diabolo*. In this regard, the redaction of the Master is undoubtedly closer to the original text. Just as God assists the individual in doing good, the devil does so in doing evil.[39] In removing the invisible power that contributes to evil, Benedict breaks the symmetry and leaves sinful individuals face-to-face with themselves.

There are two other significant modifications in the Benedictine redaction—one in the second phrase, the other in the third. First, *a Deo factum magis quam a se* becomes *Deo adplicet non sibi*. Clearly, this last statement intends to accentuate the transcendent role of divine grace in our good works. The *magis* of the Master actually seems to identify the action of God with that of the individual, therefore placing them on the same level. Understood in the sense of "more," at first glance, the correction Benedict makes to the expression seems justified. God is not the author of our deeds "more than us," he is totally and completely other. However, is it certain that *magis* has this meaning in RM? Most often the word does not mean "more" (comparative), but "rather"(adversative).[40] If this is the case here, the maxim of the Master intends to say that the monk must attribute his good works to God rather than to himself. Consequently, the idea is the same as in RB: to attribute the good not to oneself but to God. The Benedictine correction has clarified the expression and dispelled all ambiguity. It has not significantly changed its meaning.

The other notable modification of Benedict is the addition of *uero semper* in the third phrase. The conjunction *uero*, linking two separate maxims, occurs only once in the entire list, in which the conjunction *et*, of which we will speak, normally plays this role, appearing two or three times. Therefore, it seems that the *uero* of Benedict is later and that there was no conjunction in the original version of RM. The adverb *semper* seems to emphasize the responsibility of the individual for the evil deed. Such insistence corresponds with the omission of *et diabolo* by Benedict in the following phrase: the monk, and only the monk, is always culpable.

Thus the three important corrections of RB all move in the same direction. It is a matter of humbling the monk, whether by denying him all merit for good or placing all responsibility on him for evil. The tendency is clearly Augustinian. These two maxims are typical as regards the theological preoccupations of Benedict. In addition to his concern to humble the monk before God, one can mention his decreased interest in the action of the devil. This last tendency is perceptible throughout RB. While the Master employs *diabolus* thirty-seven times, Benedict uses it only twice![41]

Did Benedict know of the last two maxims of the Master on hope (RM 3.48–49) and intentionally omit them? This is difficult to answer. One can certainly guess quite easily what reasons could have prompted him to remove them. The first (*Desideria sua a Deo perfici optare*) touches on a delicate point. Are our good desires only "fulfilled" by God in response to our prayer? Are they not also first inspired by him? An Augustinian sensibility could find the maxim unsatisfying because it is incomplete. However, one will note that Benedict himself presents the matter in an equally incomplete fashion in his Prologue.[42]

The second maxim (*Substantiam suam non in solo labore manuum suarum, sed plus a Deo sperare*) indicates a reticence regarding manual labor that appears many times in RM,[43] but that Benedict does not seem to share. Its absence in RB can be connected with Benedict's acceptance of work in the fields, which the Master prohibits. Exhorting his monks to do the harvesting themselves, if necessity requires it, "because they are truly monks, *if they live by the work of their hands*, as did our Fathers and the Apostles" (RB 48.8), Benedict cannot appreciate this invitation to rely on God more than on the "work of one's hands." The maxim of the Master seems to encourage the repugnance for agricultural work that Benedict fights all around him.

One can explain quite easily why Benedict would have set aside these two maxims. But just because this explanation encounters no difficulty, it does not mean that things actually happened in this way. Nothing yet confirms that Benedict knew these maxims, which the Master could have added later. Let us see whether the rest of the list presents some particular affinity with either the two maxims proper to the Master or with Benedict's double maxim on good and evil.

The next maxims (RM 3.50–52; RB 4.44–46) are common to both Rules: "Fear the day of judgment, dread hell, desire eternal life." We have seen that, after RM 3.49, this evocation of the last things is easily understood: if Christians must expect their livelihood to come more from God than from their own work, it is because their gaze must be more on eternal than on temporal realities. *Sursum corda!* "Seek the kingdom and his justice and your Father in heaven will provide you with all that is necessary."

However, the link created by Benedict is no less satisfying: after having spoken of the good and evil accomplished by the individual (RB 4.42–43), he passes very naturally to divine judgment and eschatological sanctions. Perhaps this sequence is even simpler and more natural than that of the Master. In any case, one cannot use subsequent context to point to a lacuna in RB. It remains uncertain whether RM 3.48–49 was present in the original redaction.

The Section Parallel to the First Step of Humility

We come now to the long section parallel to the first step of humility (RM 3.50–67; RB 4.44–61). We find there four significant variants, at least three of which clearly indicate that Benedict revised the original text of the Master:

1. *Vitam aeternam omni concupiscentia spiritali desiderare* (RB 4.46). The words *omni concupiscentia spiritali* replace *et Hierusalem sanctam* (RM 3.52). They are certainly later, as we will see in comparing this section with the first step.[44] Why has Benedict omitted reference to the heavenly Jerusalem? Perhaps because he intends to replace the long description of the latter (RM 3.84–94) with some words drawn from Scripture (RB 4.77). The notation *omni concupiscentia spiritali* already denotes the concern for subjectivity that will characterize all of RB. Instead of emphasizing the object of desire, Benedict insists on the intensity and purity of desire. To desire paradise with *spiritual* longing[45] — perhaps this attributive adjective protests the tangible delicacies with which the Master fills his paradise.

2. *Cogitationes malas cordi suo aduenientes mox ad Christum adlidere et seniori spiritali patefacere* (RB 4.50). The last four words, replacing the insignificant *debere* of the Master (RM 3.56), introduce a new person whom Benedict will discuss again: "the spiritual senior" charged with receiving confessions.[46] The monastic character of his office cannot be doubted, and it is this that rends the reading of Benedict very suspect. In the entire *Ars* of the Master, one finds only one reference of a clearly monastic character — that to the abbot (RM 3.67; RB 4.61).

Chapter 5: The Treatise of Benedict (RB 4)

The additional monastic touches of RB, here and later, are all indicators that mitigate against the priority of the Benedictine text.

Undoubtedly, the maxim of the Master stems from the original list. Like the parallel passage from the Commentary on the Psalms,[47] the sole means it prescribes for rejecting evil thoughts is having recourse to Christ. Benedict adds the monastic practice of confession. In a way, he joins the fifth step of humility with the first.[48] This combination does not seem totally coherent: if the thought has already been "dashed," why manifest it?

3. *Verba uana aut risui apta non loqui* (RB 4.53). The Master writes *ex toto* after *non* (RM 3.59), which makes the prohibition more categorical.[49] One finds a similar difference on the same point at the end of the treatise on silence, but this time it is Benedict who is, at least apparently, more insistent than the Master, adding *in omnibus locis*.[50] The variant that we observe here would hardly be significant if Benedict did not let a rather remarkable confession slip when discussing Lent. He says that during this holy season, monks must cut back on talkativeness and "jokes."[51] Does this not reveal that the latter are not completely prohibited in ordinary time? Thus, in practice, Benedict seems to have made concessions in the *aeterna clusura* to which, following the Master, he had condemned these sorts of words. Perhaps the absence of *ex toto* in Benedict's maxim is explained by this. As opposed to what we have noted in other cases, Benedict would have softened the absolute expression of the Master here.

4. *Praeceptis abbatis in omnibus oboedire, etiamsi ipse aliter, quod absit, agat, memores illud dominicum praeceptum: Quae dicunt facite; quae autem faciunt, facere nolite* (RB 4.61). This sentence replaces a brief maxim of the Master: *Oboedientiam ad monitionem abbatis parare* (RM 3.67). It is certainly later, as demonstrated by its exorbitant length, the circumstantial clauses with which it is loaded, and the explicit citation with which it concludes. Incidentally, it poses a problem unknown to the Master—that of the attitude to be adopted toward a deficient superior.[52] One recognizes two characteristic traits of Benedict here: concern for the subjective difficulties of obedience and taking into account the inadequacies of the abbot.

The Last Maxims (RB 4.62–74)

Without returning to the maxim that immediately follows,[53] we move to the final group on charity that contains four sentences proper to Benedict: *Elationem fugere. Et seniores uenerare. Iuniores diligere. In Christi amore pro inimicis orare* (RB 4.69–72). These are the first and only maxims that Benedict adds to the common text.[54] He inserts them between *Contentionem non amare* and *Cum discordante ante solis occasum in pacem redire*. These two maxims, which follow one another in RM, form a proper sequence: after recommending not to love arguing, it indicates what one must do if it occurs. Therefore, the series belonging to Benedict interrupts a rather natural sequence. Yet, it does so with tact: *Elationem fugere* does not clash with *Contentionem non amare*, and *In Christi amore pro inimicis orare* is along the same lines as *Cum discordante ... in pacem redire*. However, the similarity of these last two maxims with the context is more seeming than real. First, *elatio* is not a direct sin against charity, as are hatred, jealousy, and envy. Next, prayer for enemies supposes a state of enmity that is hardly compatible with reconciliation before sunset. It is true that in RB one is reconciled with an opponent (*discordant*) rather than an enemy (*inimico*) as in RM. However, it is very possible that this Benedictine variation is aimed precisely at overcoming this incompatibility of which we speak.

Whatever the value of these connections, the fact remains that the first and last maxims are in keeping with the context. In contrast, it is immediately apparent that the two middle maxims are additions. Instead of emphasizing faults to avoid and difficulties to surmount, they focus on the peaceful relationships of brothers in community. Moreover, they have a clearly monastic character. "Revere the elders. Love the juniors": these complementary prescriptions are found together in the chapter on community rank (*De ordine congregationis*).[55] Therefore, it is less a matter of age in life than of rank in community. Like *senior spiritalis* in RB 4.50, *seniores* and *iuniores* are terms of cenobitic vocabulary. Thus, these maxims belong to the series of revisions Benedict makes in the list for non-monastic readers that was hardly modified by the Master.

Finally, the *Et* that introduces *seniores uenerare* accentuates the interpolation. Only twice in the common text does one find a similar conjunction at the beginning of a maxim.[56] In these two instances, *Et* indicates a concluding maxim. Yet, this is not the purpose of the conjunction in the present case. One can scarcely explain this *Et*, except as a sign of an interpolation. It seems to indicate that the two maxims on fraternal relations have not been written by the same hand, or at the same time, as the two maxims that they separate.

Therefore, this small Benedictine series seems to have been composed in two phases: Benedict began by inserting the maxims on pride and prayer for enemies,[57] carefully adapting them to the context, then glossed between them the maxims on reverence for elders and love of juniors, which are both considered without taking into account the surrounding maxims.

Chapter 5: The Treatise of Benedict (RB 4)

The Announcement of the Reward (RB 4.75–76)

In RB the conclusion is presented in a form that is consistently shorter than RM. The first sentence has four fewer words (RM 3.78; RB 4.75). The second is two times shorter (RM 3.79–82; RB 4.76). The description of paradise is contained in a single brief citation (RM 3.83–94; RB 4.77). Finally, the definition of the workshop has six fewer words (RM 6.1–2; RB 4.78).

We have already commented on the first two sentences.[58] It appeared then that the presentation of the Master was the original and that of Benedict later: the true name of the list was *ars*, not *instrumenta*, and it was this *ars* (created object) that must be returned to the Lord to obtain the reward. We must still compare the two versions of the second sentence:

RM 3.79–82	RB 4.76
a Quae ars sancta cum fuerit a nobis die noctuque incessabiliter adimpleta,	Quae cum fuerint a nobis die noctuque incessabiliter adimpleta
b et cum unusquisque in die iudicii Domino Deo factorum suorum operam adsignauerit,	et
a¹ tunc haec ars sancta, quae ex Dei uoluntate descendit, cum a nobis perfecta	
b¹ et inculpabiliter Domino fuerit in die iudicii reconsignata,	in die iudicii reconsignata,
c illa merces nobis a Domino repensetur, quam nobis fidelis Dominus repromittit ...	illa merces nobis a Domino recompensabitur, quam ipse promisit:

The sentence of the Master is inordinately redundant. Twice it moves from earthly life, where the *ars* (*aa¹*) is accomplished, to judgment, where the result of the latter is presented to the Lord (*bb¹*). Designating the reward *c*, one arrives at the formula *aba¹b¹c*.

The sentence of Benedict limits itself to *ab¹c*. Therefore, it avoids any impoverishing omissions as well as any repetition. It is both succinct and complete.

Which is the original redaction? It is difficult to immediately answer this question, as, at first sight, neither one of the two converse processes—expansion or contraction—is more improbable than the other.[59] But one can attempt to clarify the situation by comparing other similar situations, of which there is no lack.

First, here is a passage where the same contrast is observed between the two Rules:

RM 7.48–50	RB 5.12
a ut non suo arbitrio uiuentes uel desideriis suis et uoluptatibus oboedientes,	ut non suo arbitrio uiuentes uel desideriis suis et uoluptatibus oboedientes,
b sed ambulantes alieno iudicio et imperio,	sed ambulantes alieno iudicio et imperio,
a¹ non solum in supradictis desideriis suis et uoluptatibus coartantur et facere suum nolunt, cum possunt, arbitrium,	
b¹ sed etiam alieno se imperio subdunt	
c et in coenobiis degentes abbatem sibi praeesse non nomen ipsud sibi inesse desiderant.	in coenobiis degentes abbatem sibi praeesse desiderant.

In phrase *a*, the Master candidly acknowledges his redundancy (*supradicta*). If possible, it is even more unwieldy than the previous. Phrases *a¹b¹* (indicative) simply repeat *ab* (participle), with no new elements other than the inversion of the elements of phrase *a¹* and the merely seeming advance *solum ... etiam* added to the opposition *non ... sed*. Perhaps this veritable muddle can again be represented by the formula *aba¹b¹c*.

Benedict again presents a text that is free from all repetition. However, the relationship of the two texts is no longer quite the same as above. First, the elements that appear in RB are no longer *ab¹c*, but *abc*. Next, phrase *c* is significantly abbreviated: only *abbatem sibi praeesse* remains, without the contrasting ending *non nomen ipsud sibi inesse*, which, however, constitutes no redundancy whatsoever.[60] Finally, in the absence of phrases *a¹b¹*, *desiderant* is the only verb in the indicative, and the four preceding participles converge toward it. The relationship of the last participle (*degentes*) to the other three of the series is unclear, whether on the level of syntax (absence of *et*) or that of ideas. Consequently, the Benedictine text does not give the impression, as previously, of a completely successful discourse that flows naturally.

Chapter 5: The Treatise of Benedict (RB 4)

The two Rules are found in a similar relationship at the end of *De oboedientia*:

RM 7.71–74	RB 5.17–19
Nam cum malo animo discipulis oboedit, si non solum nobis de ore sed et Deo de corde inproperat quod malo animo facit.	Nam cum malo animo si oboedit discipulis et non solum nobis de ore sed etiam in corde si murmurauerit,
a Et quamuis inpleat quod ei fuerat inperatum,	etiamsi inpleat iussionem,
b tamen acceptum iam non erit Deo,	tamen acceptum iam non erit Deo,
c qui cor eius respicit murmurantem,	qui cor eius respicit murmurantem,
a¹ et quamuis faciat quod iubetur,	et
b¹ tamen cum malo illud animo facit, nullam et de ipso facto mercedem Dominus inputabit,	pro tali facto nullam consequitur gratiam,
c¹ cum scrutans mox Deus corda eius, triste facientis uotum in eo inuenerit.	immo poenam murmurantium incurrit, si non cum satisfactione emendauerit.

Here again, the *abcb¹* formula of Benedict corresponds to the *abca¹b¹c¹* formula of the Master, phrase *a¹* being represented by the *et* that links *b* to *b¹*.[61] This *abcb¹* formula reveals an apparent repetition of the second element (*bb¹*). However, one will note that *c¹* is replaced by an entirely different text, that, building on *b¹*, further advances the thought. As a result, *nullam consequitur gratiam* (*b¹*) does not appear to be a simple echo of *b*, but also and, more importantly, a preparation for *immo poenam murmurantium incurrit*. Thus the Benedictine redaction is nearly as free from repetition here as it was in the two previous cases.

Here then are three passages where the relationship between the two Rules hardly varies. In contrast with the insufferable redundancy of the Master, Benedict offers a text that has everything that is needed, but nothing more. However, the terseness of Benedict in the second passage results in slight damage to the substance and clarity of the text.

In sum, in spite of the data we have just mentioned, one remains quite perplexed in the face of this phenomenon that recurs three times. The question posed by the finale of the *Ars* is raised again in almost the same terms[62] in the two passages on obedience, and they contribute no truly decisive answer. One will always be able to maintain that the Master develops it or Benedict amplifies it with equal likelihood.

One must attempt to find an approach for solving this question apart from these cases where both Rules are involved. If, for example, one noticed that the texts proper to the Master present the same phenomenon of redundancy, one could draw from this a supposition in favor of the originality of the texts where he agrees with Benedict. In fact, it would appear that the Master has no need of the Benedictine text to indulge in this use of repetition: he occasionally writes thus for himself. Therefore, he could have spontaneously produced the redundant phrases that are simple in appearance in RB.

We examine the parts proper to RM to discover, if possible, some redundancies of the same genre. The first case occurs in the Prologue. As is evident, the first part of this passage consists of passages in second-person singular and first-person plural that alternate regularly.[63] The triple repetition of this alternation is accompanied by numerous additional redundancies. Each return to the second-person singular is accomplished by means of an *Ergo*, followed by an appeal to the reader in which the words vary only slightly:

Prol 1:   *O homo ... qui me auscultas dicentem ...*
Prol 5:   *Ergo auditor qui me audis dicentem....*
Prol 8:   *Ergo qui me auscultas....*

The same words and ideas constantly return, and there is little development in thought from one paragraph to the next. It is clearly the stagnation that we commented on in the long phrases of Chapters Three and Seven.

Still, it is a matter here of distant repetitions, not of redundancies within the same phrase. But it is not necessary to go very far to encounter this latter phenomenon under the specific form that interests us. The commentary on the *Pater* offers two good examples. First, a passage from the commentary on the third petition in Thp 41–42:

a   quia quomodo uersis in se oculis suis
    uultum suum respicere homo non potest,
b   sic iudex sui sibi esse non potest,
c   nisi iuste quod uidetur ab alio iudicetur.
a¹ Si ergo uultum suum uidere nemo potest,
b¹ uoluntatem suam iustam probare quomodo potest,
c¹ nisi in nobis quod uidetur ab alio iudicetur?

Chapter 5: The Treatise of Benedict (RB 4)

The variation between *ab* and *a¹b¹* is insignificant: one moves from a comparative clause (*a*) to a conditional clause (*a¹*), and from a negative clause (*b*) to an interrogative clause (*b¹*). In *c* and *c¹*, the only difference is the substitution of *in nobis* for *iuste*. Does the Master depend on a source text here that he develops by repeating? One could suppose so since the commentary on the *Pater* is probably essentially a borrowed passage. But these two exact phrases are part of a digression that clearly interrupts the commentary on the third petition.[64] Therefore, the source text has not provided one of the phrases, whose repetition would be attributed to the same interpolator who introduced both phrases into the source text. Obviously, this interpolator who repeats himself is to be identified with the redundant author of Chapters Three to Seven.

Now a case drawn from the commentary on the sixth petition in Thp 71–74:

    Ergo incessanter est praecandum ad Dominum,
a   ut dignetur adiutorii sui custodia muro nos suae gratiae circumdare
    et temptationum in nobis aditos sua munitione obstruere,
b   ut non patiatur plasmam facturae suae captiuam fieri et seruitutibus cedere inimici,
a¹   si tamen supradicti hostis temptationibus non ultro nostrum tradamus adsensum,
b¹   et uelut nosmetipsos ipsi nos captiuantes
c   hostem nostrum incipiamus magis desiderare quam fugere.

Here, the redundancy is much less evident because it is limited to the words *temptationum-temptationibus* (aa¹) and *captiuam-captiuantes* (bb¹).[65] Moreover, phrases a¹b¹ introduce a real development in thought. Therefore, the repetitions are progressive, and the case is clearly different from those we have analyzed thus far. Note that this passage seems to belong to the original text of the commentary that RM probably borrowed.

We conclude with a case that is closer to those that interest us. It is found in the treatise on silence:[66]

a   Vnde e contrario fit ut migrante de ipso domicilio anima
totum in mortuo homine desit quod
agebatur in uiuo ab anima quae migrauit,
b   et mox sua terrae mortua reddita gleba,
reuertens in natura terrae hominis terra,
absconsoque homine in sepulcro recoperta fossa,
in figura sua terra redeat pauimenti,
c   ut similis tunc fuisse terra uiuente agnoscatur in homine,
quae animae fuerat rigore erecta
et peregrinae uitae mutata ad tempus.
a¹   Ideo animae in nobis migrante rigore,
stare non potest nostri corporis terra,
b¹   sed cadens in naturam suam
abscondat in sinu suo terra facturam quam genuit.

The redundancy is very clear here. The soul departs—all life ceases (*aa¹*); dust returns to dust (*bb¹*). In addition, one will note several minor repetitions of words or ideas within phrases: *migrante ... anima* and *anima quae migrauit* (*a*); *reuertens in natura terrae hominis terra* and *in figura sua terra redeat pauimenti* (*b*). The series is almost as muddled and ponderous as RM 3.79–82. Moreover, we note that this interminable phrase has the appearance of a digression in Chapter Eight. In this respect, it must be linked with the interpolated phrases in the commentary on the third intercession of the *Pater*.[67] We will see that the commentary on the *Pater* and the introductory discourse of Chapter Eight are related, both apparently borrowed from the same source. It is significant that both also present interpolations where one recognizes the same unskilled writer, unable to develop his thought without repetition.

Therefore, this inquiry into the parts proper of the Master yields an important observation. Here, where he is alone, our author occasionally falls into the vice of redundancy just as he did when he traveled alongside Benedict. Moreover, these solitary redundancies are not based on a preexisting text even when the context is drawn from a source. They do not stem from the juxtaposition of a gloss with a glossed text. They are not composite, but simple: a single author, who is fond of or unable to extricate himself from this style, is responsible.

These conclusions shed light on the three cases where the redundant text of the Master corresponds to a sober text of Benedict. Based on Thp 40–42 and 8.12–16, it is very likely that the Master did not gloss the sober text but produced the redundant text completely independently. Consequently, it seems that the Benedictine redaction was later. The few

Chapter 5: The Treatise of Benedict (RB 4)

clues revealed in RM 7.48–50 would suggest that it is not the Master who developed RB, but Benedict who simplified the prolix phrases of RM.

The Evocation of Paradise (RB 4.77)

The sentence we have just studied is not yet complete in RM. It continues with a relative clause that indicates who the reward is reserved for: *(merces) quae paratur sanctis et Deum timentibus et haec praecepta factis implentibus* (RM 3.83). The description of paradise that follows is also closely attached to RM 3.79–82 by the gerundive *habitandi* (3.84). Thus, the Master does not separate the announcement of the reward from the designation of its beneficiaries and its description. They all form a single sentence.

In contrast, Benedict, not satisfied with merely shortening the sentence that announces the reward, interrupts it after *promisit.* The rest is a citation from Saint Paul: *Quod oculos non uidit nec auris audiuit, quae praeparauit Deus his qui diligunt illum.*[68] One will note that this scriptural citation is definitely in context: the words *quam ipse promisit* herald a scriptural text.[69] RM, in contrast, contains no citation whatsoever after the reference to the "promise." The beneficiaries of the reward are designated with words that reference no particular passage of Scripture. The description of paradise will not be drawn primarily from canonical Scripture, but from the Apocrypha *Visio Pauli*, itself utilized very freely. It is true that the authority of this Apocrypha and its counterparts was so great in the eyes of the Master that he was able to consider their eschatological descriptions as authentic "promises of the Lord."[70]

The Pauline text that Benedict cites contains two elements: first, a completely apophatic evocation of heaven (*Quod oculos non uidit nec auris audiuit*), then the designation of those for whom this happiness is reserved (*quae praeparauit Deus his qui diligunt illum*). These are the very elements that we found in RM although it placed them in the opposite order: first, a brief reference to those for whom God has reserved the reward (RM 3.83), then, the lengthy description of paradise (RM 3.84).

In making these observations, one cannot help but be struck by the original character of the Benedictine text. In fact, we assume that Benedict comes after the Master and wants to give the redaction a briefer and more biblical twist. It would have been an unusual stroke of good fortune for him to find a brief citation from Scripture that joined the exact two elements that follow one another in RM. However, this is what happens in the present case, and the citation also corresponds perfectly to the reference to the divine promise that immediately precedes it! Such good fortune is scarcely conceivable. The reverse process is better explained: the Master reads 1 Corinthians 2:9 in his source, and, desiring to develop it, revises each of the elements of the sacred text, first the phrase *quae praeparauit* ... , which he barely expands, then the two apophatic clauses, for which he substitutes a long detailed description.

Such is the interpretation that emerges when one compares the two texts as a whole. We will see if it is confirmed by a study of the details. We compare the two following clauses:

RM 3.83	RB 4.77 (1 Cor 2:9)
quae paratur sanctis et Deum timentibus et haec praecepta factis implentibus ...	quae praeparauit Deus his qui diligunt illum.

Obviously, the words *quae paratur* correspond with *quae praeparauit*. The relative is in the feminine singular in RM, with the antecedent *merces*, while it is in the neuter plural in 1 Corinthians and RB. Here again, a progression from the Master to Benedict seems less obvious than the reverse process. Benedict would have needed exceptional luck to find a Scripture text that corresponded so closely, not only to the thought, but even to the letter of the Master, while the latter could have easily adapted the scriptural text to his own context.

Next, note that the two authors differ in regard to the attitude of the elect toward God: one speaks of fear, the other of love. It is tempting to connect this contrast with an occurrence noted at the beginning of the *Ars*. There, before citing the two commandments of love, the Master enjoins his readers to "believe in, confess, and fear God" (RM 3.1). In contrast, Benedict begins immediately with the first commandment: "to love." Thus, at both ends of the *Ars*, the Master has placed references to fear that are lacking in RB. Benedict puts precepts concerning love in these places, the second of which is missing in RM.[71]

The correspondence of *Deum timentibus* (RM 3.83) with *timere Deum* (3.1) does not give us confidence in this last phrase of the redaction of the Master. The words *timere Deum* are, in fact, part of the Trinitarian confession that clearly appears to be an addition to the beginning of the *Ars*.

However, one must set this unfavorable evidence alongside two opposing facts. First, in a passage from the shared text,[72] it is clearly fear of God rather than love that merits eternal reward. Second, the expression *haec praecepta factis implentibus* reproduces one of the articles from the list that belongs to both Rules.[73] Moreover, the words *factis implere* (or *adimplere*) return many times, not only in the writings proper to the Master, but also in the first lines of the treatise on the abbot, also a shared text.[74] Thus the phrase *quae paratur sanctis*[75] *et Deum timentibus et haec praecepta factis implentibus* appears to be in continuity with the original source of our Rules. Consequently, in spite of the compelling reasons discussed above,[76] one hesitates to consider it later.

The Definition of the Workshop (RB 4.78)

We must now compare the two redactions of what is for both Rules the last sentence of the treatise:

RM 6.1–2	RB 4.78
Officina uero monasterium est, in qua ferramenta cordis in clusura corporis reposita opus diuiniae artis diligenti custodia perseuerando operari potest.	Officina uero ubi haec omnia diligenter operemur claustra sunt monasterii et stabilitas in congregatione.

Nothing could be more difficult than interpreting this table. We will attempt to at least untangle the threads that are woven between the two texts.

The Master makes a distinction between the "tools" and the "created object," which here, as above, Benedict does not recognize. In RB, only the dry and vague words *haec omnia* correspond to the *ferramenta cordis ... opus diuinae artis* of RM.

A second contrast is observed concerning the words *clusura* and *claustra*, which are clearly linked. In RM, it is a matter of an image: the enclosure is the body insofar as it contains the heart and its "tools." In contrast, in RB it is a matter of a reality: the enclosure is the monastery where one is really enclosed.[77] While the word of the Master metaphorically evokes the monk, that of Benedict specifies the exterior framework of the action: the workshop is not merely the "monastery" but the enclosure of the monastery.

One can make a similar observation concerning the parallel terms *perseuerando* and *stabilitas in congregatione.* The gerundive of the Master indicates the effort of the subject: perseverance is considered as the action and virtue of the artisan.[78] In contrast, the substantive of Benedict is presented as a defining element of the workshop, in the same capacity as *claustra monasterii*: stability, which emphasizes the specification "in community," is considered an objective condition, a constitutive element of the external framework. There is only a slight difference between the two texts, but the Master accentuates the action of the monk, Benedict, the objective condition.

We also note that the principal and relative clauses are of converse structure in the two texts: in RM, the principal, very brief, is followed by an extensive relative; in RB, the principal runs from one end of the sentence to the other and envelops the brief relative. The relative of RM is not only longer, but it also plays a more important role. Instead of being a simple explanation of *officina*, like *ubi haec omnia diligenter operemur*, it proposes a new topic, the manner of using the tools, corresponding to the second question of the title.[79] Consequently, the corresponding words of the two relatives, *diligenti custodia ... operari potest* and *diligenter operemur*, do not carry the same weight: RM is much more insistent than RB. Here again, it appears that, beyond the workshop, the Master is especially interested in individual effort.

Such are the connections and principal differences between the two texts. We must still determine which of the two is the original redaction. One will recall that the text of the Master has certainly undergone some revisions.[80] There is every indication that Benedict did not find a distinct chapter on the workshop, the long and awkward relative clause of RM 6.2, or an attempt to describe the manner of using the tools in his source. The Benedictine redaction can be considered the most faithful to the original text in regard to all of these. However, this redaction is not exempt from anomalies. First and foremost, there is that of adding "tools," represented by *haec omnia,* to *operemur*: the tools are the objects with which one works, not the objects that one produces. There is one other peculiarity to speak of: the phrase, "the workshop, that is stability." Even seen from an objective point of view, *stabilitas* can hardly serve as an attributive to *officina* and as a term matching with the concrete *claustra*.

Therefore, it seems that neither of these two texts is exactly representative of the original text. And it would be futile to attempt to reconstitute it. However, all things considered, one is inclined to think that Benedict has safeguarded the essential traits better than the Master.

Summary of the Results

The time has come to summarize the results of our comparative analysis of RM 3–6 and RB 4. The overview we began with suggested that the Benedictine redaction was situated at the beginning of the last stage of the development of the *Ars*: the text used by Benedict already contained the *merces* between the *ars* and the *ferramenta* but did not yet include the list of vices between the *ferramenta* and the *officina*. We can now add two new details to this picture: first, it seems that Benedict

Chapter 5: The Treatise of Benedict (RB 4)

did not find the Trinitarian preamble of the *Ars* (RM 3.1) in his source; second, while he probably read the introductory phrase of the *merces* in its long and redundant form (RM 3.79–82), it could be that the description of the *merces* (reward) still consisted only of the Pauline citation (1 Cor 2:9) that he himself transmitted to us.[81]

In many cases, the maxims of the list prove to be later in the Benedictine redaction. The "monastic" touches of RB 4 are particularly significant in this regard. They consist either in the omission of certain sentences inappropriate to cenobitism (those prescribing making loans, giving alms, loyalty to others, and fulfilling one's promises) or, in certain additions, referencing the "spiritual senior," the "elders," and the "young." The transformation of "Honor your father and mother" to "Honor all people" reveals the same tendency. There is also the characteristic concern of Benedictine legislation to provide for the insufficiencies of the superior that inspires the long addition on obedience to an unworthy abbot.

Other revisions of Benedict deal with maxims that probably appeared to him not in close enough conformity with the New Testament. Such is certainly the case with the change from *Non amare iurare* to *Non iurare* and probably also with that from *Non amare detrahere* to *Non detractorem*. In these cases, Benedict does not seem to have been aware of the patristic or Old Testament sources of the sentences he corrected. It is possible that *Corpus [pro anima] castigare, Inimicos [plus quam amicos] diligere,* and *Maledicentes se non [solum non] remaledicere* result from revisions of the same nature, made by a deliberate return to Scripture.

Finally, Benedict seems to have carefully revised the two maxims regarding individual responsibility for good and evil. The influence of Augustine appears indisputable on the severe doctrine of RB.

Beyond this, there remain few cases where the variants of Benedict could possibly represent the original text.[82] Overall, the *Ars* of the Master is certainly the more faithful to the original.

Endnotes

1. See *The Witness of E** in Chapter 4.
2. That is to say from RM 4 (see the following note).
3. Consequently, RM 4.T is probably in its proper place (cf. Chapter Four, nn. 128 and 139).
4. This way of preserving the last phrase is reminiscent of RB 6.8, which reproduces RM 9.51 in its entirety, while RB 6.7 simply summarizes the entirety of RM 9 in a single phrase.
5. To be complete, one would have to add the *merces* in the stage represented by RB.
6. RM 2.52; 3.78; 4.T; 6.T, and 2. Benedict uses *ferramentum* (RB 32.T–1) only on two occasions where he is following the Master (RM 17.T–1). The word is foreign to his vocabulary proper. — For the relationship of the two terms, see Cassian, *Conl.* 1.7 (*ferramentum* once, then *instrumentum* three times); 21.5 (once each).
7. The same is true of the French word *instrument,* less specific and colorful than the word *outil* (English: "tool").
8. *Ars* designates either the craft and its rules (2.51–52; 3.T; 6.T) or the object fashioned according to the rules of the craft (3.81; cf. 85.T). The expression is ambiguous in 3.78–79; 4.T; 6.2.
9. *Factorum suorum operam* (3.80).
10. Bernard Capelle, "Un plaidoyer pour la Règle du Maître," *Recherches de Théologie Ancienne et Médiévale* 12 (1940): 14–23.
11. Cassian, *Conl.* 1.7; 21.15. We take "virtue" here in the sense of *Conl.* 21.15, where the word designates charity and its daughters, juxtaposed with fasting and other exterior practices. In contrast, in *Conl.* 1.7, *uirtutes* designates the exterior practices juxtaposed with charity. One sees that although the thought of Cassian is the same in these two texts, the meaning of the word *uirtus* varies.
12. *Conl.* 6.10. Capelle, 16 (cited in n. 10) understands "instruments for the formation of virtues." However, it may be a matter of a simple explicative genitive ("the instruments that are the works"), since *uirtus* means "work" in *Conl.* 1.7 (preceding note). The same ambiguity with *uirtutum ... instrumentis* exists in *Conl.* 24.24.3.
13. Cf. RB Prol 47; 7.67–69.
14. Evagrius, *Sent.* 79: *instrumenta artis suae* (PL 20.1184a); *organa artis suae* (early version edited by J. Leclerq). The context does not indicate whether it is a matter of works or virtues.
15. *Vitae Patrum* 5.15.34: *ferramenta sunt quibus anima operatur.*
16. Pelagius, *Ad Demetr.* 25.
17. *Vitae Patr. Jur.* II.7.86.
18. Greg. Nyss., *De uirg.* 23.1; Hillary, *Vita Honorati* 17 (*officina uirtutum*).
19. *Conl.* 1.7: *ieiunia, uigiliae, mediatio scripturarum, nuditas ac priuatio omnium facultatum*; 6.10: *psalmus, oratio, lectio*; 21.15: *ieiunium.*

Chapter 5: The Treatise of Benedict (RB 4)

20 RB 9.7 (cf. 11.3).

21 *Passio Juliani* 49. In the first phrase, the reading *trinus* is proper to AS, while one finds *trinitas* in G and L as well as in the three Vatican manuscripts: *Lat. 5771, Reg. 516*, and *Arch S. Petr. A 2*. The second phrase is attested to by AS, L, and *Vat. Lat. 5771*. On the other hand, it and the "modalist" formula, *Ipse est Christus Deus aeternus, Pater in Filio est et Spiritus Sanctus* are missing in *Reg. 516* and *Arch. S. Petr. A 2*. For its part, G substitutes the formula "the one who is in heaven in the consubstantial Trinity" (203.20–21). These three last witnesses seem to reflect the unease caused by a phrase that could seem theologically incorrect. The first Trinitarian formula of *Pass. Jul.* 49 (*unus in Trinitate et Trinitas in unitate*) is missing in P (no. 51, p. 139). The second (*qui est trina maiestas et una deitas*) is significantly modified: *in quo est una maiestas et deitas*. This substitution of *una* for *trina* before *maiestas* undoubtedly stems from the same theological scruples that one detects in the reading of G and the omission of the two Vatican manuscripts.

22 Note that *haec est* is found both in the introduction of the *Quicumque* (*fides catholica haec est*) and in that of the *Ars* (*Quae haec est ars sancta*). Is this the stamp of the Creed on RM or a simple coincidence? See Adalbert de Vogüé, "Scholies sur la Règle du Maître," *Revue d'Ascétique et de Mystique* (*RAM*) 44 (1968): 266.

23 See the previous note, as well as "Scholies," 288–289.

24 See Adalbert de Vogüé, "Honorer tous les hommes," *RAM* 40 (1964): 129–138.

25 However, when it comes to Scripture citations, one must always leave open the possibility of increased fidelity to Scripture on the part of the dependent author (see n. 35 below). Some definite cases of this phenomenon are presented in RM 3.22 = RB 4.27 (see nn. 33–34 below), as well as in RM 10.88 = RB 7.67, where the two Rules align more closely with 1 John 4:18 than does the source text (Cassian, *Inst.* 4.39.3). Beyond these Rules, see also the case we have analyzed in "Ne haïr personne," *RAM* 44 (1968): 4, n. 8.

26 RB 54.1. Benedict is more severe here than Pachomius, *Reg.* 183 (*Leg.* 7), who permits loans, at least between men of the same building.

27 Basil, *Reg.* 98–99 and 185–186; RM 16.32–37.

28 The expression *fidem seruare* is also found in RM 1.7 = RB 1.7. Therefore, it belongs to the common source of the two Rules.

29 Ths. 29–30: *qui iurat proximo suo et non decepit eum, qui pecuniam suam non dedit ad usuram* (Ps 14:4–5).

30 Cf. Cassian, Inst. 5.22 and Conl. 5.16: *Noli diligere detrahere, ne eradiceris*.

31 Wisdom 1:11: *Custodite ergo uos a murmuratione et a detractione parcite linguae*. Cf. RM 78.12: *et conuersi in murmurium et detractionem tales odire incipiant peregrinos*.

32 Matthew 5:34: *Ego dico uobis non iurare omnino*.

33 This is confirmed by RM 11.66–67: *Si uero audierit multum fratrem iurantem ... Quid tantum iuras*, which cites in its support Matthew 5:34 with the gloss: *ne per iuramentum nascatur causa periurii*, an obvious allusion to the teaching of Ambrose. One will note that *multem iurantem* seems to allude to Sirach 23:12 (*uir multum iurans implebitur iniquitate*), a sentence very close to Sirach 23:9 (*iurationi non assuescat os tuum, multi enim casus in illa*), which is the text on

which Ambrose and Augustine rely (see Chapter Four, n. 72). Cf. Sir. 27:15: *loquela multum iurans horripilationem capiti statuet.*

34 Matthew 5:44; Luke 6:27. The addition of the Master has a basis in the portion of the Gospel text that contrasts love of friends with love of enemies.

35 See n. 25 above.

36 Ths 25–26 (see Chapter Four, n. 24). Compare also *a Domino fieri* (Ths 25) and *a Deo factum* (3.46).

37 The infinitive gives a *cursus uelox*, the subjunctive a *cursus tardus*.

38 A count of syllables gives respectively: 11–13–9–12 (RM 3.46–47) and 11–8–12–6 (RB 4.42–43). The maximum difference is four syllables in RM, six in RB.

39 Compare the text of Valerian of Cimiez cited in the note on RM 3.46–47. On the other hand, like the maxim of Benedict, the texts of Porphyrius and Augustine, cited by Butler, leave the individual alone in the presence of God.

40 See in particular Thp 74; 1.19, 30, 73; 7.31, 74; 13.25; 16.66; 92.46. Therefore, it is not necessary to see the expression of the Master as a "significant mitigation" of that of Benedict, as did C. Vagaggini, "S. Benedetto e la questione semipelagiana," *Studia Benedictina*, Studia Anselmiana Series (Rome: 1947), 58, n. 40.

41 As well as instances shared by the two Rules (Ths 24 = Prol 28; RM 1.4 = RB 1.4). As regards *diabolicus*, one can consider RM 7.71 (twice) = RB 53.5 as a shared text. Although the Master and Benedict both use the term twice more, only Benedict has *malignus* (RB 43.8. Cf. Ths 24 = Prol 28), while only the Master has *Satanas* (RM 93.84).

42 Prol 4: *ut quidquid agendum inchoas bonum, ab eo perfici instantissima oratione deposcas.*

43 Cf. RM 82.4–11, 16; RM 16.1–26; RM 86.3–16. See also Chapter Four, nn. 88–89.

44 See nn. 32–36 in Chapter Seven.

45 Cf. RB 49.7: *cum spiritalis desiderii gaudio* (to desire Easter "spiritually," not only for the sake of relaxation.)

46 RB 46.5 (also confession). Cf. 49.9: *patris spiritalis.*

47 Ths 24 = Prol 28. Cf. RM 8.23.

48 Note that the words *cogitationes malas cordi suo aduenientes* are found both here and in the fifth step (RM 10.61 = RB 7.44; Cassian wrote only: *cogitationes*) in the common text. Therefore, it is quite natural that Benedict finished connecting the two passages by introducing confession, a practice characteristic of the fifth step.

49 This also leads to the absence of the rhythmic clausula, while Benedict has a *cursus planus*.

50 RM 9.51 = RB 6.8. One could also interpret these words as a gloss explaining *aeterna clusura*, understood here as "exclusion" (see the commentary on RB 6 in Chapter Six, nn. 67–70).

51 RB 49.7: *de loquacitate, de scurrilitate.*

Chapter 5: The Treatise of Benedict (RB 4)

52 See A. de Vogüé, *La Communauté et l'Abbé* (Brussels: Desclée des Brouwer, 1961), 520–521 and 523–524; ET: *Community and Abbot* (Kalamazoo, MI: Cistercian, 1979 [I] and 1988 [II]).

53 RM 3.68 = RB 4.62. See Chapter Four, nn. 47–48.

54 *Non detractorem* (RB 4.40) corresponds to *Non amare detrahere* (RM 3.29), previously omitted by Benedict.

55 RB 63.10: *Juniores igitur priores suos honorent, priores minores suos diligent.* Although the term designating the elder differs, this last is also later called *senior suus* (RB 63.16), as in RB 4.70.

56 RM 3.9 = RB 4.9; RM 3.76 = RB 4.74. *Et* is missing here in many manuscripts but seems authentic.

57 In this last (RB 4.72), the words *in Christi amore* are reminiscent of RB 7.34: *pro Dei amore,* another addition of Benedict, as well as RB 7.69: *amore Christi.*

58 See nn. 8–10 above, as well as RM 3.78 and RB 4.75.

59 See a summary of the conflicting interpretations in G. Penco, *S. Benedicti Regula* (Florence: 1958), 230–232.

60 In its absence, *abbatem sibi praeesse* seems slightly hollow and inexpressive.

61 Compare the *et* shared by RM 3.80 and RB 4.76.

62 It would have been more difficult for the Master to make an interpolation in the case of RM 3.80–81 where, compared with the Benedictine text, the added phrases are ba^l, against the flow of the sentence.

63 See the initial note in Adalbert de Vogüé, *La Règle du Maître*, Sources Chrétiennes 105–107 (Paris: Cerf, 1964–65) I.288.

64 Thp 40–42 (see the note *in loco*). The case is identical to that of RM 8.12–16 (see n. 67 below).

65 Note also *supradicti hostis* (a^l) referring to *inimici* (*b*) and repeated by *hostem nostrum* (*c*). This *supradicti* is reminiscent of RM 7.49, mentioned above.

66 RM 8.12–16. See also RM 16.18–22 ($aba^l b^l$) that is part of a passage that is probably interpolated (cf. Thp 41–42 and 8.12–16).

67 Thp 40–42. See n. 64 above.

68 1 Corinthians 2:9. Benedict omits the words *nec in cor hominis ascendit.*

69 It matters little that the text had Saint Paul as its human author, who himself cited Isaiah. It is clearly the Lord himself who speaks through his apostle. The suitability of the citation is emphasized by *ipse,* as opposed to *fidelis Dominus* in RM.

70 See *La Règle du Maître* I.215–218.

71 Certainly, RB often insists on love (see n. 57 above), but the significance of *his qui diligunt illum* must not be overemphasized, since Benedict only reproduces Saint Paul. More typical perhaps is the *Deum timentibus* of the Master, especially if one concedes that it is a correction. See our remarks on RM 10.120 (*quam preparavit Deus his qui diligunt eum*) in the commentary on RB 7, Chapter 7 (nn. 127–130).

72 RM 10.11 (*uita aeterna quid timentibus Deum praeparet*) = RB 7.11 (*uita aeterna quae timentibus Deum praeparata est*). In this passage, the influence of 1 Corinthians 2:9 may explain the variant of Benedict: for him, as for Saint Paul, the one who "prepares eternal life" seems to be God himself.

73 RM 3.69 = RB 4.63: *Praecepta Dei factis cottidie adimplere.*

74 RM 2.1 = RB 2.1 Frequent in the texts proper to the Master, the expression is absent from the texts proper to Benedict.

75 Cf. RM 3.68 = RB 4.62: *Non uelle dici sanctum....* Is it by mere coincidence that this maxim immediately precedes RM 3.69 = RB 4.63, which provides the Master with the words *haec praecepta factis implentibus*?

76 We note in passing that the *paratur* of the Master is not necessarily a sign of 1 Corinthians 2:9. See the similar uses of this verb in Matthew 20:23 and 25:34; John 14:2; Revelation 12:6, etc. When the Master actually uses 1 Corinthians 2:9, he writes *praeparauit*, as does Benedict here (RM 10.120).

77 Cf. RB 67.7: *nec claustra monasterii egredi*; RM 91.3: *claustro monasterii uindicetur.*

78 Cf. RM 4.10: *perseuerantia usque in finem*; Ths 46 = Prol 50: *usque ad mortem perseuerantes.*

79 RM 6.T: *uel (quae est) operatio spiritalium ferramentorum.*

80 See RM 2.52; 3.78; 4.T; 6.T; 8.22; 17.1–4. See also n. 2 above and Chapter Four, nn. 133–135.

81 However, in addition to the previously raised objections, one will note that Benedict replaces *et Hierusalem sanctam* (RM 3.52), which seems to represent the original text, with *par omni concupiscentia spiritali* (RB 4.46). One cannot help but connect this change with that observed in the description of paradise. If Benedict removed the reference to "Holy Jerusalem" in this maxim, is it not because he intended to omit the description of "Jerusalem, city adorned with gold and gems" (RM 3.92)?

82 One of these cases is the absence of *Desideria sua a Deo perfici optare* and of *Substantiam suam non in solo labore manuum suarum, sed plus a Deo sperare* (RM 3.48–49), as well as the variant *inputare/reputet* in the preceding maxim, where the odd infinitive of the Master seems to result from the infinitives that follow — *optare* and *sperare*. The Benedictine text also seems to be closer to the original redaction in RM 6.1–2 = RB 4.78.

Part Three

Silence and Humility

Chapter Six

Silence

I. The Treatise of the Master (RM 8–9)

Like the treatise of RM on obedience, that on silence is definitely an amalgam. But, in the present case, the lack of unity is aggravated by the fact that the virtue in question first appears mixed with other forms of ascesis. It is only toward the end of Chapter Eight that the exposition on silence sufficiently develops to give the impression that one has truly entered into the subject. Immediately afterward, the chapter comes to an abrupt close. As a whole, it provides the worst possible basis for its title, *De taciturnitate*. Far from constituting a treatise on silence, one could say that its general considerations serve as an introduction to Chapter Nine. This latter corresponds perfectly to its title: *Quo ordine tacentes fratres aliquas interrogationes faciant abbati*.[1] It is only in this second chapter that the matter, in and of itself, is fully treated.

Overview of RM 8

Not only is the treatise on silence divided into two chapters, but the first chapter itself is clearly broken in two. It becomes immediately apparent if one notes the repetition of certain themes. After a discussion of the relationship between the soul and the body (8.1–16), the author proceeds to some moral applications (8.17–18). These concern first sight (8.19–20), then thought and speech (8.21–23). The touch of the hands and steps of the feet, named simply as a matter of interest, are set aside (8.24–25). Up to this point, the theme is developed coherently, without repetition. But from 8.26 forward, one returns to thought (8.27–29) and speech (8.30–37). These two functions are no longer considered conjointly but consecutively in similarly constructed paragraphs: the tempted brother begins by signing himself, then recites an appropriate psalm text. The commentary on one of these texts (Ps 38:2–3) forms the development on silence that concludes the chapter.

Thus, one distinguishes two sections in RM 8. The first (8.1–25) examines human behavior using three metaphors: a building, a tree, and childbirth. The second (8.26–37) makes no use of this imagery. The first passage contains no Scripture citations; in the second, they abound. The first passage speaks of the "human race," the "soul," and the "man." The second is addressed to the "brother," a monastic term that the first part never employs. Moreover, the first part does not seem to be intended specifically for monks. If one keeps one's gaze downcast, it is to avoid seeing objects that arouse concupiscence;[2] the sins of the hands and feet are robbery, homicide, and taking flight.[3] Finally, the first part is an exhortation in first-person plural, while the second employs a legislative style in third person.

All of these contrasts make the two parts of RM 8 two clearly different passages. The first resembles the baptismal catechesis of the *Thema* in a number of characteristics.[4] Like this latter, it may borrow its content from a collection of homilies for the laity. In contrast, the second part bears the mark of concerns proper to the Master.[5] He prescribes a very definite method of combat, apparently wishing to particularize the too vague instructions of the first passage.

The transitional sentence that joins the two texts (8.26) hides their discontinuity rather poorly. Its redactor employs the authorial "we" (*diximus*), which is at variance with the predicatory "we" of the first part.[6] In referring to "what has been said above," he distinguishes three superior faculties (*tria suprema*) that, in reality, do not correspond entirely with the schema traced above.[7] The connection with what follows is scarcely better. Not only does it fail to anticipate the *ut* that will brusquely introduce the prescriptions concerning speech, but the word *cogitatio*, which is left dangling at this point, seems to be a title that has inadvertently survived an earlier redaction. These facts lead one to think that the second passage was written independently on a separate folio[8] and subsequently inserted here with an introductory paragraph that only succeeded in tying it to what preceded it with difficulty.

The 8.26 transition presents another perplexing issue. It lists three areas that require particular vigilance: thoughts, speech, and the gaze. Yet only the two first are examined in the rest of the chapter. It is true that the gaze has already been the focus of a development in the first part of the treatise (8.19–20). But the same is true for thoughts and speech. If these last two are reexamined in the second part, why not the gaze? Therefore, one can ask if the gaze is not intentionally placed third in rank here, instead of appearing first, as it previously did (RM 8.9, 17, 19–20). Perhaps the author relegated it to this place precisely with the intent not to speak of it again.[9]

However, we note that an ascesis of the gaze will be prescribed in a digression of sorts in the middle of the next chapter.[10] Certainly, this passage does not present the same characteristics as the developments on thought and speech at the end of Chapter Eight. There are no references to temptation and combat, the sign of the cross, or a scriptural text that is to be recited. However, it is possible that the Master is thinking of these lines when he introduces *aspectum* in 8.26. More specifically, it may be that they represent the end of a longer pericope that began as the treatises on thought and speech. Having first been part of these developments, the pericope on the gaze would have been removed when the Master decided to compose the chapter *De taciturnitate*. To give greater significance and emphasis to this virtue, he would have concluded his chapter with the treatise on speech and prolonged it with a new chapter, entirely devoted to the same theme. The paragraph on the gaze would have been partially reused in this new construction. As an insertion point, the Master chose the inclination of the head that must accompany the *Benedicite* request. We will later see how this insertion is awkward and problematic. Incongruous in its present context, where it has the appearance of an added piece, the 9.21–24 digression has an even greater chance of stemming from an earlier pericope, such as the discussion on the gaze introduced in 8.26.

Whatever one thinks of this hypothesis concerning RM 9.21–24, one cannot deny that we have caught a glimpse of the origin of RM 8. The discord between the title of the chapter and its content suggests that it has been reorganized.[11] The Master wished to create a treatise on silence from a general discussion on ascesis. He was only able to do so by sacrificing a concluding passage on the *aspectus (gaze)*. In this way, he was able to give *eloquium* (speech), if not the absolute primacy suggested by the title *De taciturnitate*, at least the last word. Such is the hypothesis that seems to best account for the facts observed in RM itself. We will soon see that comparison with RB suggests another theory, which we will discuss.

The End of RM 8

As the title of the Master invites, we will now examine more thoroughly the passage on silence that concludes the chapter (8.30–37). At the heart of this text is a citation from Psalm 38:2–3: *Dixi custodiam uias meas....* The phrase of the psalmist has primarily a practical thrust. It is to be recited as an antidote to temptation. But unlike the two psalm citations used against evil thoughts (8.28–29), it will receive commentary. The Master distinguishes two types of silence, one that guards against sins of the tongue, another that humbly refrains from good words. While this latter is required in certain instances, the first is imposed *a fortiori*. And while perfect disciples are granted permission on rare occasions to speak of edifying matters,[12] brothers must never take the initiative in other topics of conversation but wait to be asked by the abbot.

Therefore, the citation *dixi custodiam uias ...* has a twofold impact. Presented as a weapon against sinful words, it also engenders a theory of silence that includes good words. Its first dimension is previously found in Cassian in the sermon of Abba Pinufius on clothing, on the page following the program of spiritual ascent that serves as the source of the ladder of humility in RM and RB. According to Pinufius-Cassian, the monk who is injured and tempted to respond in the same tone, must "unceasingly chant this verse of the psalmist in his heart."[13] The length of the citation is the same in RM and in the *Institutes*.[14] The context is very similar and the injunction to say the verse "in his heart" succeeds in connecting the Master and Cassian.[15] Therefore, it is very likely that RM 8.30–31 was written under the influence of the *Institutes*. In contrast, the commentary of the Master on the citation has no precedent in Cassian. It would seem that this theory of silence on good things belongs totally to the Master.[16]

In addition to citing Psalm 38, the Master adds two texts from Proverbs.[17] In the context of the commentary on the psalm citation, these *testimonia* are presented as theoretical proofs of the necessity for silence. The concrete situation of the tempted brother that led to this citation is no longer at issue. Finally, following the two texts from Proverbs, a concluding sentence defines the respective roles of Master and disciple. By definition, this latter is one of silence.

The Parallel Pericope of RM 9

The theory of silence that we have just analyzed (RM 8.31–37) is developed again in the following chapter (RM 9.32–40). One again finds the two citations from Proverbs as well as that from Psalm 38, the latter giving rise to an almost identical, albeit briefer, commentary. The chief difference between the two passages is that the second is not content to tersely cite the texts from Proverbs one after another, but produces them separately and paired with a brief commentary. This time, *In multiloquio non effugitur peccatum* (Prov 10:9) comes near the beginning of the passage, preceded by some words of introduction, while *Mors et uita in manibus linguae* (Prov 18:21) remains at the end, but is followed by a gloss. Between the two, the psalm citation and its commentary are still of paramount importance, but clearly less so than

Chapter 6: Silence

in the parallel passage in RM 8. Thus, the citations from Proverbs have been accentuated, while that from the Psalms has lost its prominence.

Can one discern an order of precedence between these two parallel redactions? Undoubtedly yes, if one pays heed to the textual variants of the Scripture citations:

	RM 8	**RM 9**
Ps 38:2–3	*delinquam ... silui*	*peccem ... tacui et humiliatus sum (nimis)* om. *tacui: etiam* add.
Prov 18:21	*Mors et uita*	*Vita et mors*

In all respects, RM 8 conforms more to known Scripture texts than does RM 9. *Delinquam ... silui* is in keeping with the Roman Psalter and the Vulgate, while *peccem ... tacui* is not found in any early psalter. The reason for this double variant is easy to understand. *Delinquere* and *silere* are both hapax in RM,[18] while *peccare* and *tacere* are common. In Chapter Eight, the Master simply cites the text, while in Chapter Nine, he adapts it to his own vocabulary.[19] The revision is also apparent in the omission of *et humiliatus sum (nimis)*[20] and the addition of *etiam*. The psalm citation of RM 9 is altogether less pure than that of RM 8. The same is true for the citation of Prov 18:21: it is RM 9 that diverges from the text.

These facts lead one to believe that the Master wrote the two pericopes in the order they presently appear in the Rule. He began by writing RM 8 in conformity with the scriptural texts. Then he wrote RM 9, consciously freeing himself to a certain extent from his biblical sources.[21] Consequently, it is quite understandable that RM 8 produces the three texts in the order they follow in the Bible (Ps 38, Prov 10, Prov 18), while RM 9 breaks this sequence (Prov 10, Ps 38, Prov 18). From this point of view, RM 8 also appears to be the original.[22] Finally, a previously highlighted fact points in the same direction. If, in RM 8, the psalm citation is suggested to the Master by Cassian as a weapon against temptation, it does not have this same function or connection with the *Institutes* in RM 9. Therefore, it seems that RM 8 must have been written directly under the inspiration of Cassian and that RM 9 repeats RM 8.

In sum, one can depict the evolution of the two passages as follows. The Master read *Inst.* 4.41 and wrote his prescription against evil words (RM 8.30–31). He drew a meditation on the absolute necessity of silence (8.33–34) from its psalm citation, completed it with two citations from

Proverbs (8.35–36), and provided a conclusion (8.37). Later, a sentence from Sextus inspired him to repeat the first citation from Proverbs (9.32–34), which brought to mind two other texts. This time, each citation received separate consideration and commentary.

The commentary on *Dixi custodiam uias meas ...* has a different emphasis in each passage. In the first case, the Master insists on abstention from evil or unedifying words; in the second, on abstention from good words.[23] Each of these emphases corresponds to the point of departure for the passage: in the first, the battle against *eloquium prauum* (8.30), in the second, the risks of *multiloquium* (9.32). In the second instance, the commentary is not only shorter, but also less rich in content, the same idea being repeated before and after the citation.[24]

The most noteworthy aspect of this second commentary is its conclusion: *quia etsi loquenda sunt bona eloquia, non discipulis sed magistro debetur doctrina* (9.38). The last words of this phrase, juxtaposing "master" and "disciple," correspond exactly with the sentence that serves as the conclusion for the first passage: *Nam loqui et docere magistrum condecet, tacere et audire discipulum conuenit* (8.37). But this time, the master-disciple juxtaposition is directly connected with silence on good things, an obligation ensuing from *tacui etiam a bonis* (Ps 38.3). Thus, one can guess that the sentence from RM 8.37, which does not appear to fit in its context,[25] is, in the mind of the Master, connected to what he previously said concerning "rare permission to speak of good things" (8.33), that is to say, to the *silui a bonis* of the psalmist (8.31).[26] Thus, one better understands the meaning of the motifs *propter taciturnitatem* (8.32) and *propter taciturnitatis grauitatem* (8.33) in the first text. Therefore, it is likely that the Master is thinking of the final maxim from 8.37. "For the sake of silence" comes down to saying: for the sake of the condition of the disciple that requires silence.[27]

Overview of RM 9

Not only the parallel passage studied above, but all of Chapter Nine elucidates the theory of silence found in RM 8.31–37. To better understand it, we must read through Chapter Nine once in its entirety. It contains three parts: a discussion of the rules for the *Benedicite* (9.1–26), a doctrinal rationale for these rules (9.27–40), and, finally, a case-based rationale that distinguishes between the perfect and the imperfect, the presence and the absence of the abbot, and spiritual and worldly words (9.41–51).

In and of itself, the question of the *Benedicite* consumes half of the chapter. When the abbot is present, a monk cannot speak to him without

Chapter 6: Silence

obtaining permission. To do this, he bows and says: *"Benedicite."* If the abbot does not respond, he must repeat the request. If the abbot persists in not responding, he must desist. This rule is quite simple and is introduced in a few lines (9.2–8). What requires much more space is the extensive and detailed explanation that the Master likes to give for all that he prescribes. At the end of his regulation, he notes the motives and humble thoughts of the brother who withdraws after being rejected for the second time (9.7, 9–10). Then the Master justifies the sole repetition of *Benedicite* followed by departure. From his point of view, this rule seems to offer every advantage: one remains in silence and humility (11–12); the repetition both allows the humility of the disciple to be tested and avoids the displeasure of the master, because the latter could be distracted at that time and subsequently complain that the disciple had not sufficiently attempted to get his attention (13–17); finally, the departure after the second refusal and return to silent work is recommended by the previously indicated considerations (18–19).[28]

The inclination of the head that accompanies the *Benedicite* calls for special comment. Its goal is to accustom the brother to always and everywhere keep his head lowered. This attitude, combined with silence and "sadness," leads to and manifests the remembrance and fear of God, flight from sin, and vigilance to keep oneself from all that displeases God (20–24).[29]

The concluding remark of this first part contrasts with the spiritual considerations that precede it. Its goal is not to explain the rules for the *Benedicite*, but to complete it with a particular case, that of when the brothers are at table. In this instance, one knocks on the table prior to speaking to the superior (25–26).

Before leaving this regulation, we note its connections with what is said in the treatise on obedience (RM 7.10–21). This latter specifies that the abbot should repeat both his orders (*iussiones*) and his questions (*interrogationes*) — the first to allow for the weakness of certain imperfect disciples, the second to allow for disciples who are so familiar with silence and respectful of the master that they do not immediately respond. Thus, there is reciprocity between master and disciple. Both must repeat their "queries," and the motives for this repetition are quite similar for both.[30]

We now proceed to the second part of the chapter (RM 9.27–40). It is presented as another justification for the *Benedicite* rule, but this time the detail of the prescriptions is set aside in order to provide general considerations that explain the regulation as a whole. Scripture citations, absent until here, will henceforth frame the discussion. One will recall that the last three of these come from the theory of silence developed at the end of Chapter Eight.[31] Previous to this, the Master cites Ephesians 4:29, contaminated[32] by Matthew 12:36, as well as the sentence of Sextus, *Sapiens paucis innotescit*. The first of these citations confirms the necessity of lengthy meditation upon what one will say so as to avoid sin. The second presents the injunction against *multiloquium*. Therefore, one must first be wary of rashness in speech, which leads to saying evil things (28–30), then of much talking, in which one cannot avoid sin (31–34). Finally, even uttering good words would encroach upon the teaching role of the master (35–38). Thus, the tongue appears as an organ that is so dangerous that one can never go too far in its restraint.

Concluding this general discussion, the Master embarks upon the third part of the chapter, a series of directives for specific situations. An initial distinction is made between the rules for perfect and imperfect disciples. Previously, the teaching of silence on good things was presented as pertaining only to the perfect (RM 8.33 and 9.37). This is what he seems to intend to reference here.[33] But this first distinction remains provisional without application. In its place, a second, altogether new distinction will enter into play between the silence to be observed when the abbot is present and that to be observed in his absence.

When the abbot is present, the disciples will not speak unless questioned (RM 9.42). This maxim perplexes the reader who has just read the first part of the chapter, where the manner of "questioning" the abbot is described at length, and who recalls that, previously, only unedifying words (*alia uerba*) fell under such a proscription (RM 8.34). Is the author speaking *grosso modo* here, without intending to revoke the "rarely granted permission to speak of good things" (RM 8.33) and the right of disciples to "ask questions" that the former supposes? Or are we in the presence of a formal and detailed law that contradicts what was previously stated?[34]

In the presence of the abbot, a third distinction is made between words *de uerbo Dei* and words that are "vain or secular and unrelated to God."[35] The first are authorized, provided that they are spoken softly and humbly.[36] The second must be quelled by the deans.[37] This last distinction was already proposed at the end of the previous chapter (RM 8.33–34). However, the prescriptions of the two chapters are far from equivalent.[38] To conclude, the Master authorizes the recitation of Scripture during work. Since this recitation occurs sotto voce, it requires permission.[39]

Up to this point, the Master seems to have legislated for all the brothers.[40] Now the rule for the imperfect appears. This time, the distinguishing factor is no longer the presence or absence of the abbot. One only differentiates between "secular matters" that are not concerned with spiritual edification and "spiritual matters." For the first, the monk must not only say the *Benedicite*, but also obtain permission. For the second, the *Benedicite* suffices to allow one to begin speaking immediately.[41] Note that "secular matters" are no longer paired with "vain words."[42] Instead, such words are now totally prohibited along with "jokes and speech leading to laughter" (RM 9.51).

Its absence of scriptural citations renders this entire third part similar to the first. Its prescriptions are also connected to the first part. It is a matter of supplementing the *Benedicite* rule and making it more flexible. The former supposed that the abbot was present. Here one envisions the case where the abbot is absent. The *Benedicite* rule is addressed to the perfect. Here one grants a dispensation to the imperfect. However, we acknowledge that the passage differentiating between the presence and absence of the abbot (9.42–45) fits poorly with the rest of the chapter. The Master seems to have lost sight of the *Benedicite* rule, as he even replaces it with a conflicting principle: not to speak unless questioned by the abbot. Moreover, he does not distinguish between "secular" or "unedifying" words and "vain" words, as does RM 9.49–51 explicitly and RM 8.34 implicitly. Therefore, one gets the impression that this passage did not originally belong in its present context. Like the parallel passages of RM 50.25–26 and 42–46, it reflects a rigorous doctrine that does not allow one to question the abbot or to speak of anything other than God in the abbot's absence.[43] Perhaps the Master has reemployed a fragment here from an early version of his theory of silence, previous to the more humane *Benedicite* rule.

The Legislation of the Master on Silence

After examining RM 8–9, it will be good to take a look at the group of prescriptions, often confused or contradictory, that the Master writes here and throughout the Rule on the subject of silence. We first gather together all that concerns the "question,"[44] that is to say, the query that begins the dialogue. It can originate with either the abbot or the brothers.

The Brothers Wait to Be Questioned	The Brothers Ask Questions[45]
(7.16–18: one may wait until the abbot repeats the question.)	
8.34: if it is an unedifying matter, one must wait until the abbot asks.	
	9.1–27: in the presence of the abbot, repeat the query once, no more.
9.42–44: if the abbot is present, one must wait until he is questioned; if he is absent, one may speak, but only of the word of God.	
	9.49–50: the imperfect may ask a secular question with permission, a spiritual question after they have said, *Benedicite*.
10.75: to keep silence by not speaking unless questioned.	
11.41–43: not to speak unless questioned. Keep silence until one is questioned (on all matters and even in the presence of the abbot).	
	24.19: the brothers may question the abbot on the reading in the refectory.
	50.43: if the abbot is absent, one may ask about the divine precepts.[46]

We cannot see how some of these texts can be harmonized. There is a flagrant contradiction between 11.43 (cf. 10.75), which eliminates any spontaneous speech by an inferior, even in the absence of the abbot, and 50.43, which authorizes "good" speech in the same circumstances. There is again a contradiction between 11.41–43 and 9.42–44: in this last passage, it is only in the presence of the abbot that the disciple must wait to be questioned and only when he begins to speak of unedifying

Chapter 6: Silence

matters that the deans must impose silence on him. Therefore, it seems that 50.43 and 9.42–44 belong to a later and less severe layer of texts than does 11.41–43.[47] As we have already noted, 8.34 is less demanding than 9.42.[48]

Below is a series of texts on words that are "secular," "unrelated to God, aimless, or unedifying." They are sometimes prohibited along with words that are "vain or leading to laughter," sometimes distinguished from the latter and authorized under certain conditions.

In What Conditions Secular Words Are Authorized	In What Conditions Secular Words Are Forbidden
8.34: "other" words (beyond those that are "good, holy and edifying") may only be spoken if one is asked by the abbot (rule for the perfect?).	
	9.44: words that are "vain, secular, and unrelated to God" must be curbed by the deans.
9.49: Questions that are "secular" and unconnected with edification require express permission in addition to the *Benedicite* (imperfect).	
	10.80: he must only speak of holy things.
	11.49: words that are unrelated to "edification and sanctity" (as well as words that are "vain and apt to lead to laughter") must be curbed by the deans.
	50.25: "secular matters" (as well as unregulated chatter and idle words), being aimless, must be silenced.
	50.42: "secular matters" (as well as idle words and jokes) unrelated to edification must be silenced.

The tendency of the Master is to constantly quell these sorts of words. Usually he simply includes them in the "unseemly words" reproved by Saint Paul.[49] The two times he permits them, it is only with strict restrictions. In fact, concrete life scarcely permits one to avoid them completely, as shown by several passages of the Rule itself.[50]

In this broad range of texts, one is surprised to find the *Benedicite* mentioned only sporadically. The only passages where it appears explicitly are RM 9.1–27 (the perfect) and 9.49–50 (the imperfect).[51] Likewise, the distinction between the perfect and imperfect appears only rarely (RM 8.34; 9.41, 46–50).

In sum, this legislation is not coherent in the least. Making allowances for some presentational blunders—the Master may sometimes get lost in the labyrinth of his own distinctions—one begins to wonder if our author does not simply contradict himself from one passage to another. The most sympathetic explanation is to suppose that there were successive revisions to the text. In particular, it seems certain that the 9.42–45 passage is not in its original place. The *Benedicite* rule that frames it (9.1–27 and 49–50) belongs to a different and probably more recent layer of texts. In the Rule as a whole, one can discern the following stratifications:

1. RM 10.75 and 11.1–43: never to speak without being queried.
2. RM 9.42–45 and 50.25–26, 41–46: one may speak without being asked if the abbot is absent and if it is a matter of good things.
3. RM 8.33–34 and 9.1–27, 41, 46–50: one may ask the abbot a question; *Benedicite* rule (with a distinction between the perfect and imperfect).

It is impossible to bring these three series of prescriptions together in a single schema. Therefore, we content ourselves with schematizing, as much as is possible, the teaching of the third series:

In the Presence of the Abbot	**The Perfect**	good things (8.33): ask (twice, no more, 9.1–27) and obtain permission. "other" things (8.34): wait to be asked.
	The Imperfect	good things (9.50): ask permission (without waiting to obtain it). secular things (9.49): ask and obtain permission before speaking.

Chapter 6: Silence

II. The Treatise of Benedict (RB 6)

As compared with the treatise of the Master, that of Benedict is brief and simple. Here is a schematic synopsis of the two passages:

RM		RB
8.T	*De taciturnitate*	6.T
1–30		
31–33	Psalm 38 and its commentary	1–3
34–35a		
35b–36	Proverbs 10:19 and 18:21	4–5
37	It is proper for the disciple to be silent	6
(9.T–50)	How to ask the superior a question	(7)
9.51	Never joke	8

The two texts usually correspond word-for-word. Only the penultimate passage, which we have put between parentheses, is written differently in each: a single short sentence in RB corresponds to the long development of RM.

The Psalm Citation and Its Commentary

The introduction of Benedict is abrupt, simply presenting the "prophet" as a model (Ps 38.2–3). This beginning is very similar to that of RB 16, which also corresponds to a more developed introduction in RM.[52] In both instances, Benedict uses the verb *ait*, a hallmark of his vocabulary.[53]

Therefore, Benedict ignores the first purpose that the psalm citation fulfills in RM. Following Cassian, the latter proposes Psalm 38:2–3 as a text to "repeat in one's heart" when tempted to utter an angry word. In RB, the text is not presented as a weapon against temptation, but as an example to be followed.[54] This introduction fits easily with the commentary that follows the citation in both Rules. In reading RB, one does not experience the surprise that the Master evokes when he switches from the first function of the text (practical directives to curb evil speech) to the second (reflection on the two forms of silence).

Evil Words and Good Words

The commentary on the psalm citation is the same in both authors. The only difference is that Benedict stops sooner than the Master. In RB, the phrase *Ergo quamuis de bonis ... rara loquendi concedatur licentia* (RM 8.33 = RB 6.3) is the conclusion. This clause is quite clear in its meaning: "even if it is a matter of good things ... one will rarely be granted permission to speak." Only the words *perfectis discipulis* are slightly difficult to interpret. Should they be attached to *quamuis*: "even to perfect disciples," as they are often understood,[55] or separated and understood in a restrictive sense: "at least to perfect disciples," implying that the imperfect may benefit from more frequent permission? This latter sense, which agrees better with the teaching of the Master, is also more natural from a grammatical point of view.[56] In any case, there is no doubt that *quamuis* is an adverb bearing on *de bonis ... eloquiis*, not a conjunction correlative to *tamen*, as the case appears to be in RM.

In this way, the sentence of Benedict escapes the serious difficulties raised by that of the Master.[57] One is strongly tempted to consider the Benedictine text as the original here and that of the Master as an awkward revision that has diverted *quamuis* from its original function.[58] However, the sentence of the Master has the advantage of corresponding with what precedes it. The *quamuis ... tamen* juxtaposition repeats the previous *si interdum ... quanto magis* progression (RM 8.33). In these two successive sentences, the thought of the Master proceeds from good words to evil words, from edifying aims to unedifying aims.[59] Both times the accent falls on the second type. If good words are subject to some restrictions, evil or unedifying words must be even more so. This insistence on the second sort clearly follows a line of thought that takes as its starting point the struggle against *eloquium prauum* (RM 8.30). Thus, the "awkward" apodosis *tamen ab aliis uerbis ... siliscant* (RM 8.34) has the merit of corresponding to that of the first phrase: *quanto magis a malis uerbis ... debet cessari*.[60] It draws attention to the unedifying words that one must be especially wary of.

In contrast, the Benedictine sentence has the disadvantage of stopping with good words, which modifies the theme. While the first sentence proceeds *a fortiori* from good to evil words, the second has nothing concerning the latter. The *ergo* connecting the two sentences becomes less intelligible. Thus, RB 6.3, much more satisfying in itself than RM 8.33–34, is less easily joined to what precedes it.

One can say the same of the link with what follows, that is to say, of the two citations from Proverbs. In RM, these new *testimonia* appear in a separate sentence, linked to the commentary of sentence 38:2–3 by a simple *namque*. In RB, they are appended to the last sentence of the commentary. The opening *ergo* of this sentence clearly indicates that it is a continuation of the development of the psalm text. Thus, it is somewhat surprising to find *quia scriptum est* introducing two new citations at the end of the sentence, as if the editor loses sight of the fact that he has already relied on the authority of Scripture.

Master and Disciple

The two following sentences (RB 6.6–7) very much resemble a passage from the treatise on counsel (RB 3.4–6):

RB 3	RB 6
[6]Sed sicut *discipulos conuenit* oboedire *magistro*, ita et ipsum prouide et iuste *condecet* cuncta disponere.	[6]Nam loqui et docere *magistrum condecet*, tacere et audire *discipulum conuenit*.
[4]Sic autem dent fratres consilium *cum omni humilitatis subiectione* et non praesumant procaciter defendere quod eis uisum fuerit.	[7]Et ideo si qua requirenda sunt a priore, *cum omni humilitate et subiectione* reuerentiae requirantur.

This similarity is not unexpected in the second sentence of RB 6, as it is proper to Benedict. But the first is found as it is in RM 8.37. While the Master uses *conuenit* and *condecet* separately elsewhere, nowhere else does he contrast them. Thus, it is quite striking that Benedict again uses the same contrast with exactly the same objects (*magistrum ... discipulos*) in the treatise on counsel, indicating either that he is the author of this sentence from RB 6 or that he has closely imitated the style of the Master in RB 3.[61]

One recalls[62] that in RM the maxim *Nam loqui ...* marks a return to the previously expressed idea that perfect disciples should refrain as much as possible even from good words (RM 8.33 = RB 6.3). This connection is more apparent in RB, which places nothing between the two declarations.

Questions Posed to the Superior

We now examine the phrase *Et ideo ...* (RB 6.7) and its relationship to the corresponding long text of RM 9.1–50. Instead of a ceremonial and casuistic rule, entangled in sweeping explanations and justifications, one finds in RB only a brief directive on the appropriate attitude toward a superior. Based on the only passage in RB where *requirere* reappears (RB 38.8), it seems that Benedict is thinking here of the step that RM calls *interrogatio*. Therefore, it is not a matter of "requests" but of "questions," as in RM. However, the words *requirere* and *prior* (designating the superior) are both proper to Benedict.

We have seen how the terms designating the attitude of the subject resemble those that Benedict uses in his treatise on counsel. There this "humble and submissive attitude" prohibits monks from "obstinately defending their opinions" against the decisions of the abbot. Apparently, Benedict is thinking of the same sort of objections here. This is to say, in spite of the identical vocabulary, *humilitas* and *reuerentia* do not have the same significance for Benedict as they do for the Master. In using these words in regard to silence, the latter aims for a specific deportment. Humility consists in bowing the head each time one asks a question and departing in silence at the second refusal.[63] "Reverence" is conveyed by complete silence in the presence of the abbot and slowness in responding to his questions (RM 7.17–18; 50.44). It seems that Benedict has something other than these gestures in mind. He is less concerned with combating inappropriate gestures and attitudes than with battling independence in judgment and remarks. Like the counsel given to the superior, the questions posed to him may occasion discussion and conflict. *Ne detur occasio*, Benedict will write in prohibiting such questions in the course of the meal.[64] In this passage, as in the treatise on silence, it is undoubtedly "presumption" and "disputes" that he fears. Contrary to the Master, in the refectory he nips these problems in the bud by prohibiting all questions (RM 9.25–26; 24.19). As a rule, he does not prohibit questions but asks for a perfectly humble, respectful, and submissive attitude.

Thus, the little sentence of Benedict does not correspond as closely as it seems to the long development of RM 9.1–50. Between the two there is not only the contrast between a general and imprecise directive and minutely detailed prescriptions and distinctions,[65] but also the gulf between the concerns of the two authors. While the Master thinks only of teaching his disciples good manners whether the abbot is present or not, Benedict seems concerned to avoid conflicts between superior and subjects. As we know, this is a constant preoccupation of RB.[66] Unlike the Master, Benedict unceasingly reaffirms the rights of the abbot and the duty of monks to submit. The treatise on silence offers us a new sign of this tension between superior and inferiors.

Jokes

The last sentence of the Benedictine text (RB 6.8) is also the last of the treatise of the Master (RM 9.51). The only notable variant is *in omnibus locis*, which is read only in RB. These words have the appearance of an addition. Adjacent to *clusura*, they suggest giving this latter a "local" thrust, as opposed to its original meaning. Hapax in RB, *clusura* reappears twelve times in RM, six of which are in Chapters Eight and Nine. In regard to silence, the word appears in the metaphor of the "house" of the heart, closed by the "door" of the teeth.[67] Therefore, the sense here is that jokes are condemned to perpetual reclusion, that is to say, to never leaving the mouth. In contrast, the Benedictine addition suggests that they are condemned to "perpetual exclusion," that is to say, not to be kept "anywhere." Most of the interpreters of RB have understood thus.[68] Thus, one switches from the notion of a closed mouth, probably original,[69] to that of banishment, exile, and ostracism. This *in omnibus locis* variant is all the more remarkable in that Benedict is constantly abbreviating in this chapter. If he adds these three words, it is undoubtedly because he intends to reinforce the injunction by pairing the temporal clause (*aeterna*) with a local clause.[70]

In fact, the entire sentence is more in context in RM. It has just granted the imperfect some possibility of speech in both spiritual and secular matters, with the clear understanding that the latter must not "involve sin" (9.49–50). On the other hand (*uero*), all sinful speech is absolutely forbidden (9.51). In RB, it is less clear what this last sort of speech is being contrasted with.[71] Moreover, in RM, the verbs *damnamus ... permittimus* follow from two other verbs in the first person plural: *taxauimus* (9.46) ... *relaxamus* (9.48).[72] Thus, the paragraph of the Master finishes as it began, with the authorial "we." In contrast, this first-person plural makes its first appearance here in RB. It is true that RB 6 began with *Faciamus*, but this was a predicatory "we," equivalent to "you and I."[73] Therefore, the authorial "we" (*damnamus ... permittimus*) is clearly a novelty in the Benedictine chapter. In and of itself, this does not prove that the Benedictine text is disjointed, but it must be recognized that the text of RM is more consistent. If RM 9.46–50 was an addition, it required much attention or luck for the Master to write this paragraph in a style so conformed to that of the concluding phrase. Thus, content and form alike suggest that this last phrase had its original *situs* in RM.

Overview

The two Rules present the same contrasts in the treatise on silence as they do in those on the different types of monks and obedience. On the part of the Master, a vast complex series in two chapters, inflated with redundancies and repetitions, in which neither the legislative content nor the literary aspect is homogeneous. In RB, we have a small chapter treating only speech, conformed to the title and bringing together via excerpts or summary most of the points discussed by the Master.

The dependence of Benedict on the Master is far from always being clear. If, however, relying on a certain number of serious indicators, one accepts this dependence, it appears that Benedict has taken his excerpts from the end of the chapters of the Master. He has retained nothing from the first part of RM 8, where silence is not separated from other ascetic themes. From the second part, he has preserved only what pertains to speech, omitting some details that were probably too precise for his liking.[74] Benedict shows himself simultaneously more severe and more welcoming toward RM 9 than he was toward the previous chapter. While he has reproduced only a single sentence of the text, the last, he has made a summary of all the rest. Aside from a fleeting and ambiguous reference to *perfecti discipuli*, from one end to the other, Benedict avoids all casuistry and specific regulations. His chapter on silence stays in the theoretical domain. This small treatise seems much more consistent and coherent than that of the Master. But its very brevity, obtained at the price of multiple omissions, sometimes rends the rest of the ideas rather vague.

III. Theory and Practice of Silence

We will conclude this study of *De taciturnitate* in RM and RB with a preliminary reflection on the doctrine of silence that they present. This endeavor will require us to go beyond the strict framework of the present treatise (RM 8–9; RB 6) in two ways. First, without returning *ex professo* to the treatise on obedience (RM 7; RB 5), to which we have elsewhere devoted a comprehensive commentary,[75] we must constantly keep it in mind. In fact, obedience and silence go hand in hand, and the meaning of silence is uniquely illumined when juxtaposed with obedience. Second, our study of the theory of silence will necessarily lead to the practical applications of the discipline of silence because one cannot appreciate one without the other.

Obedience and Silence

We begin with an examination of the connections between *De taciturnitate* and *De oboedientia*. The relationship of the two treatises is first an obvious literary fact. Between the "Instruments of Good Works" and the immense chapter on humility, obedience and silence are the subject of adjoining expositions, extended in RM, succinct in RB, but rather similar to one another in each Rule.

Thus connected, the two virtues are also linked by their tie to humility. In both Rules the initial phrase of *De oboedientia* affirms that obedience is the first step of humility. In *De taciturnitate,* silence is equated with

Chapter 6: Silence

humility only once in RB, but very often in RM.[76] These facts take on their full meaning when one examines the scriptural citations and notices that in steps 1–4 and 9–11, the treatise on humility reemploys texts used to elucidate the treatises on obedience and silence.[77] It then becomes evident that the Master and Benedict have recapitulated these chapters in their treatise on humility—or rather, since this latter is drawn from Cassian, that they have developed the material from *De humilitate* in *De oboedientia* and *De taciturnitate*. It is Cassian who has provided our authors with the schema for a description of humility where obedience and silence occupy the first and last "signs" respectively. Thus, the two virtues, highlighted at both ends of the ladder of humility, are of such importance that special treatises, anticipating and developing *De humilitate*, are dedicated to them.

Consequently, the meaning of the obedience-silence-humility trilogy becomes evident. These three major virtues of monastic ascesis are not placed on the same level. The third is clearly separated from the first two. In genealogical terms, one might say that humility is the mother virtue and obedience and silence her children. This shared origin in humility again connects the sister virtues.

To finish bringing them together, the Master has increased the parallels in content and form between the two treatises. The most salient is the distinction that both make between "perfect" and "imperfect" disciples, with a procedure appropriate to each category. In both instances, this casuistry invokes the same words, principles, and motives: here the abbot must repeat his orders, there the disciples must repeat their questions; in both cases, one is dealing with distractions on the part of the one being spoken to, and when he refuses or is slow to respond, his silence is to be interpreted as charitably as possible.[78]

These similarities are so numerous and accentuated that in the middle of the regulations on obedience, the Master very naturally slips in a comment pertaining to those on silence.[79] He clearly considers the two matters from the same point of view, that of the relationship between master and disciples, abbot and brothers. Obviously, such a relationship is part of obedience. On the other hand, the importance granted to it in the case of silence seems most unwarranted. In both instances, one is particularly surprised that the question is posed in such concrete terms: how many times must the master repeat his orders, the disciple his questions? But regardless of how one evaluates these regulations, it is undeniable that they correspond exactly from one treatise to the other. The directive for the disciple in *De taciturnitate* corresponds to that for the master in *De oboedientia*. Together, the two treatises seek to completely and uniformly regulate the mutual relationship between abbot and brothers.

We seek to further examine this point of view by going beyond casuistry to perceive the profound similarities of obedience and silence. For this, the best guiding principle will undoubtedly be the theme of *listening* that runs through the two treatises. "To speak and teach befit the Master, it is fitting for the disciple to be silent and listen (*audire*)" (RM 8.37 = RB 6.6). This sentence perfectly expresses the meaning of silence from the point of view that we are considering. Silence is the attitude characterizing the disciple and thus cannot be separated from *listening* to the master. One is silent in order to listen. Yet listening also plays a primary role in the theory of obedience. It is by hearing that one perceives the command of the superior.[80] This initial instant of hearing is written into the very terminology of obedience: *oboedire*, that is, *obaudire, abaudire*.[81] The Master is clearly conscious of this, as, following some versions of the Psalter, he intentionally restores the verb to its etymological form.[82] But listening is even more than an indispensable preliminary to the act of obedience. It is a veritable synonym. Like the French écouter, the Latin *audire* can, in and of itself, signify obedience. *Qui uos audit, me audit.* In this sentence of Christ, *audire* conveys more than perceiving the sound of a voice. It means to pay attention to, to hear and welcome the divine call, not merely with one's ears, but also with one's heart.[83] Thus, *audire* is equivalent to *oboedire;* to listen means to obey.[84] This equivalence, which draws its origin from the Hebrew language and the constant usage of the Bible, has the effect of attaching monastic obedience to the great scriptural theme of the divine word addressed to humanity. For the monk, to obey is nothing other than to listen to Christ who speaks to him in the voice of his abbot.

Thus, one sees how obedience and silence come together on a much more profound level than those of casuistry and regulations. Their truest tie is this: they are two modes of the same act of submission. One is silent to listen to the master, thus, ultimately to obey him. No doubt, the superior is seen from a different angle in each case: obedience rends homage to his orders, silence to his teaching. But to command and teach are two inseparable prerogatives of the same person and role, that of the abbot who speaks in the name of Christ (RM 2.4–5 = RB 2.4–5). Obedience and silence are likewise the two virtues that characterize the attitude of the disciple toward his abbot. He obeys as soon as he hears; he preserves silence in order to listen.

Using the moment of listening that is common to both obedience and silence as their link, we find virtually the same idea previously encountered in identifying humility as their common source. One will recall that this idea comes from Cassian: disciples demonstrate humility by mortifying their desires and submitting to the elder, restraining their tongues, and moderating their voices. However, the connection of the three virtues appears in a unique light in RM. In the *Institutes*, Pinufius-Cassian does not describe silence as the attitude of the disciple *in the presence of his master*.[85] The originality of the theory of RM consists in this new trait. Here, silence is presented as the veritable twin sister of obedience. Not only do these two virtues both follow from humility, but they also resemble one another in their common reference to the speech of the superior.[86] Thus, the Master has brought silence and obedience considerably closer by seeing both as a mark of voluntary submission. When he takes these two virtues from the "steps of humility," drawing them from both ends of the list to make them the subject of adjoining treatises, our author not only brings them together on the page, but also models silence on obedience, integrating it into the master-disciple relationship.

Since silence has become so similar to obedience, we are challenged to highlight what distinguishes one from the other. To obey is to act; to be silent is to renounce speech. Therefore, the two virtues affect two complementary spheres: action and language.[87] Obedience is humility in action; silence is humility in speech. Let us be clear—in speech and not in words. Already Cassian warned against verbal professions of humility: "Let him not halfheartedly declare himself the last of all, but from the depths of his heart let him believe it to be true." This "ninth sign," together with the next two that it introduces,[88] shows perfectly the true role of speech in learning and evidencing humility. To show oneself truly humble is less a matter of speech than silence.

So, while in the sphere of action, humility is positively expressed by obedience, in that of speech it consists of a negative effort of restraint, that of silence. Thus, not only are the two virtues distinguished by their respective spheres, they are also, one might say, contrasting signs.[89] The one is promptness to act, the other delay in speech. But this contrast matters much less than their complementarity. The Master's intent in highlighting both is to situate all cenobitic behavior, words and deeds alike, within the master-disciple relationship.

However, this relationship far from exhausts the matter of silence. As opposed to obedience, this latter can be defined independently of a master whose presence imposes silence. Everyone, whether or not they are under an abbot, must be silent in order to escape sin. Avoiding evil or idle words and even the prolific discourse by which one inevitably falls into sin is required in any hypothesis before the master-disciple relationship is even considered. And, in fact, this is how both the Master and Benedict open their treatises on silence. The theme of flight from sin precedes that of deference toward the abbot.

Therefore, silence proves to be more complex than obedience. Hence, the regulation also becomes more complex as one passes from one to the other. The treatise on obedience distinguishes only between perfect and imperfect disciples. That on silence takes several new variables into account: the quality of the conversation, good or evil, spiritual or secular, and the presence or absence of the abbot. Thus a subtle and rather confused casuistry is drawn up. While it is impossible, as we have seen, to bring all the elements together into a coherent schema, one can easily discern the major objectives. One of them is to eliminate, as much as possible, not only words that are evil, trivial, or likely to induce laughter, but even those that are simply secular. The intent is that the monk be occupied, both in word and thought (cf. RM 82.4–15; 86.8–16) with things above. As a consequence, one is authorized, even invited, to replace secular words with those that are edifying by "meditating" in an undertone on Scripture, posing questions on the sacred text, and conversing about spiritual matters. The other objective consists in demanding more silence when the abbot is present. This is actually a function of the master-disciple relationship. It imposes silence even in regard to edifying subjects out of respect for the "teaching" prerogative of the abbot.

One sees that, to a certain extent, the two objectives are antithetical. While the first, by a positive pedagogy, encourages "holy" words, the second prohibits or restrains them in the name of respect for the abbot. Consequently, the flight from sin and humility develop opposing demands, although both agree in advising against *multiloquium,* an inevitable source of sin.

Thus, silence is distinguished from obedience by its greater complexity. Having acknowledged this dissonance between the two sister virtues, we can now return to traits that unite them. It happens that the Master himself expresses this unity in a striking turn of phrase: *magistri ministratae doctrinae tacitus auditus discipuli factis respondeat.* The disciple is silent in order to listen and only responds by taking action (RM 11.53). Silence and obedience are two means of receiving the word of the master. In addition, the very act of obedience, which must be exempt from murmuring and a negative response, demands a certain silence (RM 7.67 = RB 5.14).

As expressions of humility, both virtues demand more than is imposed by the simple concern not to offend God. One is first placed under

Chapter 6: Silence

obedience to learn and practice the divine law, to be taught by a spokesperson for Christ. But one must also obey with humility, in the manner of Christ who was obedient unto death.[90] This latter goes much further than the former: it is no longer a matter of merely knowing and observing the divine commandments but of completely immolating one's own will, which brings to mind the martyr. The same is true of silence. If it were only a matter of observing the divine law by avoiding sins of the tongue, there would be a limit to silence. But one also remains silent out of humility, as is fitting for the disciple in the presence of the master, and this silence, like humble obedience, knows no limits.

"To speak and teach belong to the Master, to be silent and listen to the disciple" (RM 8.37 = RB 6.6). The significance of this maxim appears in its full light when one compares it with a phrase of Augustine that is perhaps its source. Addressing his flock in a sermon, the Bishop of Hippo remarks: *Non modo mihi loquimini, quia meum est loqui in hoc loco, uestrum autem tacere et audire.*[91] Augustine and the Master agree. The respective attitude of master and disciples is the same in the two texts, but the maxim has a very different scope in each. With Augustine, it is a matter of a bishop in his chair (*cathedra*), in the very act of sacred preaching; with the Master, it is an abbot in his usual day-to-day existence. The respectful silence that Augustine requires of the faithful only for the duration of his homily, the Master requires of monks for life, every time they are in the presence of their abbot! That is to say that the alternating of tension and relaxation and the sacred and secular that mark the relationship of the bishop with his flock are not part of monastic life. A bishop does not constantly speak *ex cathedra*. Outside of the church and liturgy, the faithful may freely come up and converse with the bishop, and they typically live some distance from him. The same cannot be said for the monastery. There the disciples remain constantly in the silent and receptive disposition of the faithful who are being instructed by their shepherd. Cenobitic life is living perpetually with a "master" who never descends from his chair. He is constantly engaged in teaching. Augustine said, *Modo ... in hoc loco.* These restrictions disappear in RM. For the disciples, there is no longer a time or place where the law of silence is relaxed.

From this point of view, silence again resembles obedience. The obedience of monks to their abbot extends well beyond what simple Christians give to their bishop. To be a monk is to renounce the sphere of temporal life where each of the faithful must freely apply, according to their conscience, the teaching received from the shepherd.[92] Renouncing earthly matters, the disciple grants to his "master" complete control over his life, with no earthly reality coming between them from that time forward. The sharing of life between the abbot and the brothers is total, and the obedience of the brothers is also total, in both temporal and spiritual matters. Just as obedience expands and becomes unlimited, the silence of disciples before their master will henceforth know no limits. The ties between superior and subjects are uniquely close. Beyond the secular realm that weakens the spiritual relationship that unites them, the kingdom of God has literally become their only reason to live. In every moment, they live fully their respective conditions of disciples and master in Christ.

But the similarity of these two virtues is not evidenced only on the level of these connections concerning submission to the superior. It is God himself who speaks to the disciples through the superior. Consequently, obedience and silence both ultimately refer to God. Both are methods to "listen" to God. That is their importance in the Rules that both open with the same appeal to "listen" (RM Pr 1–22; RB Prol 1). God speaks, the individual listens: after having resounded in the first words of the Prologue, this theme fills the *Thema*, whose ending is again shared by both Rules.[93] The "cry of Scripture" rings out again at the beginning of the chapter on humility (RM 10.1 = RB 7.1) and makes itself heard several times before and after in RM (RM 1.76; 86.17; 91.13.) While God speaks primarily by Scripture, he also does so by the Rule and "masters." Ultimately, it is these last, that is to say, the abbots, who, by their verbal teaching, give concrete expression to the divine word inscribed in the holy books and repeated by the Rule. *Qui uos audit, me audit.* The fundamental theme of the divine voice that speaks to the individual also leads quite naturally to obedience and silence.

Thus we discover what is undoubtedly the most profound reason for the connection that RB and RM establish between the two virtues. Their convergence is explained not only by the signs of humility from Cassian, but also stems in particular from a pedagogical necessity: obedience and silence are distinguished and glorified side by side in order to trace the double path by which cenobites will go to God. The following chapter will show that this way is also called humility. But above all, it is defined as silent attention and obedient responsiveness to the word of God transmitted by the abbot.

From Cassian to the Master: Promotion of Silence

Having shown the significance of the obedience-silence duo, one cannot help but be struck by the promotion that the second virtue has received in being considered equal to the first. While both already appear

Chapter 6: Silence

in the list of signs in *Institutes* 4.39, by no means does Cassian accord them the same importance in the whole of his works on the formation of cenobites. There, obedience incontestably plays the lead role in every respect. Throughout Book IV of the *Institutes,* one can say that, once the dispossession of material goods has been legislated, obedience is virtually the sole concern.[94] In contrast, silence appears only rarely and obliquely in these pages. Cassian notes only that one should punish conversations held outside of the cells (*Inst.* 4.16.2. Cf. *Inst.* 2.15) and also endeavor to prevent them in the refectory (*Inst.* 4.17). While Pinufius recommends "silence" in his sermon on clothing, it is only in regard to vengeful responses that come to the lips when one is insulted (*Inst.* 4.41.2). To these few comments from Book IV, one can add those of Book II. Cenobites observe perfect silence during Office, and especially during the prayers.[95] They are also silent during the manual labor that they do in common outside of their cells. To this end, the continual meditation of Scripture is essential in order that both lips and mind are occupied (*Inst.* 2.15.1–2).

Overall, the first books of the *Institutes* offer only a small number of scattered remarks on the subject of silence. On occasion, Cassian clearly states that it is observed rigorously in the *coenobia* of Egypt and the East and, in fact, even makes it one of the distinctive features of model communities, but he makes little effort to explain its meaning and to provide a rationale for it. Silence is presented as one among many regular observances rather than as one of the fundamentals of spiritual and ascetic formation that leads to perfection. In any event, there is no question of it being equal to obedience. Moreover, no tie is established between the two virtues. If Cassian happens to connect them, it is by means of contrast: the cenobite of Egypt prefers immediate obedience and common work to the silence of the cell.[96] The primacy of obedience, illustrated by this particular case, is affirmed everywhere else. There is no comparison between obedience, the cardinal virtue of cenobitism, and silence, a simple point of discipline.

Therefore, the Master has raised the stature of silence remarkably by placing it alongside obedience and dedicating an entire treatise to it. He deems it no less important in Chapter Eleven, where most of the admonitions to the deans deal with the use of speech. And when, in Chapter 50, he will regulate the order of the conventual day, he will elaborate much less on actual obedience than on silence. The first of these points seems to be self-evident (RM 50.19. Cf. 50.36 and 63). In contrast, the second is often reiterated (RM 50.19, 22–23, 29, 61) and carefully spelled out (RM 50.24–26 and 41–46). This is because the right use of speech appears as an essential means to ensure what is an obsession for the Master: innocence and the absence of sin. While hand and mind are occupied in work,[97] the lips are occupied repeating Scripture or speaking spiritual words (RM 50.46). The monk being thus totally "occupied" (RM 50.17, 23, 52, 55), sin cannot creep into his deeds, words, or thoughts. Work and silence are two inseparable allies in this battle against sin. Of course, work is done in obedience, but one is particularly interested in it as an activity that prevents idleness and wandering thoughts. Thus, in this particular context, the original pair of obedience and silence tends to become work and silence.

We have been able to note the very positive role that the discipline of silence assumes in this daily horarium. While primarily concerned with avoiding sin, the Master rightly understands that this goal cannot be attained by silence pure and simple. One can only eliminate evil words by replacing them with good words. Also, except when the abbot is present, the Master encourages brothers to recite Scripture, ask questions, and converse about the things of God. In the same vein, one reads to them as often as possible (RM 50.28–33. Cf. 53.38–41), the latter undoubtedly in its turn evoking spiritual questions and conversation. The same is true for the refectory, where the brothers may ask questions on the reading they have heard, while the abbot himself is authorized to comment on it or to secure the attention of listeners by posing impromptu questions (RM 24.19. Cf. 9.25–26). Overall, it seems that the entire day is spent in an almost incessant hum of public reading, recitation in a low voice, and questions and answers. Silence does not exclude spiritual conversation but demands it in order to guard against evil conversation.

Compared to what Cassian describes, this discipline of RM seems rather loose. Outside of their cells, the cenobites of Egypt seem authorized only to "meditate." Cassian does not speak of common reading, questions and answers, or spiritual conversations. He even expressly notes the prohibition against exchanging words with anyone who does not live in one's cell (*Inst.* 2.15; 4.16.2. Cf. 2.12.3). Likewise, in the refectory, where the total silence of the Egyptians is considered as the ideal, the "Cappadocian" practice of reading does not seem to allow any questions from listeners or commentary by the superior. Therefore, the Master has considerably relaxed the rules of silence.[98] He no longer knows conversations in the cell (the cell is replaced by the common dormitory) or regular conferences by the abbot and dean. On the other hand, he authorizes exchanges in the course of the meal and work. These conversations between superior and subjects, which may begin informally throughout the day, tend to compensate for the absence of private conversation and *ex professo* teaching.[99]

Chapter 6: Silence

Moreover, if there is a certain relaxation in comparison with the signs of Cassian, one must remember that the latter does not know the legislation of silence in the presence of the abbot, such as established by the Master.[100] On this point, RM is severe. This Rule, with *Regula Ferioli*, has written the *usque ad interrogationem non loqui* into law,[101] adding elsewhere both exemptions to the practice for the weak and conflicting comments that scarcely permit its legislation to be considered a coherent whole.

This comparison of the Master with Cassian would be incomplete if one did not take into account a particular aspect of silence that is emphasized by the one and lacking in the other. For Cassian, silence is linked with prayer. One cannot arrive at pure prayer if one has a mind filled with recent conversations and words that lead to laughter (Cassian, *Conl.* 9.13). More broadly, contemplation demands that one stay in one's cell and preserve silence there (*Inst.* 10.3. Cf. *Inst.* 4.12). The prerequisite for prayer, silence is also the mark of its more elevated states. "Prayer of fire" consists in an ineffable cry that transcends all speech (*Conl.* 9.25; 10.10. Cf. 9.15). The soul is then enveloped in a profound silence, in contemplation that rends it mute and powerless to express itself (*Conl.* 9.27). Elsewhere, without going to these sublime extremes, the simple law of the Gospel wishes that we pray *clauso ostio*, that is to say, with our lips sealed in perfect silence (*Conl.* 9.35. Cf. *Inst.* 2.10.1–2). Our own security, as well as the tranquility of our neighbors, depends on it because it prevents the devil from knowing what we ask of God in prayer.

The Master is not concerned with this silence in preparation for prayer or in prayer itself.[102] In RM, silence has no contemplative end or mystical purpose. Its only goals are to avoid sin and show the humility of the disciple in the presence of the Master. RM does not deal with the teachings of *Conferences* 9–10, restricting itself to the more modest concerns of cenobitic asceticism along the lines of the first books of the *Institutes*. Benedict only hints at the relationship of silence to prayer in discussing departure from the oratory.[103] The *summum silentium* required on this occasion is chiefly a point of communal discipline. If, in this case, he aims to facilitate prayer, elsewhere he requires silence in the refectory out of respect for public reading and during the siesta so that the brothers are able to rest.[104]

From the Master to Benedict

With these remarks we have just entered into the Benedictine legislation on a particular point. In order to situate it in relationship to that of the Master, we must consider it as a whole. An initial impression is that RB differs from RM only in some details, several of which suggest the direct influence of Cassian on Benedict.[105] RB especially diverges from RM in its omission of the long casuistic development of RM 9. As we have seen,[106] the corresponding little phrase in RB allows one to discern a slightly different concern in RB than RM. Instead of involving himself with the external behavior of the disciple desirous of questioning the abbot, Benedict is concerned to instill in him the docility that precludes debate and argument.

Moreover, nothing leads one to believe that the issue has fundamentally changed from one Rule to the other. Therefore, one must reject Herwegen's recently proposed explanation of RB. For him, the aim of Benedict was to protect the unity of teaching in the monastic community.[107] It would be a matter of barring "perfect" disciples, that is to say, those capable of teaching, from the role of master reserved for the abbot. If the "perfect" have received a spiritual charism, it is for themselves, not for others. Only the abbot has the mission to impart the word of God. He would only rarely delegate this function because the community would risk being divided by the diversity of the masters that were teaching.

One can see how this interpretation of RB should be regarded. Plausible in itself, it can scarcely be so when one takes RM into account. For both Benedict and the Master, the problem is not communal but one of individual ascesis. The "perfect" disciple is not the one who the *Pneuma* empowers to teach others but the one who has become entirely master of himself. It is not a matter of him renouncing a teaching role in the community but of conducting himself as a true disciple in relationship to his abbot.[108]

This is not the only point where RM helps to interpret RB. In its brevity, RB leaves us unaware of the important practice of *meditatio*. In the light of RM, it seems almost certain that this rumination of Scripture in the course of work was customary in the milieu of Benedict, as it was in all of ancient monasticism, east and west. It is less certain that Benedict allowed the spiritual conversations authorized by the Master in the same circumstances, about which Cassian says nothing. In any event, the questions of disciples are categorically forbidden in the refectory, while brief commentary by the abbot is authorized. Here the Benedictine norm is midway between the leniency of the Master and the rigor of Cassian.[109] Likewise, in the dormitory, keeping silence at night and during the siesta is urged more forcefully than in RM,[110] although in prescribing that the brothers exhort one another when rising, Benedict appears to forget the significance of *Domine labia mea aperies* as the end of night silence.[111]

Chapter 6: Silence

In general, it seems that the monks of Benedict, like those of the Master, are not usually bound to a rigorous silence. The strict rules announced for the refectory and dormitory suppose that the discipline is more relaxed elsewhere. This is also suggested by the treatise on Lent, which enjoins being less talkative and inclined to jokes during this holy season.[112] To this specific note of RB, one can add the distinction between *horae competentes* and *incompetentes* (RB 31.18; 48.21). The first are those times during which one can ask for and receive necessary items, the second those in which one must avoid all conversation, as is the case during the time of *lectio*. Thus, whether in the course of the year or in the course of the day, Benedict envisions some high and low points that the Master does not distinguish between.[113] In silence, as with the fast,[114] one moves from a rather uniform regimen to a more differentiated observance.

But this is clearly not the principal contrast between the two Rules. More significant are certain new comments of Benedict on good and evil speech. The Master knew well that lying, anger, and words, pointless or otherwise, can lead to sin in speech. To completely eliminate these faults, he instituted silence and continual surveillance by the deans. This general attitude is not found in RB, but Benedict considers several specific instances in which one must be especially vigilant about what one says. Upon returning from a trip, the monk must be on guard against recounting anything that he has seen or heard outside the monastery.[115] When the cellarer receives an unreasonable request, he must not disdainfully dismiss it but humbly and reasonably refuse it in a manner that does not sadden the supplicant.[116] Several lines later, a similar exhortation is made to the same officer: if he is unable to fulfill a request, let him give what is more precious than all: a kind answer.[117] *Rationabiliter cum humilitate*: the tone that has just been prescribed for the cellarer will also be the criteria for assessing the observations of the visiting monk.[118] It is reminiscent of the eleventh step of humility. Recall that there, Benedict writes *rationabilia* instead of *sancta* (RB 7.60 = RM 10.80). This variant says much in and of itself. For the Master, it is a matter of replacing evil, unnecessary, or secular words with "holy" words. Benedict has a different concern—monks should speak reasonable words. What is important to Benedict is not the spiritual quality of the topic under discussion but the appropriateness of the words for the matter at hand and the person taking part in the conversation. His pedagogy aims less at raising speech to a "spiritual" level than at promoting its right use in concrete situations where it is necessary to speak.

The same preoccupation to improve ordinary speech comes to light in the chapter on the porter.[119] With remarkable care and warmth, Benedict describes the way in which the porter is to respond to whomever knocks at the door. Gentleness, fear of God, eagerness, and fervent charity must all be conveyed in his speech. This is because "to respond" to another is never a perfunctory matter for a monk. Whether porter or cellarer, the monk's right use of speech in addressing his neighbor takes precedence over all other assigned duties.

These original comments on the manner of speaking lead us into the area of fraternal relations. It is evident that this is a sphere that scarcely concerns the Master and to which Benedict makes a major contribution.[120] Without entering into it again here, we must at least acknowledge that this concern for fraternal relations and the common life reinvigorates the theme of speech in RB.

Chapter 6: Silence

Endnotes

1 Especially in its first part (9.1–26) and at the end of the third part (9.50).

2 In other words, women (RM 8.19–20. Cf. 8.9). Compare Orientius, *Commonitorium* I.435–436 (PL 61.987): *Ergo puellares uultus firmasque decentes Aut uerso aut merso despicies capite.* The motives of RM 9.20–24 and 10.8 are different and more "monastic."

3 It is true that RM 3.3 prescribes *non occidere*, but, from all appearances, it is a borrowed passage. Cf. RM 14.87, etc., as regards robbery and flight. However, the evocation of "chains," the "judiciary sentence," and "fetters" indicates a secular rather than monastic context here.

4 The embellished style of the Parable of the Spring is reminiscent of that of RM 8.1–25. The comparison of the human body with a *machina* is found both in Thp (52 and 77) and 8.1, in both cases joined to Genesis 2:7 (Thp 52 and 8.5). Another citation, Psalm 136:9, also reappears with the same allegorical exegesis in Ths 24 and 8.23 (cf. 3.56). The borrowing of these two instructions for seculars from a collection of ecclesial homilies is even more likely as the Master demonstrates a constant interest in Church matters. Once more he will adopt what clerics have said to Christians of the world for monastic use.

5 Compare RM 8.27–30 and 15.53–56. Both contain the same strategy against evil thoughts.

6 That is to say, "you and I." See below, n. 73.

7 Compare RM 8.26: *tria suprema … id est cogitatio, eloquium et aspectum*, and 8.8: *duo … supremos … ramos* (only sight and speech).

8 Cf. RM 13.60, an abrupt beginning that does not even commence with an introduction. See my study on the Penal Code: Adalbert de Vogüé, *La Règle de Saint Benoît,* Sources Chrétiennes 181–186 (Paris: Cerf, 1972), V.729, n. 18. Henceforth, this entire six-volume work will be referenced as *La Règle* plus volume (I–VI) and page number.

9 Likewise, in RM 8.17, one finds *aurium … auditum* in third place without a corresponding development in what follows. This similarity between 8.17 and 8.26 leads one to think that the author of 8.1–25 also composed the bridge of 8.26. Must we conclude that the Master adapts an instruction *that he himself authored* for seculars (see n. 4 above) for monastic purposes? We would thus envision a unique figure who would have simultaneously or successively had ecclesiastic and monastic responsibilities, having charge of souls both in the monastery and in the world. We note in passing that the treatise on obedience frequently presents this virtue as a matter of "listening": *auditus* (RM 7.12, 15); *auditores* (7.20); *obaudire*, etc. This may explain to a certain extent the absence of a development on hearing in RM 8.

10 RM 9.20–24. See n. 29 below.

11 It is true that other chapters of RM have a prologue of a general nature (Adalbert de Vogüé, *La Règle du Maître,* Sources Chrétiennes 105–107 [Paris: Cerf 1964–65] I.197–198), but none of them present such disproportion between the general theory and the particular theme announced by the title. Moreover, in this instance, the particular theme remains mixed with that of "the thoughts," even in the second part of the chapter, after the prologue has concluded with "we."

12 The words *perfectis discipulis propter taciturnitatis grauitatem rara* must be considered as a sort of digression if the *quamuis* that opens the phrase opposes the following *tamen*. In fact the antithesis *quamuis ... tamen* demands that the emphasis in the first clause be placed on the positive element represented by *loquendi concedatur licentia*. In the second clause, this permission to speak of good things is juxtaposed with the silence imposed on other subjects. In the context of this interpretation, the words *perfectis ... rara* necessarily appear as a parenthetical restriction. One must admit that the construction of the first clause becomes extremely difficult. Hence, the temptation to consider the text of RB 6.3 original, where the absence of the second clause beginning with *tamen*, permits *quamuis* to be interpreted not as a conjunction but as an adverb pertaining to *bonis ... eloquiis*. See n. 57 et seq. on this subject. Considering only the text of the Master, it is hardly possible to thus isolate *quamuis*, to which *tamen* appears to be the natural correlative (cf. RM 7.72–73; 11.58; 27.36; 33.22, and 54).

13 *Inst.* 4.41.2: *semper hunc psalmistae uersiculum in tuo corde decantans.*

14 Although only the Master omits the second hemistich of the first verse: *dum consistit peccator aduersum me.* In Cassian, these words were more in context since the text was placed in the mouth of the monk injured by another. On the other hand, the Master adds *nimis* after *humiliatus sum*.

15 In contrast, the presence of Psalm 17:30 (*A te eripiar a temptatione ...*) in both RM 8.29 and *Inst.* 12.17.2 is insignificant (different scope and context).

16 Augustine, Arnobius, and Cassiodorus do not have anything in their commentaries on Psalm 38:2–3 that corresponds exactly.

17 Proverbs 10:19 and 18:21 (RM 8.35–36).

18 One also finds *siliscant* in RM 8.34, but this derivative is probably suggested by the *silui* of the citation (8.31). Elsewhere, it is accompanied by the words *in taciturnitate* so as to clarify the meaning. The Master utilizes only the substantive *delictum* (Th 22 and two citations) from the root *delinquere*.

19 Immediately after the correct citation, 8.32 already substitutes *taceri* and *peccati* (*poenam*) for the two unfamiliar words.

20 This time it is apparently not a matter of removing words that seem less in context than in Cassian (see above, n. 14) but of a simple abridgment.

21 See *La Règle du Maître* I.205 (cited in n. 11).

22 Obviously, the sequence of RM 8 could be the result of a simple coincidence. However, one will note that in each pericope, the first citation is introduced by the previous context: battle against temptation (RM 8.30), contrast between *paucis* and *multiloquiis* (RM 9.31).

23 In spite of the formulas *tam a malis quam a bonis* (9.35) and *tam de malis quam de bonis* (9.37), which would lead one to instead believe that the accent is placed on *mala eloquia*. *Tacui a bonis* is emphasized by *etiam* (9.36) and the significance of *bona eloquia* becomes clear in 9.37–38.

24 RM 9.35 and 37 (see previous note).

25 *Nam* may be causal (because) or adversative (on the other hand).

Chapter 6: Silence

26   *Perfectis discipulis* (8.33) is picked up again with *perfecto discipulo* (9.37), which reinforces the parallelism of the two passages.

27   Note the presence of *discipulus* in 8.33 and 8.37.

28   This last phrase is strange. *Ideo enim diximus* (9.18) normally calls for a final-consecutive clause opening with *ut* (cf. 9.11). Was the expected apodosis forgotten or removed? As it is, the phrase could be considered a conclusion to 9.6–10, and 9.11–17 an interpolation. However, one encounters a group of words in 9.18–19 that are previously found in 9.12 (*repetitur et post ipsam mox a nolente disceditur*), such that it also seems to recapitulate 9.11–17.

29   Again a passage that leaves one wondering. How does the Master get from the transitory gesture of the inclination of the head, a sign of humility before the abbot, to the permanent attitude of a downcast gaze, a sign of the remembrance of God? The link that the present text establishes between these two terms seems quite artificial. This occurrence likely confirms the hypothesis proposed above (n. 10) on the origin of 9.21–24. The introductory phrase of the paragraph (9.20) could be a later bridge similar to 8.26 (see nn. 6–8 above). In any case, it returns to the *Benedicite* as the only exemption from silence (cf. 9.11).

30   It is true that we suggest only a single motive for the master (to presume that the disciple is too respectful …) and two for the disciple (to presume that he is judged unworthy and to avoid angering the distracted abbot), but the second motive proposed to the disciple corresponds to what is indicated for the abbot in RM 7 regarding the repetition of *iussiones*: compare 7.12 (*surdo stupore hebescere … cogitationibus*) and 9.15 (*cogitationibus obstupescens … surdis auribus*). Thus the two chapters both speak of two motives: to presume such and such an intention in the one whom is being addressed, and to deal with his distractions. One need only link the *iussiones* with the *interrogationes* in RM 7 to obtain complete agreement with RM 9. Moreover, the two passages are written with entirely the same vocabulary: compare *praeceps in lingua* in 7.19 and 9.28, etc.

31   See nn. 18–27 above.

32   RM 9.30. The Master replaces *sermo malus* with *uerbum uanum*. On the other hand, he substitutes *si quis est* for *si quis bonus*. Thus, the contrast is no longer between "good" and "evil" speech, but between "vain" and "edifying" speech (Incidentally, this last term appears in the Pauline original). Compare RM 8.32: *bonis … malis*; 8.33–34: *bonis et sanctis et aedificationum eloquiis … aliis uerbis*; 9:43–44: *de uerbo Dei … de inanibus aut de saecularibus uel quibusuis uerbis quae ad Deum non pertinent*; 9.49–50: *de saecularibus inquirendis, quae ad aedificationem spiritalem non pertinent … de aliquo spiritali interrogando sermone.* See nn. 38 and 49–50 below on these contrasts that do not perfectly correspond.

33   RM 9.41. However, *hanc tantam taciturnitatis districtam custodiam*, very vague, seems to refer to the whole of the rule of silence.

34   Cf. 50.44, where this complete silence in the presence of the abbot is juxtaposed with the permission granted to "ask questions regarding the divine precepts" and to "speak an edifying word about God" when the abbot is absent (50.26, 43, 45). There is not a single reference to the *Benedicite* in all of RM 50 (see n. 51 below).

35   RM 9.43–44. Compare the parallel distinctions (see n. 32 above and nn. 49–50 below).

36 Cf. 11.46–48 regarding tone of voice. Regarding permission to speak, the present passage seems to disagree with 11.41–45, which presumes that one must always wait to be asked. One will note that *lente et humiliter non clamosa uoce* is based on RM 10.80, or at least on Cassian *Inst.* 4.39.2.

37 Unlike the exception for good things found here, in 11.41–45, the deans must quell *all* words spoken by a brother who has not been questioned. However, here there is no question of waiting until one is asked, as in RM 11. All this is less coherent than it seemed.

38 First, the *alia uerba* in 8.34 are not comparable with the *inania* in 9.44 ("vain" words can only be sinful, therefore absolutely forbidden. Cf. 9.30). Then 8.34 mentions the abbot who is assumed absent in 9.43–44. Finally, the prescribed behavior is different: for speaking of good things, permission being granted rarely (8.33) vs. speech in a low voice (9.43); for other matters: waiting until asked (8.34) vs. being silenced by the deans (9.44).

39 RM 9.45. Cf. 50.26 and 43, which mention the recitation before the "words on God," not after as here.

40 In fact, in spite of the reference to the perfect in 9.41, it does not seem that 9.42–45 is addressed to them in particular. Compare 50.25–26 and 42–46, exactly parallel texts in which no reference occurs. Just like 8.26 and 9.20 (see nn. 6–8 and 29), 9.41 is a later addition, not necessarily related to the paragraph it introduces. 9.46–47, another new addition, is remarkably similar to 9.41. The only innovation is *praesente abbate*. This clause does not necessarily refer to 9.42 because the *Benedicite* rule (9.1–27) already presupposes the constant presence of the abbot. Therefore, it is probable that *Hanc ... clusuram* designates the beginning of the chapter (9.1–27) and not what immediately precedes it (9.42–45). Consequently, the 9.46–47 addition appears to be a duplicate of 9.41.

41 This point does not reappear elsewhere in the Rule.

42 As they are in 9.44 and 50.25, 42. Compare the tolerance of 8.34 for *alia uerba*.

43 At least as indicated by *incoauerint* (9.44): "to begin speaking without having obtained permission" (cf. 9.49). But then, why does one find no reference to the *benedictio* in the entire paragraph?

44 It is not simply a matter of "posing some questions."

45 One could place 8.33, which presupposes the *interrogatio* of the disciples, in this column.

46 Or say something that is good (50.26) or about God (50.45).

47 Perhaps one should not push 10.75, a spiritual text without legislative significance, too far. If need be, 11.41–43 could be seen as emerging from the same genre, which would dispense one from taking it literally.

48 RM 8.33–34. See n. 34 above.

49 *Quae ad rem non pertinent* (Eph 5:4). The expression is reproduced in RM 50.25 and adapted in RM 9.44 and 49; 11.49; 50.42. In our table, we render each instance with "unrelated with.... "

50 See the questions of the brothers in RM 9.11 and 18; 61.1; those of the abbot in RM 85.2. Cf. also the *interrogatio discipulorum* of the chapter titles.

51 The *Benedicite* seems implicit in 8.33 and 50.43.

Chapter 6: Silence

52 RB 16.1: *Ut ait propheta*. Cf. RM 34.1–3.

53 One only finds *ait* in RM 47.2; 48.5 and 14, where the Master probably copies a source.

54 Augustin Genestout notes that "the use of the word *faciamus* to introduce a citation that is a discourse is not particularly appropriate" ("La Règle du Maître et la Règle de S. Benoît," *Revue d'Ascétique et de Mystique [RAM]* 21 [1940]: 76). Are the *decantans* of Cassian and *dicens* of the Master more so? It would seem to me to that the simple fact that the Master agrees with Cassian here, something that has not previously occurred, is more convincing in regard to the priority of the Master.

55 Thus Paul Delatte, *Commentaire sur la Règle de saint Benoît* (Paris: 1913), 108. ET: *The Rule of Saint Benedict: A Commentary*. (Latrobe: Archabbey Press, 1950); G. Penco, *S. Benedicti Regula*. Biblioteca di Studi Superiori 39 (Florence: 1958), 51, etc.

56 *Quamuis* normally applies only to what immediately follows it (*de bonis ... eloquiis*). This is the interpretation of L. Sansegundo, G. Colombás, and O. Cunill, *San Benito: su vida y su regla* (Madrid: La Editorial Católica, 1954), 367; J. McCann, *The Rule of S. Benedict* (London: 1952), 37; B. Steidle, *Die Regel St. Benedikts, eingeleitet, übersetzt und aus dem alten Mönchtum erklärt* (Beuron: 1952), 121.

57 Beyond the major difficulty analyzed above (n. 12), one will note the following: (1) the shift from *mala uerba* (RM 8.32) to *alia uerba* (8.34), these last not actually being evil but only "unedifying"; (2) the shift from *perfectis discipulis* (8.33) to *fratres* (8.34): are they the same? (3) the clumsy contrast between *loquendi concedatur licentia* (8.33) and *non interrogati ... siliscant* (8.34): it requires analytical effort to find the point in each term on which the contrast bears, that is to say, the opportunity given or refused to the disciples to "question" the abbot; (4) *taciturnitas* first reserved only for good words (8.32–33), then applied to "other" words (8.34). Thus, 8.34 so spoils the text that one is tempted to see it as an interpolation. One will note that nothing there corresponds to RM 9.37–38. The pair *fratres ... fratribus* of RM 8.34–35 interrupts a text where, before and after, it is a question of "disciples" (8.33 and 37). Compare the opposite phenomenon in 11.53–54. All of these unfavorable factors in the long text of the Master would be decisive if these stylistic weaknesses were not typical of him even when there is no parallel text of Benedict on which to base a suspicion of interpolation. The entire RM is full of similar awkward instances. Consequently, those we have pointed out here serve to authenticate rather than disqualify the text. However, one can ask if Benedict had knowledge of this passage before the Master spoiled it by adding 8.34–35[a]. Cf. Th. Payr, "Der Magistertext in der Uberlieferungsgeschichte der Benediktinerregel," *Regula Magistri—Regula S. Benedicti, Studia monastica, cura B. Steidle*. Studia Anselmiana 44 (Rome: 1959): 52.

58 It seems to us that Genestout, 76–77 (cited in n. 54) and Penco, 239–240 (cited in n. 55) are overly optimistic concerning the quality of the text of the Master and its claims to priority over that of Benedict.

59 Not without a curious shift from *mala* to *alia* (see above n. 57).

60 In both instances, *a ... uerbis* in the second phrase corresponds to *a bonis ... eloquiis* in the first.

61 A reversal of thought is hidden beneath the apparent similarity of the formulas. On this subject, see Adalbert de Vogüé, *La Communauté et l'Abbé* (Brussels: Desclée des Brouwer, 1961), 201, n. 1; ET: *Community and Abbot* (Kalamazoo, MI: Cistercian, 1979 [I] and 1988 [II]). On the other hand, one will note that Benedict does not employ *condecet* elsewhere. The imitation of a formula of the Master would not be an isolated case: compare RB 63.13 and RB 2.1–2 (= RM 2.1–2); RB 19.1 and RB 7.26 (= RM 10.37); RB 55.4 and RB 39.1 (= RM 26.1).

62 See nn. 25–27 above.

63 RM 9.3, 6, 9, 10, 12, 14, 16, 17; 50.44. In RM 9.43, humility is conveyed by moderating the tone of voice (cf. 10.80).

64 RB 38.8. Cf. 43.8 (*et datur occasio maligno*); 54.4 (*ut non detur occasio diabulo*). Among the five other uses of *occasio*, we note *occasio scandalorum* (69.3) and *praesumptionis occasio* (70.1).

65 Compare the simplification that Benedict accomplishes in RB 5 = RM 7; RB 51 = RM 61. The omission of ceremonial prescriptions is reminiscent of RB 64 (cf. RM 93).

66 *La Communauté et l'Abbé*, 518–521 (cited in n. 61).

67 RM 8.22. Cf. RM 9.10, 27, 29, 46.

68 We cite Delatte, 111 (cited in n. 55), Penco, 51 (cited in n. 55), Ph. Schmitz, *S. Benoît, La Règle des Moines* (Maredsous: 1945), 22; McCann, 37 (cited in n. 56); B. Steidle, 121 (cited in n. 56).

69 As the rest suggests: *non aperire os permittimus*. We cannot be certain whether Benedict realized that he risked altering the image when he added *in omnibus locis*.

70 Cf. RB 7.13 = RM 10.13: *omni hora ... omni loco*. Benedict intentionally uses *omnis*, especially in the *cum omni ...* formula (cf. 6.7).

71 Cf. F. Cavallera, "La *Regula Magistri* et la Règle de S. Benoît. Le problème littéraire," *RAM* 20 (1939): 229.

72 Cf. RM 8.26 (*diximus*); 9.11, 18 (*diximus*); 9.27 (*constituimus*).

73 This "we" is frequent in the first part of RM 8 (1, 5, 7, 11, 17, 20, 21, 24) and sporadic in RM 9 (22, 32, 35).

74 Thus 8.30 (method for resisting temptation) and 8.34 (to wait to be questioned on *alia uerba*) are omitted.

75 *La Communauté et l'Abbé*, 207–288 (cited in n. 61 above).

76 RB 6.7 and RM 8.31; 9.10, 12, 14, 16, 17, 43 (cf. RM 8.5, 19; 9.3, 6, 20).

77 See *La Communauté et l'Abbé*, 207–211.

78 RM 7.10–21. See n. 30 above.

79 RM 7.16–19 (questions of the abbot). Cf. RM 9.1 (questions of the brothers).

80 RM 7.4: *audierint* (to which *fuerit* corresponds in RB 5.4).

81 See A. Ernout and A. Meillet, *Dictionnaire étymologique de la langue latin* (Paris: 1959), 455. *Oboedire* seems to be a composite of *audire*. Festus notes the *oboedire-abaudire* equivalence.

Chapter 6: Silence

82 RM presents six *obaudire* as opposed to seven *oboedire* (of which five are participles). *Obaudire* is attested to by Apuleius and Tertullian. One also finds *obauditu ... obaudiuit* (Ps 17:45) in several early psalters. On the other hand, *abauditu ... abaudiuit* seems proper to RM, indeed only to manuscript P*.

83 As the antithesis *qui uos spernit, me spernit* shows.

84 See RM 87.13–14 (*audias = sequi*); 91.43–46. Cf. Ernout-Meillet (cited n. 82 above), 55, under the word *Audio*.

85 One only finds something that comes close to the views of the Master in Cassian, *Conl.* 14.9.4–5 (see n. 100 below).

86 It is in this spirit that the Master will transform the ninth sign of Cassian into his ninth step, according to which silence must be kept *usque ad interrogationem* (until the superior asks). See RM 10.75 = RB 7.56. Cf. RM 8.34; 9.42; 11.41–44; 50.26, 43. See also Chapter Seven, nn. 91–94.

87 As P. Delatte rightly indicates, *Commentaire*, 105 (cited in n. 55 above).

88 In making the eighth sign his seventh step, the Master has broken the ties that join the signs/steps about speech. However, by its citations, the eighth step of the Master also announces those that follow. See RM 9.24, 45; 50.8–17, 26, 43, 62–69; 57.1–3. See also Chapter Seven, nn. 84–85.

89 Although obedience also has a negative aspect: the renunciation of self-will.

90 See *La Communauté et l'Abbé*, 266–288 (cited above in n. 61). Unlike the two facets of silence, these two aspects of obedience are not clearly differentiated by the Master.

91 Augustine, *Serm.* 211.5, PL 38.1057.

92 See *La Communauté et l'Abbé*, 152–153.

93 RM Th 9–23; Ths 6–39 = RB Prol 9–39.

94 See especially *Inst.* 4.23–29.

95 *Inst.* 2.10.1. The same expressions are used regarding silence in the refectory in *Inst.* 4.17.

96 *Inst.* 4.12. In *Inst.* 11.3, the *in taciturnitate, in oboedientia, in humilitate* sequence seems to echo *Inst.* 4.39.2.

97 RM 50.3–5 and 38. Cf. Cassian, *Inst.* 2.14 and 10.23–24 (in *Inst.* 2.15.1, it is *meditatio* that occupies the mind).

98 Even at night, exchanges in a low voice are not completely prohibited (RM 30.17–22). On a trip, only the Office incontrovertibly interrupts conversations (RM 57.2–10).

99 The monks of Egypt were familiar with group discussions or conferences after instruction from the superiors (Jerome, *Ep.* 22.35; Pachomius, *Reg.* 20–21). Strictly speaking, the Master provides neither but gives something equivalent to the conference throughout the day.

100 According to Cassian, *Conl.* 14.9.4–5, only the youngest are exhorted to preserve silence and not even to ask questions in the presence of the elders in the course of conferences. This text makes no official prescriptions and is not specific to cenobites.

101 RM 10.75; 11.43. Cf. Ferreolus, *Reg.* 29 (see n. 108 below).

102 At the most, he prohibits *multiloquium* in prayer and *oratio prolixa* (RM 48.5 and 10–11). Cf. Cassian, *Inst.* 2.7.2–3 and 2.10.2–3; *Conl.* 9.36.

103 RB 52.2–3 and 4–5. This point is missing in RM and calls to mind Cassian, *Inst.* 2.10.2. On the various aspects of silence, see P. Salmon, "Le Silence religieux. Pratique et théorie," *Mélanges Bénédictins* (Sainte-Wandrille: Éditions de Fontenelle, 1947), 11–58.

104 RB 38.5 (*summum fiat silentium*) and 48.5 (*cum omni silentio*).

105 Compare RB 38.6–7 (signs in the refectory) and Cassian, *Inst.* 4.17; RB 52.2–5 (silence in the oratory) and Cassian *Inst.* 2.10.2 (see n. 103 above).

106 See nn. 63–66 above, as well as RM 7.17–18 and 50.44; RM 9.25–26 and 24.19.

107 I. Herwegen, *Sinn und Geist der Benediktinerregel* (Einsiedeln: 1944), 113–119.

108 Cf. Ferreolus, *Reg.* 29: *taciturnitatem tibi praesentia abbatis uel etiam alterius senioris imponat, ita ut nisi interrogatus ab eo uel iussus silentium irrumpere non praesumas.*

109 This moderate position of Benedict leads one to think that he follows Cassian and precedes the Master. However, the fact that he categorically prohibits questions proves that he is aware of this practice. The latter is allowed by RM. Thus, it seems that Benedict returns to the rigor of Cassian after the concessions of the Master. Ferreolus (*Reg.* 29) also prohibits questions in the refectory.

110 Compare RM 30.13–27 and RB 42.8–11: Benedict adds a penal sanction and grants exceptions only to the guestmasters and abbot. Silence during the siesta (RB 48.5) is not mentioned in RM 50.56–60 (cf. 29.1).

111 See Adalbert de Vogüé, "Comment les moines dormiront," *Studia monastica* 7 (1965): 37–38 and *La Règle* V.662–664 (cited in n. 8).

112 RB 49.7. This remark supposes that *scurrilitas* is not completely eliminated, in spite of RM 9.51 = RB 6.8.

113 In RM 53, Lenten restrictions pertain only to the diet. Daily reading (RM 50) is not done individually but as a group.

114 Compare RM 28.1–7 and RB 41.2–6.

115 RB 67.5–6. For a similar reason, one must not speak to guests (RB 53.23–24).

116 RB 31.7: *non spernendo eum contristet, sed rationabiliter cum humilitate male petenti deneget* (cf. 31.16).

117 RB 31.13–14: *Humilitatem ante omnia habeat et ... sermo responsionis porrigatur bonus.*

118 RB 61.4: *Si qua sane rationabiliter et cum humilitate caritatis reprehendit aut ostendit....* In these three texts, "humility" in speech does not consist so much in speaking softly, as the Master undoubtedly intended in the eleventh step (RM 10.80 = RB 7.60. Cf. RM 9.43; see Chapter Seven, n. 98), as in responding reasonably and encouragingly to the one with whom one is conversing.

119 RB 66.2–4. These comments are entirely original in comparison with RM. See *La Communauté et l'Abbé*, 458–459 (cited in n. 61).

120 See *La Communauté et l'Abbé*, 439–503.

Chapter Seven

Humility

I. The Treatise of the Master

We partially explored this vast treatise of the Master in a previous work.[1] There it was a matter of studying the elements that corresponded to the treatise on obedience (RM 7). This thread led us to consider, in particular, steps one through four, five, and eight. At present, we must complete this exploration by examining, in particular, steps six, seven, and nine through eleven (abasement and silence), as well as the twelfth and final step whose close relationship with the first will require us to consider the top and bottom of the ladder together.

Structure of the Introduction

In fact, the Master very quickly indicates the relationship that he establishes between the two ends of the ladder and the treatise on humility. The introduction of the chapter (RM 10.1–9) is entirely his own work. The influence of Cassian only begins to be slightly felt in the first step. The initial citation (Lk 14:11) provides the structure for the whole passage. With fluid coherence,[2] the Master comments successively on the two parts: *Omnis qui se exaltat humiliabitur* engenders a meditation on pride and its punishment (RM 10.1–4), while (*omnis*) *qui se humiliat exaltabitur*[3] produces an exhortation to climb to heaven by humility (RM 10.5–9).

The two parts of the Gospel maxim are interpreted with the help of texts from the Old Testament, the first with citations from Psalm 130:1–2 (*Domine non est exaltatum cor meum* ...), the second with a paraphrase of Genesis 28:12 (Jacob's ladder). Both of these texts allude, directly or indirectly, to two parts of the human person. The psalmist says: *Domine non est exaltatum cor meum, neque elati sunt oculi mei* (RM 10.3 = RB 7.3). In its turn, Jacob's ladder has two sides, which the Master emphasizes that he wishes to be understood as "our body and soul" (RM 10.9 = RB 7.9). Thus, pride and humility must be confronted both within and without. The disciple in search of humility must guard both heart and eyes, both soul and body.

These facts are read in RB as well as RM, but there is an entire parallel missing in RB. Only the Master tells us that the ladder represents *humiliato corde et capite suo* in our earthly life. Benedict removes the last words and retains only *humiliato corde* (RM 10.8. Cf. RB 7.8). The indication of the Master is clearly attached to those that we have just highlighted. After *cor/oculi* and before *anima/corpus,* the *cor/caput* pair shows once again the division of the human being into two parts. We list these three pairs one after another in order to better show their connections.

RM 10.3: *"non est exaltatum cor meum neque elati sunt oculi mei"*

RM 10.8: *uita ... quae humiliato corde et capite suo ...*

RM 10.9: *Latera ... credimus nostrum esse corpus et anima ...*

Obviously, the second phrase is simply the positive counterpart of the first. In contrast, the third is clearly separated from both by the terms employed (*corpus et anima*), the order in which these terms appear, and by the absence of a verb corresponding to *exaltatum, elati,* or *humiliato.* Thus, although the pair *cor/caput* (RM 10.8) appears apropos to the thought of Jacob, thus belonging to the second part of the introduction, it is nonetheless attached to the first. It is only a recollection of Psalm 130 that suggests this remark to the Master. He does not yet connect it to any image relevant to the ladder metaphor. It is not until the following sentence that he will decide to find an image of the two parts of the human person in the *latera scalae.*

Introduction and Steps

These observations already throw a certain light on the way in which the Master has constructed his ladder. In fact, most of the antithetical terms we have just encountered (*cor/oculi, corde/capite, corpus/anima*) also appear at the other end of the chapter, in the twelfth step of humility:

RM 10.82: *non solo corde, sed etiam ipso corpore*

RM 10.83: *inclinato semper capite, defixis in terra aspectibus*

RM 10.85: *(dicens sibi in corde) ... fixis in terris oculis ... leuare oculos meos ad caelos*

Only the word *anima* is missing. Here, instead of the pair *anima/corpus* from RM 10.9, one finds the antithesis *corde ... corpore,*[4] the second term then being clarified by *capite* and *oculis.*[5] This passage clearly corresponds to the statement from the introduction. It is here that we witness the second phase of implementation of the scriptural program:

Chapter 7: Humility

Non est exaltatum cor meum, neque elati sunt oculi mei. Lowering the "eyes" or — what amounts to the same — bowing the "head," reflect humility of the "body," as opposed to that of the "heart."[6] The twelfth step is certainly not a matter of simple external comportment. This corporal comportment is accompanied by a constant awareness of the sins that one has committed. One sees oneself already standing before God the Judge and unceasingly repeats in one's heart the humble words of the publican and psalmist. But by thus describing the internal face of the twelfth step,[7] the Master does not retreat from his original purpose: what he prescribes here is above all the comportment of the head and eyes, or, in a word, the body.

Humility of the "body" is juxtaposed with that of the "heart." This indication invites us to search in previous steps for one or more passages that describe interior humility. There is nothing of this sort in the steps immediately before, which from nine to eleven deal with the tongue,[8] laughter, and manner of speech. Neither is anything found in the eighth step, where it is a matter of "deeds." But in the seventh step, it appears that we have found what we are looking for: "not content to merely declare with his *tongue* that he is the last and most vile of all, the disciple also believes it in the inmost depths of his *heart, humbling himself* and saying...." The reference to the tongue clearly alludes to the fifth step, where disciples are encouraged to reveal their evil thoughts and actions "by a *humble* confession of the *tongue*." Consequently, humility of the tongue, if one can so speak, ends in humility of the heart. The first is not enough. Disciples must pass from an exterior confession of faults to the inmost conviction of their own wretchedness. But the seventh step not only completes the fifth, it announces the twelfth. After progressing from the exterior to the interior, from "tongue" to "heart" (steps five to seven), disciples remake the journey in the opposite direction, from the interior to the exterior, from "heart" to "body," that is to say to the "head" and "eyes" (steps seven to twelve). Both going and returning, middle rungs separate the points of arrival and departure: going, the sixth step, and returning, the ninth to eleventh steps. These steps play no intermediary role whatsoever between the contrasting terms. Unrelated to the play of antithesis that frames them, they even make it difficult to recognize. If the Master, nevertheless, keeps them in their place, it is undoubtedly because he wishes to cause no further disruption to the already very distorted signs of Cassian. This concern to show the utmost respect for the structure of *Inst* 4.39 explains in particular the placement of the twelfth step, a description of corporal humility that is totally lacking in Cassian, after the series of steps corresponding to the signs.

But we return to the introduction. The announcement of two forms of humility, that of the heart and that of the eyes or head (RM 10.3 and 8), seems perfectly realized in the seventh and twelfth steps.[9] However, it is possible that the Master instead has the first step in mind in regard to the "heart."[10] Likewise, there is no doubt that, in the most general of terms, the introduction of the *latera scala*, image of the body and soul (RM 10.9), concerns steps seven and twelve,[11] but it may also apply to the contrast established between steps five and seven.[12] In addition, it is very possible that the Master is thinking of the first step, where he will successively examine the thoughts, tongue, hands and feet,[13] as well as steps nine to eleven, which address speech and laughter, therefore, the "corporal" aspects of humility.

However, one hesitates to pursue this direction because the metaphor of the sides of the ladder is difficult to reconcile with a classification of steps in which some are considered corporal and others spiritual. In fact, taken literally, this image suggests that *each* step is inserted into *both* sides, into both body and soul. Yet only steps one and twelve present a rather clear two-part structure, having both internal and external aspects.[14] Must one conclude that when the Master speaks of rungs inserted "into body and soul," he is thinking only of these two specific steps?[15]

Connection of the First and Twelfth Steps

In any event, one will not be mistaken in seeing the first and twelfth steps as two closely connected passages. When the Master converts the list of signs from Cassian into a ladder, he places these two steps, which do not correspond to any sign, at top and bottom. Symmetrically framing the ten steps drawn from the *Institutes*, they are similar in their shared independence from Cassian. While this independence is total in the twelfth step, it is only slightly curtailed in the first by the fact that the "fear of the Lord" previously appears in the introductions of *Inst.* 4.39.1. One need only compare this brief reference from Cassian with the vast development that the Master composes for the first step to see that it owes almost nothing to *Inst.* 4.39.1, which will be the source of the following steps. As was noted by A. Borias,[16] the Master instead looks for the various themes developed here in an earlier passage of his own work, namely the *Ars Sancta*. Therefore, the first step is as much a veritable creation of the Master as the last.

To this common origin, one can add the similarity of form and ideas. From the first reading, one is struck by the insistence with which the Master repeats *semper* and *omni hora* in the first step.[17] These same repetitions return with the same frequency in the twelfth step,[18] while

Chapter 7: Humility

one finds *semper* only once in between.[19] One can say the same for the words *extimet* or *existimet*,[20] *dicat sibi in corde*,[21] and *iudicio*.[22] But this last word leads to a more important observation. It appears at the very end of the first step where the Master concludes his exhortation to "be vigilant" in the present by anticipating what God will say *in futuro iudicio*: "You did these things, and I was silent." Therefore, the judgment appears here in the distant, although already daunting, future. It is precisely this distance that will be abolished in the twelfth step. There the disciple "believes that he already stands (*repraesentari*) at the terrible judgment." The eschatological event has become a present reality. The faith of the disciple and his continual awareness of his sins create this frightening anticipation in his mind. Thus, the twelfth step picks up where the first step left off, actualizing a threat that previously hovered in the future.

This relationship between the two steps is even more apparent if one considers certain themes that run through both, such as fear, the presence of God, and sin. The "fear of God" is not merely the opening note of the first step in keeping with a statement from Cassian[23] but remains latent throughout this long text,[24] whether it is a question of divine commands, warnings from Scripture, the last things, or the gaze and presence of God—all daunting thoughts[25] that summon the disciple to continually "guard against" his sins and vices (RM 10.12, 19, 35, 40), in anxious expectation of the judgment to come. In its turn, the twelfth step employs the descriptor *tremendum*, applying it specifically to the judgment. Thus, the "fear of God" of the first step is crystallized in the twelfth by the fear of divine judgment being realized.

The concomitant theme of presence evolves in the same way. In the first step, God is seen as being present to our thoughts, deeds, wills, and desires. In the twelfth, he is no longer so much the witness of our earthly life who is "present" to the conscience of disciples but already the judge who will pronounce the ultimate sentence. One has passed from the theme of the "presence of the Lord" to that of the judgment.

Finally, both steps speak of sin, but, in this instance, the shared theme establishes a paradoxical sequence between them. In the first step, disciples are encouraged to constantly guard themselves *a peccatis et uitiis* (RM 10.12). In the twelfth, they constantly see themselves as *reum de peccatis suis* (RM 10.84). Thus, disciples constantly guard themselves against sin only to constantly feel themselves sinners! At first glance, this is a surprising progression, but it conforms to the experience of the saints as well as to the dialectic of the ladder of humility where one can only ascend by descending. The battle against sin sensitizes individuals to the sin dwelling within them, and their awareness of being sinners increases. Moreover, at this twelfth step, disciples are not far from the perfect charity by which the Holy Spirit will make them *mundum a uitiis et peccatis*,[26] "pure from their vices and sins," which, in the first step, they guarded against in fear. But before this reversal occurs, it is necessary that all these joint sentiments from the first step—fear of God, consciousness of being under his gaze, terror of his judgments, and dread of the sin that he hates—reach a sort of climax in the twelfth step. Thus, this last step of the ladder appears as the sequel to the first and as the final development of the dispositions that were required at the point of departure for the ascent.

The First Step and the Ars Sancta

For the most part, the various threads that are woven throughout the first step are not only found at the other end of the ladder, but, as we have noted, also appear in a series of items from the *Ars Sancta*. A synopsis of this passage and of the first step will highlight their connections:

RM 3.50–60	RM 10.10–14, 20–21
[58]Diem iudicii timere.	... [10]timorem Dei ante oculos sibi semper ponens (cf. ne dicat nobis in futuro iudicio in 10.41) ...
[51]Gehennam expauescere.	[11]ut quomodo et gehenna ... incendat, et uita aeterna
[52]Vitam aeternam et Hierusalem sanctam desiderare.	quid timentibus Deum praeparet, animo suo semper reuoluat.
[53]Mortem cottidie ante oculos suspectam habere.	
[54]Actus uitae suae omni hora custodire.	[12]Et custodiens se omni hora a peccatis et uitiis ...
[55]In quouis loco a Deo se respici pro certo scire.	[13]extimet se ... a Deo ... respici ... omni loco ...

Chapter 7: Humility

RM 3.50–60	RM 10.10–14, 20–21
[56]Cogitationes malas cordi suo aduenientes mox ad Christum allidere.	... [14]in cogitationibus nostris ita Deum semper esse praesentem ostendit ...
[57]Os suum a malo uel prauo eloquio custodire. [58]Multum loqui non amare.	[20]Ad linguae uero eloquia ita agnoscimus Deum nobis esse praesentem ...
[59]Verba uana aut risui apta non ex toto loqui.	([21]De uerbo uano reddetis rationem).
[60]Risum multum aut excussum non amare.	

The parallelism of the two sequences is interrupted here: while the first step shifts from sins in speech to sins in deeds (hands and feet), the *Ars Sancta* inserts four articles concerning reading, prayer, confession of past faults, and their amendment in the future (RM 3.61–64 = RB 4.55–58). But the two texts then parallel a final time, though inverting the corresponding terms:

[65]Desideria carnis non perficere.	[38] Voluntatem uero propriam ... facere prohibemur ...
[66]Voluntatem propriam odire.	[31]In desideriis uero carnis ...

The inversion observed here is a curious occurrence that leads us to examine the last two developments of the first step more closely. Were they originally arranged in the same order as the two corresponding articles in the *Ars Sancta*? In fact, examination of the citations seems to indicate that desires of the flesh originally preceded self-will in RM 10. Here is how these citations follow in the final redaction that we have in front of us:

Self-Will	RM 10.30	Sir 18:30b
	31	Mt 6:10
	32	Prov 16:25
	33	Ps 13:1
Desires of the Flesh	34	Ps 37:10
	35	*Passio Seb.* 14
	36	Sir 18:30a
Conclusion	37	Prov 15:3
	38	Ps 13:2
	39	*Vis. Pauli* 7
	40	Ps 13:3
	41	Ps 49:21

Such a sequence is abnormal in two ways. First, the two halves of Sirach 18:30 are separated and inverted, the second appearing at the beginning of the first paragraph and the first at the end of the second. Next, the first verse of Psalm 13, utilized in regard to the will, is also found far removed from the two following verses of the same psalm, which form the framework of the conclusion. This double anomaly disappears if one places desires of the flesh before self-will:

Desires of the Flesh	RM 10:34	Ps 37:10
	35	*Passio Seb.* 14
	36	Sir 18:30a
Self-Will	30	Sir 18:30b
	31	Mt 6:10
	32	Prov 16:25
	33	Ps 13:1
Conclusion	37	Prov 15:3
	38	Ps 13:2
	39	*Vis. Pauli* 7
	40	Ps 13:3
	41	Ps 49:21

In this reconstructed sequence, the two halves of Sirach 18:30 follow one another in proper order and without interruption, in such a way as to closely tie the development on self-will to the paragraph on the desires. The sacred text forming such a bridge, one understands why the second passage opens with a citation that begins with *Et*. Likewise, Psalm 13 forms a bridge between the second passage and the conclusion.

Therefore, one obtains perfect order in the citations of RM 10 by reestablishing the sequence of material indicated by RM 3. In a single stroke, one also obtains a better thematic and stylistic connection within this

Chapter 7: Humility

series in the early part of the first step. In fact, unlike the introduction and first development (on the thoughts), the subsequent three paragraphs (on words and on the actions of the hands and feet) deal only with God's presence to our works, without speaking of our vigilance against sin. Moreover, their presentation is almost stereotypical:

RM 10.20: Ad linguae *uero* eloquia *ita nobis agnoscimus Deum semper esse praesentem, cum dicit* per *prophetam* uox Domini ...

RM 10.23: *In* opere *uero* manuum *nostrarum ita agnoscimus Deum nobis esse praesentem, cum dicit propheta* ...

RM 10.24: *In* gressu *uero* peduum *nostrorum ita agnoscimus Deum nobis semper esse praesentem, cum dicit propheta* ...

After such a homogeneous series, the paragraph on self-will appears doubly disparate: first, because, apart from the phrase *praesente Domino*, it does not discuss the presence of God but forbids the accomplishment of our will; second, because it begins quite differently:

RM 10.30: Voluntatem *uero* propriam *ita*, praesente Domino, facere prohibemur, *cum dicit* scribtura nobis ...

In contrast, the beginning of the development on the desires of the flesh is in perfect continuity with the theme and style of the preceding series. It discusses the presence of God and begins like the others:

RM 10.34: *In* desideriis *uero* carnis *ita nobis Deum* credimus *semper esse praesentem, cum dicit propheta* ...

It is strange that a passage that so clearly continues the speech-hands-feet series is separated from it by the divergent development on self-will. On the other hand, the latter fits perfectly after the paragraph on desires, which concludes with a warning against evil desires. The following schema shows that the sequencing of the themes of resistance to sin (a) and divine presence (b) becomes more satisfactory if one places self-will after the desires of the flesh:

First Step According to the Present Order (Later)		First Step According to the Restored Order (Original)	
Words: theme Hands: Feet:	b b b	Words: theme Hands: Feet:	b b b
Will:	a	*Desires*:	b a
Desires:	b a	*Will*:	a

It is apparent that, according to the present order, the paragraph on the will, which develops only theme (a), is poorly inserted between two paragraphs on theme (b). In contrast, according to the restored original order, everything fits together and follows harmoniously,[27] the passage from one theme to the next occurring *within* the paragraph on desires.

Thus, consideration of both the sequence of citations and the connection of themes and formulas leads us to believe that the subject order at the end of the first step originally consisted in the desires-will sequence. This is precisely the order presented by the *Ars Sancta* (RM 3.65–66). The reverse sequence, which we find in the current redaction of RM 10, seems to be the result of a revision. What was the reason for it? One cannot answer with certainty. Perhaps the author intended that, like the first, the last of the five paragraphs should present the complete b + a bipartite structure, so as to form an inclusion of sorts. In fact, the introduction before the first paragraph and conclusion following the last present this structure in a + b or b + a order:

First Step According to the Present Order (Later)		First Step According to the Restored Order (Original)	
Introduction: theme	a b	Introduction: theme	a b
Thoughts:	b a	Thoughts:	b a
Desires:	b a	*Will*:	a
Conclusion:	b a	Conclusion:	b a

Chapter 7: Humility

From a symmetrical point of view, one notes that the present order presents a certain advantage over the previous one. Perhaps it is this that made it the preferred sequence. Regardless, one will note that the correction was carefully made: the list of RM 10.12 presents the will before the desires, in other words, in the later order.[28]

Consequently, comparison with the *Ars Sancta* shows itself to be particularly evocative as concerns these last two paragraphs on the will and desires. We must now complete our study of the conclusion of the first step, whose citations and themes have already been envisaged, and then provide an overview of the two texts. First, we observe that this conclusion, and, with it, the entire first step, finish on the note of the judgment (10.41) with which the section of the *Ars Sancta* (3.50) began.

This is an initial difference between the two passages. There are others: nothing in RM 10 corresponds to the article on death (3.53);[29] for its part, the *Ars Sancta* does not speak of remembrance of the commandments of God (10.11),[30] the relationship with the angels (10.13), etc. However, the two texts follow one another too closely for their correspondence to be coincidental. The *Ars Sancta* presents as separate articles most of the thoughts that, woven together in a coherent discourse, will constitute the first step. The Master is accustomed to these couplets. Later, the ladder of humility offers a beautiful example that we have examined in a previous work.[31]

In the present case, it is not easy to discern which of the two parallel passages was conceived first. However, we will attempt to begin by examining the *Ars Sancta*. There we find the three "last things" (judgment, hell, and eternal life) enumerated first, each rousing a particular sentiment (fear, terror, and desire). Judgment comes at the beginning of this trio in accordance with the chronological order. At the end, one turns back to consider "death" and the "deeds of life." This time, the words do not express emotions, but an attentive reflection (*ante oculos suspectam habere, custodire*), which suffers no relaxation (*cottidie, omni hora*). The following article, which speaks of the "gaze of God," presents the same characteristics: the action is more intellectual (*pro certo scire*) than affective and an adverbial phrase (*quouis loco*) emphasizes its continuity.

These three last articles can therefore be grouped under a heading such as "continual vigilance." From the sentiments of fear and hope aroused by eschatological perspectives (3.50–52), one moves to the temporal vigilance that such views continually impose (3.53–55). The transition from one group to the other is perfectly prepared by the article on death, the latter being the threshold that separates eschatology from the present life. The series is constructed with a care that is revealed even in its number of syllables: the judgment and hell, both objects of fear, are referenced with nine and eight syllables respectively, while the article on the desire for eternal life represents seventeen syllables, or the exact sum of the two that precede it.[32] The same number seventeen is found in the articles on death and the gaze of God, as indeed was previously encountered and will be encountered again later.[33] Carefully prepared or spontaneous, this series of articles of equal length is undoubtedly not the result of chance. It denotes an ear sensitive to cadence.[34] But what particularly interests us here is the relationship thus established between the first three articles that we are examining. In reality, whether one considers the rhythm or the themes, this first group is not made up of three clauses of the same importance, but of two equal stichs:

[50]*Diem iudicii timere,*[51] *gehennam expauescere,*
[52]*Vitam aeternam et Hierusalem sanctam desiderare.*

While there are clearly three verbs, the first two (*timere, expauescere*) express varying nuances of the same sentiment, fear.[35] Desire (*desiderare*) corresponds to fear, both sentiments having a double object: either judgment and hell, or eternal life and the holy Jerusalem.[36] Such a carefully written construction leaves no room for doubt as to the attention with which these phrases were constructed. In particular, it is clear that the reference to the judgment, which nothing corresponds to in RM 10.11, plays a necessary role here. Comparison with RM 10.11 could lead one to believe that this tiny article was added extraneously for no compelling reason. This is not the case. *Diem iudicii timere* is intimately linked to the following articles, with which it forms a compact and well-constructed whole. That is to say, that the *Ars Sancta* follows naturally here and does not appear to be an adaptation of the first step.

Could the first step be instead an adaptation of the *Ars Sancta*? It is theoretically possible, given that the comparative study on the treatise on obedience and the first four steps of humility led us to see these latter as a reprise of RM 7.[37] If the ladder of humility reemployed some preexisting elements in that instance, it is probable that it does the same in the present case. This hypothesis shows how the Master composed his first step.

Interactions between the Ars Sancta *and Cassian*

The foundation is provided by Cassian: *Principium nostrae salutis eiusdemque custodia timor Domini est. Per hunc enim et initium conuersionis et uitiorum purgatio et uitiorum custodia his qui imbuuntur ad uiam*

Chapter 7: Humility

perfectionis adquiritur (*Inst.* 4.39.1). Cassian has adapted and developed this from the well-known biblical definition: "The fear of God is the beginning of wisdom" (Prov 9:10; Ps 110:10). Fear has become "the beginning of salvation" and "the beginning of conversion." Moreover, this initial role is extended. Twice, Cassian speaks of *custodia*: fear is not only the beginning of salvation but also its "protector," because it brings about purification from vices and "protection" of virtues.

One will recognize here several keywords from the first step. The fear of God is also "first" for the Master, although it now opens the way to "humility," rather than to "wisdom," "salvation," or "conversion."[38] It is also a question of "vices" and of a "guard" in RM, but the Master brings these two terms, separated by Cassian, together in an original manner. The *custodia* of Cassian consists of "guarding salvation and the virtues," while the Master intends that one be "constantly on guard against sins and vices" (there is no question of virtues in the first step). On the other hand, a verb replaces the substantive (*custodia* becomes *custodiens se*). The Master no longer simply contrasts the initial and ongoing roles of fear. He requires that disciples engage in continuous effort, combat without truce, and unceasing vigilance over themselves, which they maintain by actively cultivating a series of daunting thoughts.

There is no question of this battle and activity in Cassian.[39] These create the interest and novelty of the first step. The Master replaces a simple declaration on the place of fear in the spiritual life with a description of individuals who are voluntarily permeated with this sentiment and who strive to let it fill all their deeds. It may be that Cassian's descriptive comments, known as the "signs of humility," inspire the Master to so modify his material. But the Master does not write his first step only in the style of those that follow, which he will draw from Cassian. He also recalls the *Ars Sancta*, in which each article defines an attitude or action. Admittedly, the brief propositions of RM 3.50–60 are taken up in a single long phrase here,[40] where the monotonous succession of infinitives gives way to a play of participles, main verbs, and coordinate and subordinate clauses.[41] But this change of presentation does not affect the substance of the discourse. Instead of speculating on the characteristics of the fear of God, both texts establish a program for acting in accordance with this virtue.

Therefore, the first step is much closer to the *Ars Sancta* than to the *Institutes*. The *Institutes* have, however, influenced its writing and contributed to distinguishing it from the *Ars Sancta*. In RM 3.50–51, fear has the Day of Judgment and hell as its object. Here, as in Cassian, one speaks of the fear of God.[42] There is only discussion of judgment in the conclusion of the step (RM 10.41). Hell still appears contrasted with eternal life here, but these two last ends are no longer linked with fear and desire. A continual contemplation (*animo suo semper reuoluat*) that encompasses both objects is substituted for these two opposing sentiments. The two last ends, granted very unequal treatises in the *Ars Sancta*, are now presented in two equal phrases that mention the types of persons for whom they are reserved — those who despise the Lord and those who fear God. Thus, where the *Ars Sancta* appeals to the emotions, the first step instead invites reflection.

This same meditative attitude, predominantly intellectual, is also recommended as concerns the fear of God and the divine precepts. Strictly speaking, the Master does not prescribe "fearing God," but to "keep the fear of God always before your eyes." Suggested in part by Psalm 35:2, and quite awkward, the formula puts no less emphasis on the continual attention by which one endeavors to sustain the fear. A complementary formula repeats the same idea in the negative: one must "flee forgetfulness at every moment."[43] The precepts of God must also be the object of "constant remembrance." This series of almost equivalent verbs and adverbs that crown *animo suo semper reuoluat*, express the same effort to remain unceasingly aware of the truths of faith.

It is worth noting the order and sequence of these objects of contemplation: first, God as the master that one "fears"; then "all that has been prescribed" by this divine master; finally, the fate determined by whether one fears God and observes his precepts or shows contempt for God and sins. Only this last object, that is to say, the last things, appears as such in the *Ars Sancta*, and it is at the beginning there. Cassian provides the first (God as the one to be feared) of the two previous elements that the Master notes here. The second (what God has prescribed) is the Master's own invention.[44] At the same time, he sets aside the reference that the *Ars Sancta* makes to death. He turns directly from eschatology to the present life.

In the *Ars Sancta*, the article "to be vigilant at every instant over the actions of one's life" is followed by a single precept on the thoughts and four concerning speech and laughter. The plan of the first step is different. The sins of the tongue cease to occupy a privileged place, the paragraph that refers to them being even noticeably shorter than the one dealing with evil thoughts. Moreover, a series of developments concerning the hands, feet, self-will, and the desires of the flesh is added to these two first categories. As a result, the relative importance attributed to speech further declines. Laughter is out of the question.

Another innovation of the first step is to establish a constant link between the presence of God and the vigilance of individuals over themselves. This relationship is stated in the introduction (10.12–13), recalled in speaking about several aspects of the human being (10.14–36), and finally reaffirmed in the conclusion (10.37–41). One cannot express more clearly the implicit relationship of the two successive articles: *Actus vitae suae omni hora custodire* and *In quouis loco a Deo se respici pro certo scire* (3.54–55): vigilance to avoid sin is based on the awareness of the divine gaze, attention to one's self is awakened and preserved by attentiveness to God.[45]

Overview of the First Step

After having developed at length these two adjoining themes, the first step finishes with an evocation of the judgment, heralding the twelfth step. Thus the Master presently ends where he began in the *Ars Sancta*. Still formidable, the judgment no longer appears in company with hell, but separately, contrasted with the benevolence that God manifests in sparing us here below. A day will come when the silent witness to all our deeds will become the judge who pronounces his sentence.

This conclusion (10.37–41) assumes an unexpected form: that of a sermon. Actually, it is possible that after the introduction, the Master shifts imperceptibly from the descriptive style to the hortative.[46] In any event, the hortative style clearly resounds there in regard to evil thoughts and desires.[47] Thus the first step combines three genres: description, scriptural testimony, and exhortation. These three genres are found to varying degrees in the subsequent steps, but here they actually characterize distinct passages: the description of the man who cultivates the fear of God (10.10–13), the scriptural testimony to the divine presence (10.14–36), and the exhortation to keep watch over oneself (10.37–41). There is no comparison between this all-embracing and well-constructed series and the modest precepts that Cassian and the *Ars Sancta* offer. This great passage is one of the best conceived of RM.

The Source of the First and Twelfth Steps: Basil

However, these two keystones do not constitute the only materials used by the architect of the first step. At the center of the edifice, a long dissertation is found that establishes that God is present to all the interior and exterior movements of an individual (10.14–36). This five-point scriptural proof-text[48] focuses specifically on the presence of God, whereas the introduction and conclusion speak of his gaze, along with the report of the angels (RM 10.13, 37–38). But these are only three aspects of the same idea, divine omniscience. This idea is absent from the text of Cassian that serves as the basis of the first step.[49] In the *Ars Sancta* it is only a matter of the divine gaze.[50]

Does this mean that the comments on the report of the angels and especially the well-developed theme of the divine presence are the Master's own creation? One must answer in the negative, as the report of the angels is described in the *Visio Pauli* (7, 10), one of the Master's favorite texts, and the presence of God is a frequent theme in the *Regula Basilii*.[51] What is even more significant is that Basil often associates the divine presence with the divine gaze.[52] The brothers must believe,[53] be certain,[54] and constantly keep in mind[55] that this presence and gaze scrutinize the kidneys and the heart.[56] It is by this that they will be able to avoid anger, laziness, distractions, and vanity—in a word, all sin.[57] All of this is curiously similar to the first step of the Master. In addition, Basil is no less insistent in prescribing that the remembrance of God and his will must be perpetual:[58] another parallel with the first step.[59]

Conforming to Scripture, Basil already makes the fear of the Lord the beginning of wisdom,[60] as Evagrius, Cassian, and the Master will subsequently do. But Basil seems to consider it unworthy of those who have renounced all for the service of God. It is love rather than fear that befits them. We will return to this important difference between Basil and the Master.[61] For the moment, we must primarily note that the central element of the first step—to unceasingly believe in the divine presence and gaze[62]—seems to stem from the *Regula Basilii*. The Master has only capitalized on this idea of Basil by searching Scripture for evidence that God is present to each specific type of human action.

The Master may again recall Basil in the twelfth step when he asks disciples to demonstrate humility to those who see them by their corporal bearing.[63] According to Basil, it is the elders who must so preach by example, their comportment demonstrating that their mind is unceasingly occupied with the presence of God. For the Master, it is no longer a matter of those who are elders by age, but of disciples advanced in perfection, their comportment indicating that they believe themselves to be already present at the judgment. The idea of these slight distinctions is the same. It is not surprising that the *Regula Basilii* appears to underlie both the first and twelfth steps, since we know that they are closely connected.

The Connections between the First and Twelfth Steps and RM 8–9

This connection again becomes apparent if one compares the ladder of humility with the chapters on silence (RM 8 and 9). Recall that, in

Chapter 7: Humility

these chapters, the Master twice discusses different aspects of the human person that require particular vigilance. In an initial review (8.1–25), he successively considers the eyes, thoughts and speech, and hands and feet. Then, beginning a second review, he proposes to discuss the thoughts, speech, and gaze (8.26), but actually deals with only the first two (8.27–34), although the eyes later reappear in the middle of the development on speech (9.20–24).

These two reviews of RM 8–9 both resemble the ladder of humility. In fact, the first step, like the first part of RM 8, considers in succession the thoughts, tongue, hands, and feet. And while the eyes are not represented, they become the object of the twelfth step. However, the final place assigned to the eyes in RM 10 is opposite that which falls to them in RM 8.1–25, where they appear first. The second review of RM 8–9 offers a less consistent parallel with the ladder since there is no reference to the hands and feet. On the other hand, the final position occupied by the eyes makes one think of the twelfth step. A table will better show this series of similarities and differences:

RM 8.1–26	RM 8.27–34 (cf. 9.20–24)	RM 10 (Steps One and Twelve)
Eyes Thoughts and speech[64] Hands and feet	Thoughts Speech Eyes	Thoughts Speech[65] Hands Feet Eyes

The comparison of RM 8–9 draws our attention to the absence of the eyes in the first step. Why this omission? Perhaps because the Master has not found biblical texts demonstrating that God is present to our gaze? But a deficiency of this sort does not prevent him from speaking of self-will (RM 10.30–33). Therefore, there may be another reason for the omission of the eyes: the Master foresees that he will discuss the gaze in the twelfth step and does not wish to anticipate it. It is true that the same rationale would exclude the paragraph on speech from the first step as it anticipates steps 9–11. But those will be imposed on the Master by Cassian. It is not certain that the Master had the same method in mind when writing the first step as he did when writing the twelfth, which is his own work. We know that in many respects the twelfth step continues the first. Why not also in this regard?

In any event, given that the first and twelfth steps review all the organs that have already been mentioned once or twice in RM 8–9, it is interesting to compare what is said here and there on the same subjects. RM 8.24–25 envisions very coarse faults for the hands: robbery and homicide. The first step appears to substitute a more delicate and "monastic" fault for these secular crimes: the neglect of work. Already, the first words of RM 10.23 warn us: it is no longer the "touch of the hands" that will be at issue, but the "work of the hands."[66] And the text promises follow-up: if this work remains unfinished (*imperfectum*), God will see it.[67]

An analogous substitution is probable regarding the faults of the feet.[68] But the change is particularly apparent in regard to the eyes. In the first text in which he discusses them,[69] the Master requires that the eyes be kept lowered so as not to afford entry to concupiscence by looking at "evil" objects. For this rather vague rationale, apparently more appropriate for laity than monks, the second text substitutes a group of considerations that announces the first step of humility:[70] the brothers must keep their heads and gazes lowered everywhere so as to "never forget God" and be "constantly vigilant to flee from sin, fear God, and guard themselves from all that God detests" (RM 9.24). Finally, the twelfth step gives a new significance to this same attitude: the publican of the Gospel, conscious of being a sinner, is the model for those who bow their heads and fix their eyes on the ground. Like him, disciples see themselves charged with their sins at every instant and judge that they are unworthy of raising their eyes toward heaven. Thus, it is no longer fear of committing sins that inspires this gesture but awareness of having previously committed them.

Only this last reason appears in RB, which does not preserve the two passages from RM 8–9 dealing with the lowered gaze. But if one takes these passages into account, it appears that "custody of the eyes" may have an altogether different meaning than what we are accustomed to. The attitude we consider characteristic of the twelfth step receives an interpretation in RM 9.21–24 that ties it instead to the first step.[71] This again confirms the intimate connection of these two steps in the thought of the Master.

The Twelfth Step and Those That Precede It

The second text on the eyes also provides us with a clue that is helpful in better understanding the twelfth step. The Master depicts an observer

Chapter 7: Humility

who, surprised at the attitude of the brother, poses this question to him: "Why are you silent and sad, and walking with your eyes cast down?"[72] The last (*inclinato ambulans uultu*) of the three characteristics noted is found in the twelfth step. The first two (*tacitus et tristis*) correspond with steps nine to eleven on speech and laughter. Thus this little sentence presents the last four steps of humility in a nutshell. It suggests that the Master establishes a relationship between the twelfth step and the three that immediately precede it. They are complementary aspects of the same attitude.

Therefore, the twelfth step is not only linked to the first, but also continues steps 9–11. One sees here the effort made by the Master to combine his own developments, inspired by Basil, with the elements that he draws from the list of signs in the *Institutes*. If, although the twelfth step is meant to extend the first, it is placed opposite it, it is in part because the Master wishes to link it with the last signs of Cassian. We know from RM 8–9 that the speech-gaze sequence is familiar to the Master. He intends to reestablish it here by adding a final step on modesty of gaze to the signs related to the use of speech.[73]

The Sixth and Seventh Steps

Having lingered with the first and twelfth steps that are proper to the Master, we will now rapidly review the sixth to eleventh steps, which he borrows from Cassian. As we have done elsewhere for the previous steps,[74] we will juxtapose the text of RM with that of its source each time. First, here is the sixth step, drawn from the seventh sign.

Septimo *si omni uilitate contentus sit ad omnia se quae sibi praebentur uelut operarium iudicarit indignum.*	[66]Sextum ... *si omni uilitate* uel extremitate *contentus sit et ad omnia quae sibi praebentur uelut operarium malum se iudicet* et *indignum.*

There is little to say about the new redaction, which comes close to leaving that of Cassian intact. The Master is content to augment *uilitate* with *extremitate*, an intensification that prepares for the following step. The pronoun *se*, which separated the relative from its antecedent in Cassian, is moved to a less unusual place. Beyond this simple correction, there is nothing to indicate a disturbance of the clausula. Without reflecting on its reasons and grammatical effects,[75] we note that by substituting the present subjunctive (*iudicet*) for the perfect subjunctive (*iudicarit*), the Master has removed a small fault from the text of Cassian, attributable to the *cursus*. In fact, Cassian puts the verb in the present subjunctive in eight out of ten signs. If he twice prefers the perfect subjunctive (sign two and here), it is apparently to obtain a more satisfactory clausula.[76] Again, the Master removes this unusual form,[77] but by restoring the present subjunctive and adding *et*, he obtains an excellent *cursus uelox*.

Scarcely edited, the sixth step is also one of the most poorly supplied with citations. The Master has found only a single psalm text (Ps 72:22–23) to illustrate it, which only happens again in the eleventh step. Overall, the sixth step seems to hold a very limited place in the concerns of the Master.

The seventh step, drawn from the eighth sign, is more carefully prepared:

Octavo *si se*metipsum cunctis *inferiorem non* superficie *pronuntiet* labiorum, *sed intimo cordis credat affectu*.	[68]Septimum ... *si* omnibus *se inferiorem* et uiliorum *non* solum sua lingua *pronuntiet, sed* etiam *intimo cordis credat affectu,* [69]humilians se et dicens ...

Like the previous step, the Master intensifies the simple expression of Cassian: he adds *et uiliorem* to *inferiorem*. But this addition does not simply give the phrase a breadth and rhythm similar to that of the sixth step. *Viliorem* is intentionally chosen to call to mind *uilitate*, a term characteristic of both the sixth step and the seventh sign. Therefore, the Master wishes to establish a link between the seventh step and the one that precedes it. After having accepted the most "vile" treatment, disciples must regard themselves as such in the depths of their hearts. Thus, a repetition of words highlights the very discrete progression that Cassian may have intended to establish between the corresponding signs.[78]

But the seventh step is not only a development of the sixth, it is also an interiorization of the fifth. Recall how, in writing this latter, the Master transformed the simple manifestation of thoughts into an actual confession of faults.[79] This confession *per humilem linguae confessionem* is recalled here by the words *sua lingua* that the Master intentionally substitutes for the *superficie labiorum* of the eighth sign. At the same time, he establishes a progression, changing the *non ... sed* juxtaposition from the text of Cassian to *non solum ... sed etiam*. Cassian contrasts convictions of the heart with half-hearted declarations. For the Master, conviction must *complement* the declarations of the tongue that occurred in the fifth step. Thus "to believe oneself to be the last of all" is the extension of the "humble confession" recommended above. The connection of the two steps is further emphasized by *humilians se* (seventh), which is reminiscent of *humilem* (fifth). Literally questionable, this way of using humility to define humility will be found a final time in the eleventh step.[80]

Thus, the seventh step is strongly linked to both the fifth and sixth steps. The Master intends to create a sort of summit toward which its two precursors converge. At the same time, he has provided it with abundant scriptural illustrations: two pairs of psalm citations.[81]

The Eighth Step

We could now omit the eighth step since it has already been the focus of a commentary on the Rule.[82] But this commentary considered it only from the point of view of the teaching on obedience, which it is linked to by several characteristics. Yet it not only calls to mind the steps of obedience (2–4), but also those of silence (9–11). Let us recall the content:

| Sexto *si nihil agat*, nihil praesumat, *quod* non uel *communis regula uel maiorum cohortantur exempla*. | [72]Octauum ... *si nihil agat*, nisi *quod communis* monasterii *regula uel maiorum cohortantur exempla*, [73]dicens cum scribtura: "Quia lex tua meditatio mea est" (Ps 118:77), [74]et "cum interrogat patrem suum, adnuntiabit ei, seniores suo et dicent ei" (Deut 32:7), id est per suam doctrinam abbas. |

First, note that the Master omits the words *nihil praesumat*. Perhaps he recalls having already written something to this effect in the third step and wishes to avoid repetition.[83] In any event, this omission tends to weaken the phrase of Cassian. Instead of intensifying the expression as in previous steps, the Master simplifies it. The least that one can say is that he does not insist at all on the practical conformity demanded of the disciple. On the other hand, the two scriptural citations added by the Master recommend that the disciple "meditate" on the divine law (Ps 118.77) and "question" his father (Deut 32:7), that is to say, the abbot. Therefore, it is not only a matter of conforming to received norms, but also of actively inquiring about what to do by drawing from the sources—the law of God and the teaching of the abbot.

To grasp the significance of the first citation, one must recall that in RM, *meditatio* always means the oral repetition of a reading learned by heart. This "meditation" first occurs during the three hours that are allotted for it each day (RM 50.8–17, 62–69; 57.1–3), but it continues throughout the day in the course of manual labor (RM 9:45; 50.26,

43). The text thus ruminated on is normally the "law of God," Scripture.[84] Therefore, the citation that the Master makes here cannot help but call to mind the daily exercise of *meditatio* in the course of work. Yet this exercise occurs in a whisper, and as such constitutes a significant infringement of the law of silence, such that in order to permit it, the Master sees himself obliged to make express reference to it in his guidelines on silence.[85]

So this first citation already introduces the theme of speech, which will become the object of the ninth step. The second citation clearly enters into this domain, counseling to "inquire" from the abbot and welcome his "teaching." This "inquiry" is one of the points that the Master regulates most carefully in his treatise on silence (RM 9.1–26). He sometimes uses this word in reference to questions posed by brothers to the abbot (RM 9.1–27, 49–50; 24.19; 50.43), other times in reference to those the abbot poses to the brothers.[86] It is the first type that is our focus here. The second will be mentioned in the ninth step. Is it by chance that *cum interrogat patrem suum* so precedes *usque ad interrogationem non loquatur*, and that the eighth step advises that the disciple inquire from the abbot, while the ninth prescribes that he not speak before being questioned?

It is possible that this verbal connection implies a progression. In fact, one knows that the Master proves himself restrictive even towards "good, holy and edifying" words (RM 8.34). While the imperfect can be content to say *Benedicite* before asking about these matters (RM 9.50), the perfect must await express authorization, which is sometimes denied them (RM 9.1–27). Perhaps the Master thinks of these severe principles here. It is good to question the abbot according to the rules,[87] but it is still better to say nothing and to wait to be questioned. Thus, as has occurred several times in this ladder, especially in steps five to seven, the ninth step would progress from its predecessor. The eighth step would come to occupy this place not only because it was driven forward by the displacement of the second sign (step five),[88] but also because the citations provided by the Master introduce, as it were, the question of silence, which will become the objects of steps nine to eleven. After having humbly practiced "meditation" and "inquiry,"[89] two forms of legitimate speech, the disciple will advance further in humility by not allowing himself to speak until he is questioned.[90]

The Ninth and Eleventh Steps

We must now examine this next step, the ninth. Both it and the eleventh step are drawn from the ninth sign of Cassian:

Chapter 7: Humility

Nono *si linguam cohibeat*	[75]Nonum ... *si linguam* ad loquendum pro*hibeat* et taciturnitatem habens usque ad interrogationem non loquatur ...
uel *non sit clamosus in uoce.*	[80]Undecimum ... si cum loquitur, leniter et sine risu, humiliter cum grauitate uel pauca uerba et sancta loquatur et *non sit clamosus in uoce* ...

In contrast with the modest additions to the previous steps, the size of the redaction of the Master here is striking. The two brief notes of Cassian each engender a separate sentence. In the first case, the Master places his additions after the text of Cassian, in the second, before. Thus, the sentence of the *Institutes* is stuffed, so to speak, with the views of the Master, to say nothing of the added Scripture citations.

The first of these views of the Master is well known to us from the treatise on silence: the disciple must not take the initiative in speaking (RM 8.34; 9.42). Such a principle goes much further than what was suggested by Cassian. It is not only a matter of "restraining the tongue" (*cohibeat*), but of "forbidding speech" (*ad loquendum prohibeat*).[91] The sentence of Cassian could be understood as a simple effort not to speak too much.[92] That of the Master proposes complete silence. The specification *usque ad interrogationem* further accentuates this stringency. We are no longer in the presence of a rather vague "sign" that each may fulfill in their own way but of a rigorous test that cannot be avoided. Thus, the general suggestion of Cassian is particularized, reduced to the dimensions of a well-defined practice.[93]

This practice is surprising in its severity. In the passages of *De taciturnitate* that forbid one to speak before being questioned, the Master is careful to specify the circumstances in which one is bound to practice the rule: if the subject of conversation is secular (RM 8.34) or if the abbot is present (RM 9.42. Cf. 50.26, 43). Here all delineation of this sort disappears. It is true that a spiritual treatise such as the ladder of humility does not demand such details. But we note the same imprecision in the first warning that the deans must address to their monks (RM 11.41–44): "speaking without being questioned" appears as an inexcusable breach of the Rule. To take this warning literally, it would seem that the ninth step does not formulate a simple spiritual counsel, to be followed insofar as it is possible, but an imperative prescription, applicable in all circumstances.[94]

While the ninth step narrows and specifies the material from the *Institutes*, the eleventh tends to complete it. Only the first (*leniter*) of the six qualities that the Master requires of speech is almost equivalent to the *non sit clamosus in uoce* of Cassian.[95] The rest are original touches invented by the Master. The group forms a series of three pairs, constructed with a certain elegance: *humiliter cum grauitate* corresponds to *leniter et sine risu*, while *pauca uerba et sancta* has a unique ring to it.[96]

These words are not only distinguished from those previous by their sonority. Instead of describing how to speak, they are concerned with the quantity (and type) of words that one utters. In this they stray from the theme proposed by Cassian in the second phrase of the ninth sign, which is the mother-cell of the eleventh step: *non sit clamosus in uoce*, and rejoin the first part of the ninth sign, the starting point for the ninth step, *linguam suam cohibeat*. One can even say that *pauca uerba* perfectly translates the idea of "restraint" that *cohibeat* expresses. Thus, having changed *cohibeat* to *prohibeat* and substituted rigorous silence *usque ad interrogationem* for sobriety of language, the Master now sees himself obliged to reintroduce the notion of restraint that he removed. This notion even becomes predominant, owing to the fact that the only citation for the eleventh step concerns precisely the "small number" of words: *paucis uerbis*, from the Sentences of Sextus, reiterates *pauca uerba*, while the six other remarks remain without scriptural references.

In sum, the eleventh step presents a curious construction. The first four qualifiers, grouped two by two (*leniter et sine risu, humilter cum gravitate*), indicate how one must speak. The next two (*pauca uerba et sancta*) indicate what must be said. Then the phrase borrowed from Cassian (*non sit clamosus in uoce*) returns to the manner of speech and repeats the first qualifier (*leniter*) in negative form. Finally, in its turn, the Scripture citation returns to repeating what must be said (*paucis uerbis*). The series appears disorganized and overfilled, but it could hardly be otherwise, seeing that the modifications added to the ninth step oblige the Master to bring together here all that he has said on the proper use of speech.

Various passages from RM permit us to somewhat clarify the meaning of this collection of notes. Several of them, including one which comes from Cassian, are found in RM 9.43: *Absente uero abbate, si de verbo Dei, sibi tamen lente et humiliter, non clamosa uoce loquantur, quia omnis lente locutio ab humilitate descendit*. Without retracting the equivalence of *lente, leniter*, and *non clamosa uoce*,[97] we note here the link that the Master establishes between *lente* and *humiliter*. The second adverb does not designate a different way of being than the first but indicates only

Chapter 7: Humility

the moral basis of the exterior behavior that it represents. In other words, to speak "humbly" is to speak "softly." The lowering of the voice comes from humility and the former expresses the latter.[98] This explanation clarifies the relationship between the two adverbial assonances of the eleventh step. *Humiliter* adds nothing to *leniter* on the level of concrete description but simply expresses the spiritual content of this exterior trait.

Just as these two adverbs complement one another as external and internal facets of a single reality, *cum grauitate* picks up on and further develops *sine risu*. Above all, gravity excludes laughter.[99] But this virtue has wider applications: beyond laughter, it forbids many words (RM 8.33; 9.3. Cf. 84.3) and thoughtless behavior (RM 11.86; 50.22; 54.2; 55.2, 10). Thus, *cum grauitate* not only takes up *sine risu* in a positive form,[100] but also expands it somewhat by already suggesting the concision that the Master will emphasize next (*pauca uerba ... paucis uerbis*).

"To speak little." This recommendation appears in the *Ars Sancta*,[101] as well as in the treatise on silence,[102] either in its positive form or as a condemnation of *multiloquium*. We know what the Master intends by "to speak of holy things." It is a matter of conversing about subjects that are "good, holy, and edifying; concerning God, the word of God, or the divine precepts" (RM 8.33; 9.43, 50; 50.26, 43, 45). This list of permitted topics constitutes not only a prohibition of clearly sinful words and speech that "is vain or leads to laughter," but also, insofar as possible, the elimination of merely "secular" speech, namely everything that does not formally and explicitly aim at spiritual edification or sanctity (RM 9.44, 49; 11.49; 50.25, 42).

This is to say that, in the eleventh step, *sancta* is as emphatic as *pauca* in limiting the use of speech. The one prohibits an entire series of subjects, the other demands that one converse briefly on permitted matters. *Sancta* appears particularly restrictive when one thinks of another passage where "secular" words, while subjected to stricter regulation than spiritual, are not completely prohibited (RM 9.50). Like the ninth step, the eleventh ranks among the harshest texts of the Rule (RM 9.44; 11.49; 50.25 and 42), in which spiritual demands reach an almost inhuman rigor.

Before leaving the ninth and eleventh steps, we must consider the link that the Master establishes between the two. The ninth sign of Cassian consists in a certain restraint of tongue and voice: those who are recognized as humble speak neither too profusely nor too loudly. The Master has separated the two elements of this sign and drawn from them the two points of his teaching on speech: first, humble disciples only speak when questioned; next, when they begin to speak, they do so softly, seriously, briefly, and without departing from edifying matters. The articulation of these two points is strongly marked by the repetition of the verb *loqui* in each step.[103] One cannot fail to realize that the eleventh step only continues the ninth, as the prescriptions on right speech complete the specification of circumstances in which one may speak. Thus a slightly different relationship is established between the two steps than the one that joins the two parts of the ninth sign. In Cassian, "to restrain one's tongue" and "guard against all shouting" do not seem to have to be two consecutive actions. These two efforts could occur simultaneously every time one speaks although the first can and must be exercised without the other when keeping silence. In contrast, the two behaviors recommended by the Master can only be observed separately and consecutively. The link between the ninth and eleventh steps is a much more sequential relationship than that between the two parts of the ninth sign.

One recognizes the penchant of the Master for stages, which is revealed many times in the organization and formulation of the steps. It is no accident that he chooses to transform the list of the *Institutes* into a ladder. Faithful to this metaphor, he does not miss an opportunity to create or accentuate a progression. Sometimes this attempt to systematize remains artificial or imperfect. Here, on the other hand, he attains his goal: the eleventh step is the natural and necessary counterpart to the ninth.

To create this progression, the Master has to split the ninth sign of Cassian. This is an exceptional occurrence in the ladder of humility, where, typically, a single step coincides with each sign. This splitting of the ninth sign corresponds to another anomaly: the combining of the fourth and fifth signs in the fourth step.[104] One of these occurrences necessitates the other if one wishes to have ten steps stemming from the ten signs of Cassian. Two new steps, one on each end, bring the total to the sacred number of twelve. Correlatives, the new steps have the effect of equalizing the number of steps of obedience (2–4) and silence (9–11). Between these two series, the steps of abasement (5–7) also contain three units. This balance in the three principal parts of the ladder is clearly intentional. Only the eighth step stands slightly alone, but we have seen that, in some ways, it introduces the steps of silence,[105] while in others, it extends the section on obedience.

The Tenth Step and Its Original Place after the Eleventh

The tenth step, corresponding to the tenth sign, is inserted between the two steps drawn from the ninth sign:

Chapter 7: Humility

Decimo si non sit facilis ac promptus in risu.	[78]*Decimum ... si non sit facilis ac promptus in risu,* [79]quia scribtum est ...

Here the Master is content to pin two Scripture citations onto a principle of Cassian that he leaves completely intact. This is a unique case. Everywhere else, the Master at least slightly adds, cuts, or modifies.[106] He would have absolutely nothing to say about this step if its place did not require an explanation. Why, in fact, does the Master insert the tenth sign of Cassian between the two passages from the ninth? Perhaps, to keep the number of the sign — thus, the tenth sign becomes the tenth step, just as the ninth sign became the ninth step. Previously, in the section on obedience, the Master kept two successive signs in order.[107] It may be that he is subject to the same protective tendency here.

Another possible reason appears when one examines the citations from each step. The eighth, ninth, and tenth steps each have two citations that are presented uniformly.[108] In contrast, the eleventh step has only one citation.[109] Does the Master become aware of this insufficiency? Does it incite or encourage him to relegate this less complete step to last place, so as not to interrupt a well-established series?

Finally, one will note that laughter is mentioned in both the tenth and eleventh steps. In the first, Cassian wishes that one not be *promptus in risu*. In the second, the Master requires that one speak *sine risu*. The second comment is more categorical in form than the first[110] and thus comes better at the end. Perhaps the Master intends it as an increase in strictness from the prohibition of Cassian reproduced in the previous step, following the law of progression that we have observed many times.

Such are the reasons that likely contributed to the position of the tenth step.[111] Whatever their significance, they hardly compensate for the drawbacks resulting from the dissociation of the ninth and eleventh steps. The final order of the ladder forcefully separates these two steps that were clearly written to follow one another. But it is possible that this order does not go back to the origins of the redaction. We even have a striking indication of its later character in the following chapter, where the admonitions for the deans repeat and take into account the teaching of RM 3–10. Here, in fact, is how these admonitions are arranged:

RM 11		**RM 3–10**
11.41 (1st admonition)	Speaking without being questioned	10.75 (9th step)
11.46 (2nd admonition)	Speaking loudly	10.80 (11th step)
11.49 (3rd admonition)	Vain speech, speech leading to laughter, unholy speech	3.59 (cf. 11th step)
11.54 (3rd admonition)	Evil speech	3.57
11.63 (4th admonition)	Lying	3.33
11.66 (5th admonition)	Swearing	3.32
11.69 (6th admonition)	Anger	3.31 (?)
11.75 (7th admonition)	Laughter	10.78 (10th step)
11.81 (8th admonition)	Cursing	3.37 (cf. 4th step)
11.85 (9th admonition)	Frivolous attitude	10.86 (12th step)

This synopsis of RM 11 and RM 3–10 is not exhaustive. Clearly, some additional traits merit being highlighted, especially the relationship of the last admonition to the first step of humility.[112] But our table shows quite clearly the method the Master follows in writing his admonitions: the first two correspond to steps nine and eleven; the next four invert a series of articles from the *Ars Sancta*; in the last three, one recognizes steps ten and twelve, separated by an admonition against cursing that belongs to both the *Ars Sancta* and the ladder of humility.

On one hand, the Master associates steps nine and eleven,[113] on the other, ten and twelve. While the admonitions corresponding to these latter do not directly follow one another, their connection is emphasized by the words *cum grauitate* in both (RM 11.76, 86). Thus, the Master seems to have had a ladder of humility in mind in which the steps proceeded in the following order: 9–11–10–12. It is likely that at the time when he wrote Chapter Eleven, the Master had not yet fixed the final order of the last steps as we now know them (9–10–11–12). As in Cassian, the two comments on speech (steps nine and eleven) still preceded the remark on laughter (step ten), and this latter led to the personal remarks of the Master on bodily comportment (step twelve).

If this were indeed the original order of RM 10, one better understands why the twelfth step, in spite of its affinity with the first, came to be placed at the opposite end of the ladder.[114] It is because the notion of "gravity" also excludes "thoughtless" behavior and laughter. Consequently, the remark on laughter that concludes the list of signs calls for an additional comment on comportment. In virtue of this association of ideas, it was natural that the twelfth step be joined to the last excerpt from the list of Cassian. The later displacement of this step on laughter (ten) leads to the separation of not only the two related steps on speech (nine and eleven), but also of the two related steps on gravity (ten and twelve), although the comments *sine risu ... cum grauitate* (eleven) reestablish a sort of tie between the two.[115] One can schematize the successive versions of RM 10 as follows:

Original Version (cf. RM 11)[116]	Final Version
Step 9: speech (sign 9ª)	Step 9: speech
Step 11: speech (sign 9ᵇ)	Step 10: gravity
Step 10: gravity (sign 10)	Step 11: speech with gravity
Step 12: gravity	Step 12: gravity

Origin of the Eleventh Step

The inversion that characterizes the second version seems to have been linked with a development of the eleventh step. Its original nucleus is the remark from Cassian: *et non sit clamosus in uoce* (ninth sign).[117] From this starting point, the Master began by writing the words *pauca uerba loquatur* and the corresponding citation: *Sapiens paucis uerbis innotescit*. At this stage, the eleventh step still followed the ninth. Undoubtedly, the Master later decided to add the two pairs — *leniter et sine risu, humiliter cum grauitate*[118] — in which the second element of both recalled the tenth sign. However, no citation corresponding to these new remarks was added to that of Sextus. By so inserting the references to laughter and gravity into this step, the Master took it upon himself to summarize the step on laughter. No doubt this is the source of the inversion that brought the eleventh step to its final place.

The Conclusion of the Chapter

After exploring the last steps, we must still examine the double conclusion. First, one finds the conclusion of the passage from Cassian, adopted without great changes (RM 10.87–91). Then the Master adds an eschatological finale, which contains a long descriptive passage borrowed from the *Passio Sebastiani* (RM 10.92–122).

There exists a flagrant disproportion between these two passages: the second is five times longer than the first. That is to say that the Master gives much more importance to the conclusion that he invents than to the one provided by Cassian. According to the latter, humility leads to charity, the perfection of Christian life here below.[119] Without neglecting this summit, the Master looks further. He is much more interested in the heavenly "reward."[120] From his introduction onward, he has clearly situated the summit of the ascent of humility in heaven: it is in light of heavenly exaltation that one uses a ladder, which, after death, "will have its end raised to heaven" as in the dream of Jacob (RM 10.5, 6, 8). In contrast, there is no reference to charity in the introduction. This is what confirms the dominant, or even exclusive, interest of the Master in the second conclusion. The metaphor of the ladder, whose presentation becomes the object of the introduction, aims precisely at taking to its eschatological end the spiritual path whose end Cassian seemed to fix in this present life. Humility, with its ten signs, culminated on earth with charity. Henceforth, with its twelve steps that one climbs in the present, it will reach to the regions of eternity (RM 10.118–119).

This heavenly end is even the only goal expressed by the metaphor of the ladder. Charity has no particular place in it. One need only examine the bridge placed between the twelfth step and the first conclusion: there the Master declares that "once disciples have climbed all the steps of humility, they have properly traveled the *ladder of this life* (RM 10.87) in the fear of God." This bridge is missing its end. Instead of showing charity as the fruit that the humble receive from this life, it presents the ascent of humility as an effort that takes an entire lifetime, until death. Obviously, the Master already has the actual terminus of the ladder in mind, that is to say, the heavenly reward.[121] Moreover, he will not say otherwise when beginning the second conclusion at the beginning of the next paragraph.[122] Thus, the Master fails to find a place to insert charity into his ladder. This is because he sees this ladder as coextensive with earthly life and as leading to heaven. While Cassian intends that humility also attain charity, for the Master, this is only a tangential and abstract point that remains outside the entire metaphor.

Is this to say that the two fruits of humility — charity here below and blessedness in heaven — simply remain juxtaposed in RM 10? If one considers only the first conclusion and the beginning of the second, it seems that the Master has not established any link between love and eschatology. But at the very end of the second conclusion, one can almost hear an echo of the first. It is actually a matter of love for God, the observance of his commandments, and purity of heart, three elements that previously follow in the same order, and sometimes in the same terms, in the course of the first conclusion.

Chapter 7: Humility

First Conclusion	End of the Second Conclusion
10.88: caritatem ... Domini	10.120: his qui diligunt eum[123]
10.89: quae ... obseruabas ... incipiet *custodire*	10.121: et *custodiunt* mandata eius
10.91: *mundum* a peccatis	10.122: et *mundo* sunt corde

Of course, one cannot prove that the Master thinks specifically of the first passage while writing the second. However, it is likely that he intends to summarize the first conclusion while finishing the second, especially as he has just recalled the ladder of humility at the beginning of this final sentence.[124] In essence, the Master is attempting to summarize the entire chapter here. As is his habit,[125] he begins by having the ladder of humility lead directly to heaven,[126] but once arriving there, he envelops it with a last look at the conditions for admission to eternal beatitude. It is then that he glimpses the charity that leads one to observe the commandments and purify the heart. This rapid synthesis establishes a relationship between love and eschatology at the point of death, without returning to the fear-humility-love sequence. The reader is summarily informed that once the steps of humility are climbed, the path of eternal blessing also passes through charity.

The significance of this comment becomes fully apparent when one connects it with the little phrase, quite similar in appearance, that introduces the eschatological description at the end of the *Ars Sancta* (RM 3.83). We arrange these two clauses in parallel form:

3.83: *quae paratur* sanctis et Deum timentibus et haec praecepta factis implentibus ...	10.120–122: *quam praeparauit* Deus his qui diligunt eum et custodiunt mandata eius et mundo sunt corde.

In both instances, the Master uses the same scriptural sentence to describe the eternal reward.[127] In both instances, he uses three terms to designate the elect. Does *sanctis* correspond in thought to *mundo corde*? In any event, the two other terms in each phrase obviously correspond. The one expresses an affective attitude toward God, the other, faithful observance of the divine commandments. In the first case, it is a question of *fearing* God,[128] in the second, of *loving* him. The Master is probably indebted to Cassian for this change. The latter has drawn his attention to the role of love in the advance toward heaven. In the first step of humility, as at the end of the *Ars Sancta*, eternal life was still prepared "for those who fear God."[129] But after having copied the conclusion of Cassian on charity, the Master is ready to make the Pauline formula his own: God has prepared the reward "for those who love him."[130]

So, as modest as is its place in RM 10, the first conclusion nonetheless has a real influence on the thought of the Master. Our final task will be to examine the content of this passage in the Master and in his source.

Institutes 4.39.3	RM 10.87–90
Talibus namque indiciis et *his* similibus *humilitas* uera dinoscitur. Quae cum fuerit in ueritate possessa, confestim te *ad caritatem, quae timorem* non habit gradu excelsiore *perducet, per quam uniuersa quae prius non sine* poena *formidinis obseruabas, absque ullo labore uelut naturaliter incipies* custodire, *non iam* contemplatione supplicii uel *timoris* ullius, *sed amore ipsius boni et delectatione uirtutum*.	[87]Ergo *his* omnibus *humilitatis* gradibus a discipulo perascensis, uitae huius in timore Dei bene persubitur scala [88]et mox *ad caritatem* illam Domini *peruenientes*,[131] *quae* perfecta foris mittit *timorem*, [89]*per quam uniuersa quae prius non sine formidine obseruabas, absque ullo labore uelut naturaliter* ex consuetudine *incipiet custodire*, [90]*non iam timore* gehennae *sed amore ipsius* consuetudinis *bonae et delectatione uirtutum*.

Beyond modifications in detail,[132] three significant changes merit further consideration. To begin with, the first lines are completely transformed. Cassian noted that his list of signs was not exhaustive (*et his similibus*). Moreover, he insisted that these signs were only tests of authenticity that humility was genuine (*uera ... in ueritate possessa*).[133] For the Master, the twelve steps constitute a complete path, which must be traveled in its entirety. It is no longer a matter of acquiring a virtue, recognizable by certain signs from an open-ended list, but of accomplishing point-by-point an obligatory and developmental program.

The second fact of note is the manner in which each author uses 1 John 4:18. Interestingly, it is RM that reproduces the scriptural text most accurately: *perfecta foris mittit timorem* is more literal than *timorem non habet*.[134] Thus, the Master perfectly grasps Cassian's allusion to this text and changes it to an actual citation.[135]

But the most important change is the double addition *ex consuetudine ... consuetudinis* in the last sentence. The word *consuetudo* is not only absent from *Inst.* 4.39 but is also missing from the long developments that Cassian elsewhere dedicates to the love of the Good for its own sake.[136] Therefore, the Master is solely responsible for the word and the idea. For him, ease in accomplishing good comes "from habit" (*ex consuetudine*), and it is "good habit" that one loves in charity (*amore ipsius consuetudinis bonae*).

At first glance, this last expression diverges only slightly from the language of Cassian, who also speaks of "loving virtue." Is virtue not defined as good habit acquired by repetitive acts?[137] However, it must be acknowledged that *ex consuetudine* explains in rather rudimentary fashion the "natural" ease obtained by the one who loves.[138] No matter how accurate, such a banal explanation somewhat denigrates this sublime finale by emphasizing the formation of habit at the expense of love. And when the Master repeats this word a little later, one wonders whether this overly pragmatic mind has not again succumbed to the tendency that previously led him to change the list of signs into a developmental ladder. In both instances, he tends to reduce the profound and lively spirituality of Cassian to a practical method.

II. The Treatise of Benedict

The modifications that Benedict makes in this treatise almost all tend to abridge.[139] While some of these abridgements are almost mechanical and devoid of significance,[140] others have literary value or doctrinal importance.

The Introductory Formulas of the Steps

The Master introduces all twelve steps with the same formula: (*Primum*) *humilitatis gradum in scala caeli*[141] *ascendit discipulis si* ... The formulas of Benedict are briefer and also more varied, the most simple being (*Primus*) *humilitatis gradus est si* ... (steps 1, 4, 5, 7, and 10). One sometimes finds the additions *quis* (steps 2 and 3) and *monachus* (steps 6, 8, 9, 11 and 12).

These additions clearly correspond to the need to give an express subject to the conditional clause. No similar need exists in RM, since the conditional clause has the same subject as the principal that precedes it: *discipulus*. But this word disappears from RB with the long formula of the Master, and *gradus*, which replaces it as the subject of the principal clause, no longer functions as the subject after *si*. It is therefore necessary to invent a new subject for the conditional. Benedict could reemploy the *discipulus* of the Master for this purpose, but systematically avoiding this word in the rest of the chapter,[142] he cannot think of reinstating it here. So, he vacillates among three options throughout the ladder: leaving the subject unspecified,[143] replacing it with *quis*, or replacing it with *monachus*. These variations, to which he adds the change of *si* to *ut* in the third step,[144] make the Benedictine redaction appear somewhat indecisive.

The Eschatological Finale and the Introduction

In addition to its length, the content of the formula of the Master may also be displeasing to Benedict. We have just seen that he no longer finds *discipulus* acceptable. The same can be said for *scala caeli*. It seems that, although not completely successful, Benedict seeks to keep the ladder of humility in the realm of spiritual progress here below by closing its openings to heaven as much as he is able. In this regard, the most salient fact is that RB has nothing that corresponds to the long eschatological finale of the Master. Benedict stays with the first conclusion that describes the state of charity attained here below.[145] Due to this, the Benedictine treatise does not have a conclusion that adequately corresponds to the introduction of the chapter. In both Rules, the introduction announces that the ladder will lead "to heavenly exaltation via humility in the present life."[146] Yet this eschatological end is not mentioned at all at the conclusion of RB 7.

Perhaps Benedict was somewhat embarrassed about this shortcoming. In any event, we will see that he omits several references to the last things in the introduction, as if he wishes to correct the imbalance between the beginning and end of the chapter. The Master says that the ladder appeared to Jacob to be "raised to heaven."[147] These words are absent from RB. The ladder of the Master represents "the present time," and it has "death as its final end."[148] These details are also missing in RB.[149]

But we return to the conclusion. When the Master proclaims, after the twelfth step, that the disciple "has finished traveling the ladder of this life" (RM 10.87. Cf. RB 7.67), one is not surprised to find nothing in RB corresponding to this phrase. By omitting it, Benedict avoids a serious error that mars the redaction of the Master.[150] In RB, as in Cassian, humility simply leads to charity without it being necessary to combine (with varying degrees of success) this accomplishment on earth with the heavenly reward. But while the finale of the chapter becomes simpler and more harmonious, it no longer maintains any relationship with the introduction. The expected "heavenly exaltation" is replaced with a flowering in charity that nothing foretold. The comparison of this incomplete conclusion with that of RM leads one to think that the Master, rather than Benedict, invented the metaphor of the ladder presented at the beginning of the chapter in both Rules.

Chapter 7: Humility

Minor Oversights

Several other omissions cause certain connections that seem to belong to the original framework of the treatise to disappear from RB. Thus, when the Master writes in his introduction: *humiliato corde et capite suo* (RM 10.8 = RB 7.8), it is easy for us to recognize in "the humbling of the head," an echo of *neque elati sunt oculi* and the announcement of the twelfth step. The removal of *et capite suo* in RB betrays a lack of attention to these allusions.

One can say the same for the removal of *iudicio* at the end of the first step (RM 10.41 = RB 7.30). This reference to the judgment is one of the characteristics that connect the first step to the twelfth. To omit it is to gloss over a connection that clearly was established by the author of the text.

Finally, the removal of *linguae* (RM 10.61 = RB 7.44) in the fifth step also suggests an unmistakable oversight on the part of Benedict. In fact, this word foreshadows the seventh step, where it will be intentionally repeated. In its absence, the fifth step ceases to appear as the step where one practices humility of the tongue before descending into the depths of the heart.

Benedict Subsequent to the Master

Furthermore, these inadvertent oversights do not surprise us as we discover clear evidence of a much larger omission in the first step: three paragraphs on the tongue, hands, and feet (RM 10.20–29). In removing them, Benedict is not careful or concerned not to abandon an announcement made a little earlier in the chapter (RM 10.12 = RB 7.12). The Benedictine redaction is unquestionably later on this point.

The priority of the Master is equally clear when one compares the two Rules to Cassian. This fact has already been solidly established for a long time.[151] It is such an important argument that we must explain it again here. Here, then, are the three texts in synopsis:

Cassian, *Inst.* 4.39	RM 10	RB 7
patientiaeque constantiam	[52]*patientiae constantiam*	[35]conscientia *patientiam*
praebentur	[66]*praebentur*	[49]iniunguntur
obseruabas	[89]*obseruabas*	[68]*obseruabat*
amore ipsius boni	[90]*amore ipsius consuetudinis bon*ae	[69]*amore* Christi et consuetudine[152] *ipsa bona*

Four times, the text of the Master comes closer to that of Cassian. The hypothesis according to which the Master, departing from the Benedictine redaction, returns to the source-text would merit attention if the latter were a universally known passage of Scripture.[153] But this is not the case here. Moreover, this explanation would hardly be satisfying in regard to the fourth and final passage.[154] Better to recognize, as B. Capelle dutifully does, that "the Cassian, Master, Benedict genealogy is perfectly obvious, while the Cassian, Benedict, Master succession proves impossible." In other words, "the text of the Master is the direct source of the text of Benedict."[155]

III. The Meaning of the Treatise: The Fear of God and Humility

We have just completed a careful study of the structure of the treatise of humility. It is now a matter of going deeper into its meaning.[156] However, our method will remain the same. We will again start with Cassian in order to highlight the thought of the Master and Benedict on humility.

It is, indeed, to Cassian that RM and RB owe their most important teaching on this point. A paraphrase of the talk of Abba Pinufius in the *Institutes* is found at the heart of their chapters on humility (*Inst.* 4.39). Identifying what they add to and subtract from the teaching of Pinufius-Cassian will be the best way to learn what they themselves teach. Consequently, our pursuit must begin with a detailed examination of this fundamental text from the *Institutes*.

The Teaching of Cassian

In addressing a postulant who is taking the habit, Pinufius sets before him a way toward perfection. This perfection consists in charity, which accomplishes good for its own sake—naturally, easily, and without any fear. Opposite this end is the point of departure, which is the fear of the Lord. Between these two ends, Pinufius enumerates two stages, both rather complex. First, an initial fear leads "to contempt for everything, forgetting one's family, and loathing the world." This first stage is also described as "scorning and rejecting all possessions." Then comes a second stage: humility. This latter is recognized by ten signs taking in various domains, from obedience and patience to controlling the voice and laughter.

From this list of signs, it is clear that the second stage is situated in the heart of cenobitic life. In contrast, the first is placed at the entrance of the cenobium, at the moment where, aspiring to perfection, the soul, filled with the fear of God, decides to leave the world and embrace poverty. Although the word is not used here, the first stage represents what Cassian elsewhere calls disappropriation (*nuditas*, *Inst.* 4.43).

Disappropriation and humility are intimately linked as two stages of a single movement of abasement (*Inst.* 4.3–5). To disappropriate oneself of all that one has is already to be put in a condition of dependence and humility, especially as, not content to leave anything at their disposal, the monastery does not accept any offerings from its new members. Therefore, postulants keep nothing in their possession and bring nothing to the common fund. They are both without resources should they, weary of vexations and austerities, be tempted to flee, and without superiority in relationship to their brothers who come from the lowest social class. Indistinguishable from them in the common habit, they now truly "descend to the poverty and humility of Jesus Christ," becoming the equal of the poorest to whom Jesus became brother, and, with them, receiving what they need to live from the monastery. Thus, poverty comprises an objective state of humility, which establishes the most appropriate framework to become truly humble of heart. When one is abased exteriorly by becoming the poor of Christ, one is ready to receive the rugged formation in humility that constitutes the year of probation and the entire cenobitic life.

It is this relationship between poverty and humility that Pinufius thinks of when he affirms that "one acquires humility by contempt for and loss of all one's resources," or, more briefly, "dispossession engenders humility."[157] It is true that in his discourse, the renunciation of material goods is presented as a spontaneous act of the ascetic, springing from compunction, rather than as a law that the cenobitic society imposes on all its members. But whether it is adopted from an individual or communal point of view, one finds the same sequence constituting the obligatory way to perfection. Paphnutius teaches in the *Conferences* that while the first renunciation is to abandon material goods, the second consists in disappropriating oneself of one's interior "riches," or vices, alone truly evil (*Conl.* 3.6–10). It is these two successive renunciations, the one material, the other spiritual, which Pinufius describes under the titles of "dispossession" and "humility."

When one has so identified these two stages, one begins to glimpse how, according to Pinufius, the second "leads immediately to charity." The first insight resulting from their respective definition is that "true" humility leads to charity. In fact, as Pinufius understands it, humility is nothing other than the *abrenuntiatio secunda* of Paphnutius, in other words, the renunciation of all vices.[158] We know that Cassian, with most of the ancients, sees charity as the summit of all the virtues so that one attains it by renouncing the vices (*Conl.* 1.6–7. Cf. 3.7). Considered as the expression of this renunciation, humility is therefore rightly the door to charity.

One can shed more light on this general explanation, which illumines *Institutes* 4.39 with *Conference* 3, by comparing *Inst.* 4.39 with what Pinufius will say to conclude (*Inst.* 4.43). In fact, the conclusion of his discourse presents a new way of perfection, or rather a new schema of the same way, leading from fear to love. This second schema is both more sober and more developed than the first. Instead of two complex stages, described at some length, Pinufius now lists seven, characterizing them precisely and briefly. Between fear and love, there are (we italicize the new stages): *compunction*, renunciation or "disappropriation," humility, *the mortification of the desires, the eradication of all vices, the flowering of the virtues*, and *purity of heart*. Most of the five new terms that appear here in different stages figure previously in various places and titles of the first list. "Compunction" is the fear of the Lord "penetrating the mind of the individual," spoken of by *Inst.* 4.39.1. One recognizes the first "sign of humility" in the "mortification of the desires." The "purification of the vices" and "safeguarding of the virtues" previously appear as the long-term effects of the fear of the Lord. Only "purity of heart" appears for the first time. Equivalent to the *apatheia* of Evagrius,[159] it is presented as the crowning of the *praktikè* and the precursor of charity.[160]

For our purposes, the most important aspect of this second schema of Pinufius is the first of the four stages placed between humility and charity. Instead of "leading immediately to love," humility first engenders the mortification of the desires, and it is by this that one continues to progress. Thus, the mortification of the desires no longer appears as one "sign of humility" among others, as it originally was, but as the very point where humility attains victory over the vices by the flowering of the virtues and charity. This emphasizes the importance of this moment in spiritual growth. Cassian explains it at the beginning of the book in describing the formation of a young monk (*Inst.* 4.8). If the elder begins by teaching the latter "to conquer his desires," it is because experience has shown him that one cannot defeat the various passions if one does not first achieve mastery in this realm.

What is it to "conquer the desires?" It is to submit to someone in total obedience. The superior will have the power and duty to command even what is repugnant to his disciple. By total obedience, the latter will not only demonstrate true humility, but will also be trained to master every kind of disordered impulse. Thus, one becomes obedient to a person in order to become accustomed to obeying God. In this education, the will of the elder symbolizes the Divine Law. How can those who do not obey a person that they see submit to God whom they cannot see? And just as the person who commands symbolizes the God of the conscience and Revelation, the "desires" that must be overcome represent the vicious passions. They are actually the innocent and banal manifestations of the same fundamental tendencies that lead to sin. To restrain and renounce them is to prepare to oppose every evil appetite.

Thus, humility leads to charity, whether one considers it very broadly as embracing the entire battle against the vices or one envisages it more specifically as the state of soul that makes possible the "mortification of the desires" or obedience, the true key to progress. Alongside this, there is, however, another fruit of humility that plays a primary role combating vices: the manifestation of thoughts. Although the second schema of Pinufius says nothing of it, his first schema makes confession of thoughts to the elder and submission to his judgment the second and third "signs." Obviously, it takes a good dose of humility to practice these. Yet, Cassian has previously shown that there is no more reliable means to achieve victory over all temptations.[161] Again in this respect, humility proves itself the mother of obedience[162] and mediator of perfection.

To finish delving into the teaching of Pinufius, we must comment on each of these two goals of the ascent. As we have noted, the fear of the Lord not only evokes the compunction that leads to renunciation, but according to Inst. 4.39.1, this initial role is connected with a long-term effect that Cassian calls *custodia salutis* and even *uitiorum purgatio et uirtutum custodia*. The word *custodia*, which appears twice, probably alludes to Isaiah 33:6: *diuitiae salutis sapientia et scientia, timor Domini ipse et thesaurus eius*, a text that Cassian cites and discusses in the *Conferences* (*Conl.* 11.13.2). To him, this verse of Isaiah seems to contain a teaching on the loftier fear that is inspired by love and remains forever: "the riches of our salvation that consist of true wisdom and the knowledge of God can only be preserved (*seruari*) by fear of the Lord." Thus fear is found in different forms at the beginning and end of "wisdom"; at the beginning, following Proverbs: *principium sapientiae timor Domine* (Prov 9:10); at the end, following the prophet, because it is a "treasury," that is to say, a "protector" of salvation, of which wisdom is one of the riches.

Not only does this play of correspondences explain why "salvation" appears in place of "wisdom" in one of the schemas of Pinufius and beside it in the other.[163] It throws particular light on the role attributed to the "fear of the Lord" in *Institutes* 4.39.1. This fear, which has the effect of "safeguarding salvation" and "safeguarding the virtues" is not the servile fear of beginners, but the loving fear of the perfect. In other words,

Pinufius combines the two types of fear here.[164] He primarily intends to speak of the first. He mentions the second only in passing, perhaps to qualify what he will say later when he notes the disappearance of fear (obviously, servile!) in the perfect. In any event, the "purification of vices" and "safeguarding of virtues" appear in an anticipatory role at the beginning of the first schema. More rigorous, the second assigns them their true place: after the mortification of the desires, before purity of heart and charity. To extinguish the vices and to establish and preserve the virtues[165] is actually the entire ascetical agenda, which we know can only be accomplished on the solid bases of renunciation and humility.

The very least that we can retain from the first schema is that fear is found beyond the beginning of the ascent.[166] To the degree that fear is freed from its servile motives, other higher motives, related to filial love, take over. Thus, with a certain amount of ambiguity, one can say that fear envelops the entire ascent. Preceding and giving rise to humility, it also has the role of "guarding" all the virtues.

Our second remark concerns the other end of the path: charity. This end, it is important to note, is situated in the present life. Although charity remains without end in the world to come (*Conl.* 1.11), Pinufius considers only its earthly effects here. Those who are perfect obtain the ability to accomplish the commandments, observed since the beginning, in a new way. On this side of judgment, one remains in the realm of obedience to the Divine Law.

Thus the ascent from fear to love is accomplished entirely here below. Not only are the last things beyond the end of the ascent and therefore outside the limits of the plan, they even cease to operate as motives for spiritual work along the way. At the beginning, fear of hell is sovereign; in the end, all "consideration of punishment or fear has disappeared." We know from Conference Eleven that what Pinufius says here of fear also applies to hope. The desire for reward is characteristic of those who are progressing. In those who are perfect, it gives way to pure satisfaction in the Good.[167] Consequently, it seems that eschatological perspectives, favorable or foreboding, suffer a sort of setback[168] when charity floods the soul.

The Master and Benedict: The Eschatological Perspective

This last remark will permit us to highlight, here and now, the most salient difference that distinguishes Cassian from RM and RB, especially RM. As we have noted,[169] for them, the ascent by humility does not end here below in charity but leads to "heavenly exaltation." This is affirmed from the beginning, in the prologue of the chapter common

Chapter 7: Humility

to RM and RB. Quite logically, the Master finishes his treatise with an eschatological epilogue that corresponds to the prologue. And it is not only the *chapter* on humility, but also the *ladder* of humility that so opens and closes with a view of heaven. The thought of the last things is all-powerful in the first and last steps of humility. Thus, eschatology takes hold of the treatise on humility like a clamp.

Moreover, as opposed to what we noted in Cassian, eschatological motives do not weaken as one ascends, but, on the contrary, acquire a new force, to the point of becoming haunting. The fear of judgment, suggested at the end of the first step, becomes the central theme of the twelfth. One no longer portrays the judgment as a coming event, one believes that one is already standing before the judge: the future has entered into the present.

It is true that the Master and Benedict reproduce the conclusion of Cassian where the fear of hell is dispelled by love. But, in RM, this passage is followed by the aforementioned eschatological epilogue. Placed between the last step and the actual conclusion of the treatise, it appears as a simple fragment from the discourse of Pinufius that, for better or worse, is incorporated into the structure of the Master. The internal logic of the Master requires that one pass directly from the twelfth step to the epilogue, from supreme humiliation to heavenly exaltation, from fearfully anticipated judgment to the reward of eternal life.

In order not to have to sacrifice the conclusion of Cassian, the Master has broken this natural sequence, so natural that as soon as he writes the twelfth step, the author is already turned toward eternity.[170] The first conclusion has the effect of an unwarranted intermission between the anticipated appearance before the judge and eternal blessing. It brings a history that has entered into eternity back here below. Its relationships with what precedes and follows it are equally problematic. How does love suddenly banish a fear that has just reached its climax? And why elaborate on the eternal reward when it is no longer desire for it, but love of the Good that has become the motive for action? Of course, the passage of the *Institutes* copied by the Master is content to contrast love with fear, without mentioning the contrast between love and hope. But if he escapes a definite contradiction, the Master shows at the very least that the teaching of Cassian on this point, such as developed in *Conference* 11, remains foreign or irrelevant to him. His thought, completely focused on the last things, has no interest in that pure love that replaces hope of the future life with a satisfaction tasted here below.

Thus, the sudden emergence of eschatology is the first distinctive trait of RM and RB as compared with the treatise of Cassian. Need one say how biblical and Christian this is? A theory of spiritual perfection here on earth is replaced by a ladder to be climbed to heaven. Following Evagrius and Clement,[171] Cassian proposed a philosophical ideal presented in scriptural terms. Without obstructing this view, the Master and Benedict frame it in the Gospel message of eternal life. The same Christian instinct also leads them to attribute the transforming effects of charity to Christ acting through the Holy Spirit.[172] Benedict will further accentuate this Christianization by substituting *amor Christi* for the *amor ipsius boni* of Cassian, which became *amor ipsius consuetudinis bonae* in RM.[173]

Recourse to Scripture

Furthermore, it is not only the ends of the treatise and ladder that are rendered more Christian. A similar effect results from the constant recourse to Scripture to illustrate and justify each of the steps. The "signs" of Cassian were presented as simple observations: these criteria for true humility were based on experience. The steps of the Master and Benedict claim to be more: an obligatory and sequential program founded on Holy Scripture.[174] Owing to this, the ladder of humility acquires a religious aspect that is missing in the list of signs. To climb it is to respond to God's call, to obey his word. In addition, a specifically religious, even Christian, motive often emerges from these citations. While a few set out simple wisdom sayings on the level of common experience,[175] most contain an explicit reference to the God of Revelation or to Christ. Thus, it is "in imitation of the Lord" that one will obey, "because of him" that one will endure affliction, "to accomplish his precept" that one will turn the other cheek, "to him" that one will confess one's faults, and, "in his presence" and "with him" that one will remain steadfast in humiliation. Sometimes this relationship with the Lord is even expressed by the familiar "you" of the prayer.[176] But whether or not it has this character, the reference to God transforms the ascetic behaviors described by Pinufius into expressly religious attitudes.

The Theological Aspect of Humility

Owing to a primary trait that is absent from Cassian, the humility of RM and RB is also religious. We refer to the presence of the "fear of the Lord" in the first and twelfth steps of the ladder. One recalls that this fear previously appeared in the schema of Pinufius but separate from humility, which it preceded and elicited. In contrast, in RM and RB, the fear of the Lord is inserted into the first step of the ladder. Therefore, both it and the dread of the judgment that pervades the twelfth step are

Chapter 7: Humility

integral to humility. Owing to this, humility is enriched by a theological dimension that was lacking in the analysis of Pinufius. None of the ten signs of Pinufius contained a reference to God. Mother of obedience, patience, effacement, and restraint in speech and laughter, humility is presented as a group of attitudes and sentiments relating to the neighbor.[177] In transferring this series of behaviors into his own ladder, the Master adds two steps (the first and the last) expressly related to God.[178] Disciples become aware of being creatures and servants of their Lord before humbling themselves before their superior and brothers or sisters. The excessive length of the first step further emphasizes the importance of this primordial step: together, it and the twelfth step are almost as long as the other ten steps combined.

Thus, the Master has radically broadened the scope of humility. The new series of attitudes is no less varied than what was described in the ten signs: to fear God, remember his commandments, meditate on the last things, believe that the divine gaze is present in every hour and every place, guard against sin by always standing in the presence of God, dread the future judgment, continually remember one's sins, not dare to raise one's eyes towards heaven, and see oneself already brought before the divine tribunal. Although all of this is incorporated into two steps, it is no less ample and complex than the material that constitutes the rest of the ladder. The phenomenology of humility toward God created by the Master is in no way inferior in richness of content or actual importance to the humility toward others borrowed from Cassian.

While the Master invents almost everything in these two steps, he must at least model them on the original idea of the fear of the Lord that inaugurates and safeguards salvation. But in appropriating this theme, he has modified it profoundly. According to Pinufius, divine fear precedes and engenders humility, which he describes only in relationship to other individuals. In contrast, for the Master, fear constitutes an intrinsic and fundamental aspect of humility. To be humble is first to fear God, to adopt an attitude of reverence and submission toward him.

To properly contextualize this teaching, it is important to remember that Cassian distinguishes two sorts of pride, and, in consequence, also two types of humility.[179] Carnal pride consists in glorifying oneself in the presence of others. This is the common form of pride. Spiritual pride is much more rare because it arises only in the perfect. It consists in rising up against God by attributing the virtues and charisms one possesses to oneself rather than to divine assistance. Humility towards God, which contrasts with this second form of pride, will therefore consist in recognizing and proclaiming the role of divine grace in our progress toward perfection.

One sees immediately what separates this form of humility from what the Master analyzed in his first step. It is different in two ways. First, the humility that Cassian speaks of is reserved for the perfect and spiritual, while that of the Master appears at the beginning of the ascent.[180] Next, the tenor of the two states of soul is completely different: in Cassian, one acknowledges the good that God has accomplished in oneself; in RM, one is preserved from evil by unceasing effort. Divine grace, the recognition of which is the very object of humility for the perfect, is not mentioned in the entire first step of the Master.[181] Conversely, none of the themes developed by the Master — the presence and gaze of God the Judge, remembrance of the commandments and the last things, guarding oneself in every encounter — appear in *Institutes* 12. If, in both instances, humility is connected with God, it is so in different ways: in one instance, one confesses God's healing and perfecting action; in the other, one fuels in oneself the salutary fear of his judgments. The form of pride that Cassian is combating is, from all appearances, the Pelagian pride of a naturalistic asceticism. The pride that the first step of the Master does away with is located on a much more ordinary level, that of the sinful person who lives in ignorance, forgetfulness, or practical contempt of God.

There is nothing in the divergence observed between Cassian and the Master that should surprise us. In composing his treatise on humility, the Master is inspired solely by the treatise of Pinufius (*Inst.* 4.39). This contains no allusion to the spiritual pride that Cassian analyzes in Book Twelve of the *Institutes*. Has the Master read only *Inst.* 4? Nothing proves it. In any event, his immediate source offers him no information relative to the "humility of the perfect." What Pinufius describes as humility is simply the virtue that opposes carnal pride.[182] The Master develops a distinctly theological humility based on the "fear of the Lord." This new construct is entirely his own work and responds to completely different concerns than those of the last book of the *Institutes*.

Perfection: Fear or Charity?

In fact, the Master does not address highly advanced religious, but the flock of cenobites who are taking their first steps in the way of salvation. It must be noted that, for them, the first step already represents a very high ideal. In a sense, it constitutes *perfection* even in the eyes of the Master. One notices this when the Master, speaking of silence, reserves the strict observation of this virtue "to the perfect, those who

Chapter 7: Humility

have a pure heart, who are purified from sin, who fear the undying fire of Gehenna and seek the immortal riches of eternal life,"[183] or again, "to those who are perfect before God, who never allow themselves to be caught off guard by forgetfulness of God, but zealously seek to guard themselves from vices of the tongue, being entirely pure like the angels" (RM 9.46–47). One recognizes here, attributed to the "perfect," several of the manifestations of the fear of God described in the first step. Thus, it is not merely an elementary teaching for beginners, but a veritable program of perfection. That the Master sets forth a high ideal is shown indirectly in other passages of the Rule where he prescribes that the brothers who travel or work far from the gaze of the deans "be those who are capable of fearing the presence of God more than that of human beings" (RM 11.37–39; 18.6); those also who have cast away motives of temporal interest that oppose supernatural motives tied to consideration of the last things (RM 92.42–43, 46–47). Clearly, the Master considers a good performance to be doing a good deed for the sole reason that God sees us and will punish or reward us for our deeds. This is uncommon virtue, reserved for the small number of the "perfect." For most, the down-to-earth realism of the Master does its utmost to find very human helps and incentives, from the continual surveillance of the deans to the lure of abbatial succession.

Thus, he intends a ladder with totally different values than those of Cassian. For Cassian, the fear of punishment and the hope of reward are inferior motives, good for beginners and those progressing, while the perfect have been freed to act from pure charity. In contrast, for the Master, the consideration of eschatological destiny, fortunate or unfortunate, is envisaged as a very noble motive, so noble that it does not suffice to lead ordinary souls. Thus, what Cassian regards as a departure point, the Master sees as a summit.

It is true that, following the author of the *Institutes*, the Master will *also* speak of "perfect charity that casts out fear." But this breakaway to a disinterested spirituality remains an isolated phenomenon in RM. We have already noted that the passage that describes it has been poorly inserted in its context. In addition, it must now be emphasized that its teaching remains foreign to the thought and personal vocabulary of the Master. For him, *caritas* usually designates love of neighbor, indeed, completely exterior manifestations of this charity.[184] Aside from this passage influenced by Cassian, the word is never strictly applied to the charity of Christians toward God.[185] There is no further trace anywhere in RM of a contrast between fear and love. On the contrary, *timere Deum* and *hunc diligere* are linked as two equivalents in the first article of the *Ars*

Sancta (RM 3.1). And what one notes there about the fear of God, one also observes in an even more striking manner concerning the fear of his chastisement. At the beginning of the treatise on obedience, *nihil sibi a Christo carius aliquid extimantes* is explained by *propter metum gehennae uel diuitias uitae aeternae* (RM 7.2–3). Clearly the Master does not have the same contrast between interested and disinterested motives. To fear, to desire, to love are all one for him, and he only sees different aspects of the same state there, that of the "perfect."

These observations suffice to show that the Master has not deeply assimilated the teaching of Cassian on charity. But it becomes even more apparent if one takes a look at the whole of RM 10 and its source. The entire treatise of Pinufius rests on the *timor-caritas* contrast: one advances from one to the other by humility. By incorporating fear into humility, the Master has considerably softened this contrast. From now on, a sort of imbalance exists between his two terms: the second remains outside of the ladder while the first is included. Furthermore, while fear is still mentioned at the beginning of the first step, this reference is far from having the depth that it has in Cassian, either because it appears in a simple participial clause (*timorem ... ponens*), or because it follows long developments where the word *timor* is not mentioned. Moreover, the length given to the explanations of the steps that follow again tends to diminish the importance of fear, causing one to forget that it was encountered at the starting point. The little effort made by the Master to emphasize fear suggests that he has scant interest in contrasting it with love.

It is true that he will mention it again in the introductory phrase of the conclusion,[186] but so clumsily that his incomprehension of the thought of Cassian will only become all the more manifest. To say, in fact, that the ascent of "the ladder of this life" is made "in the fear of God" is to make it a constant of earthly existence. Therefore, this nullifies at the outset the teaching of the conclusion on "the love that casts out fear." The only way to overcome this contradiction would be to suggest a distinction between two fears here, servile and filial, the one temporary and cast out by charity, the other imperishable and derived from charity itself. But if we are justified in recognizing this teaching in certain allusions of Pinufius, nothing indicates that it is present here in the thought of the Master.[187] Especially where the latter is expressing himself independently, he seems to ignore the notion of a purely servile fear such as the Alexandrians developed from certain texts of the New Testament.[188] For him, the fear of the Lord remains the simple and undifferentiated notion that it usually was in the Bible. And this reality is very highly regarded. Far from being viewed as a sign of imperfection, it appears, on the contrary, as the flower and sum of wisdom.[189]

Departure from the Path of Cassian

When one has thus noted that the contrast of fear and love remains exterior to the thought of the Master, one begins to glimpse that, for him, the path traced by Cassian has entirely lost its meaning. In fact, not only do the points of departure and arrival no longer correspond in RM 10, but the two principal stages are no longer recognizable. "Dispossession" is not mentioned, and the renunciation of goods is purely and simply relegated to another section of the Rule. Humility likewise disappears as a stage although for the opposite reason. In fact, the very importance that it is given prevents it from playing an intermediary role. Henceforth, instead of passing from fear to love, it encompasses fear. Moreover, it envelops all of life. It is no longer a matter of a spiritual evolution in which the acquisition of humility is only one point. Coextensive with earthly life, the ladder of humility necessarily embraces all asceticism.

That being the case, can one still speak of a spiritual path? In transforming the signs into steps and establishing or emphasizing certain progressions between them, the Master has presumably created a sense of motion in his treatise. But it only appears as such. Upon close examination, it becomes evident that the Master has not successfully reestablished a true progression throughout his ladder. In particular, while fear is placed at its base, one also finds it in its last step, and the Master specifically notes that it accompanies the entire ascent. Therefore, the idea of a journey toward perfection by distinct stages is radically eclipsed, if not totally lost.

Such is the fate of the treatise of Pinufius. His four-stage sequence is confused. Movement slows so that humility, artificially introduced into the description of one of the points, becomes the sole object of the new treatise. As doubtful as it may seem, in some regards, this transformation extends the evolution that one observes between *Inst.* 4.39 and 4.43, the parallel treatises of Pinufius. One recalls that 4.43 distinguishes nine points, while 4.39 contains only four, which bring together many of the traits that characterize the other five. In its summary, *Inst.* 4.39 joins compunction, the battle against vices, and the preservation of the virtues to the fear of God, while the mortification of the desires is absorbed by humility: mortification is no longer a distinct stage but a simple "sign." In his turn, the Master pushes the same unifying tendency to the extreme: not content to absorb what follows it, humility envelops the fear that precedes it, and, with it, the battle against vices. Only charity preserves its independence.

By this process of amalgamation initiated by Pinufius and completed by the Master, humility gradually acquires a unique importance in the mapping of the spiritual life. According to the analytic schema of *Inst.* 4.43, it was only one of seven intermediate steps between fear and love. In that of 4.39, joined to "dispossession," humility becomes one of only two great stages that remain. Already it tends to include all the spiritual and interior elements proper to asceticism, of which "dispossession" is only the preliminary exterior step. Finally, by omitting "dispossession" and including fear, the Master will explicitly recognize this preeminent role. Henceforth, the entire spiritual life will be built around one central idea, summarized in a single word: humility.[190]

The Elevation of Humility

Although clearly in the line of Cassian, this elevation of humility is indicative of a personal view of the Master, engendered by meditation on Scripture: "He who humbles himself will be exalted." It is this word of Christ, proclaimed at the beginning of the chapter, that suggests to the Master the basic concept of ascending to heaven by humility. From this unfolds his entire reflection on this virtue and its triple character—eschatological, religious, and preeminent.

Given that this scriptural text is so important in the genesis of RM, we cannot finish this commentary without attending to the other parts of the Rule where this same theme resounds. "To humble oneself in order to be exalted." This idea does not appear in the Prologue, the *Thema*,[191] or the *Ars Sancta*,[192] but it is affirmed in the treatise on the abbot. Here the Master gives the superior the example of the child that Christ brought into the midst of the Apostles, saying to them: "Whoever wishes to be first among you, here is what you should be."[193] While the Scripture passage invoked in this circumstance is not *Qui se humiliat exaltabitur*, the theme remains fundamentally the same: to become great, one must make oneself little. In accordance with this principle, the abbot will wash the feet of the porters and have them eat at table with him.[194] But it is especially in relationship to abbatial succession that the idea reappears at the other end of the Rule. Here the Master will cite the same texts: the lesson given to the Twelve[195] and *Qui se humiliat exaltabitur* (RM 93:55, 73) adding, "The last will be first" (RM 92.55; Mt 20:16). Under these various forms, the Gospel paradox of exaltation by humility is constantly present in this long treatise.

Thus the Master uses the idea in two different contexts: the treatise of humility and the treatises on the abbot and abbatial succession. These two series of variations on the same theme present a curious contrast.

Chapter 7: Humility

On one side, humility leads to heaven; on the other, it procures or preserves the abbacy. Thus, in the last chapters, the eschatological end of RM 10 is brought back to earth. This reduction to an earthly scale, suggested by Scripture itself,[196] is unequivocally affirmed by the Master in several passages. According to him, the hope of temporal honors can legitimately replace the thought of future judgment as a motive for action (RM 92.43) because "human nature is generally created so that it loves what it sees more than what it hopes for without seeing."[197] We have already spoken of this earthly realism that so surprised us regarding the contrast between fear and charity, in which actions motivated by considerations of the life to come appear as a type of "perfection" reserved for a small number. What we must now emphasize is that this teaching ends in an unexpected application of *Qui se humiliat exaltabitur*. In RM 10, the Gospel maxim established a personal asceticism of humility, accomplished under the gaze of God for the sake of an eternal reward. In RM 92–93, it justifies a demeanor of outward humility by which one strives to merit, in the judgment of the abbot in charge, the honor of succeeding him.[198] However strange and contradictory a motive for humility this may be, it must be remembered that this virtue must be practiced in an exemplary manner not only by candidates for the abbacy and by the "second," but also by the abbot himself. Thus, the effort at humility required by the abbatial competition appears to be an apprenticeship in abbatial humility.

The Idea of Perfection in RM

And since we have been led to review the last chapters of the Rule, we will conclude by observing that the idea of "perfection" is no longer the same as in the ascetical chapters, in which the treatise of humility was the crown. The words *perfectus, perfecte, ad perfectum,* and *perfectio* crop up often in RM 92.[199] The context of the competition for the abbacy gives them a particular color. Here, "perfection" is the impeccable accomplishment of what is prescribed in Scripture and the Rule — especially in matters of exterior humility, but without regard for the motive that leads one to act. This latter can be the drive for achievement and power. The entire pedagogy of the competition even strives to exploit such sentiments.

This totally materialistic interpretation of the vocabulary of "perfection" marks a decline as compared with RM 7–9. There, one recalls, the Master presented the state of soul of the first step of humility, with its eschatological motives, as characteristic of the "perfect." The supernatural motives of the fear of hell and hope of eternal life, although self-interested, formed an integral part of "perfection." One sees how this notion has deteriorated in passing from the ascetic chapters to those on the succession of the abbot. Here, it is a downgraded "perfection," a perfection for the imperfect that is proposed to all.

Thus, the idea of perfection assumes three forms in RM. In its highest form, it consists of acting rightly in pure love without any fear. At a lower level, it admits self-serving but supernatural motives: the hope of reward and the fear of eternal punishment. Lower still, it makes the best of any motive, even a temporal interest. Strictly speaking, the highest ideal does not belong to the spiritual world of the Master: it is Cassian who inspires it. In contrast, the two lesser forms constitute the two stages of his personal thought, born from the confrontation of the religious ideal with the disappointing reality of a quasi-infantile humanity.

Two Traits Proper to Benedict

Such is the mental universe in which Benedict mapped his own way. Two major characteristics mark the chapter of Benedict. First, in RB, the treatise on humility does not have an eschatological finale. Owing to this, the conclusion of Cassian regains its importance, and charity again appears as the end of the ascent. It matters little that this manner of concluding does not correspond with the purpose expressed in the introduction of the chapter[200] or that Benedict, by a shortsighted addition, anticipates the ascent to charity in the third step.[201] What matters is that, at the top of the ladder, charity has rediscovered the shining radiance that it possessed in the treatise of Pinufius.

The second notable characteristic is that Benedict does not have any special program for the "imperfect." The very idea of a distinction between the "perfect" and the "imperfect" is absent from his work.[202] Henceforth, the ideal of the fear of God is proposed to all without distinction. No motive of human ambition will replace supernatural motives. In theory, these must suffice for all.[203]

Thus, while the absence of heavenly portraits highlights charity at the end of RB 7, the severe doctrine of the first step also gains importance because no overly human pedagogy competes with it at the other end of the Rule. The remaining particularities of RB are only occasional touches and passing nuances.[204] All in all, the path of Benedict diverges little from that of the Master. Heirs of Cassian, but neglecting his path from fear to love, the two authors concur in extraordinarily magnifying humility, making it the way of eternal blessing, the habitual attitude toward God and others, and the summit of Christian spirituality.[205] Pushed to its limits, the Gospel teaching on exaltation by humility leads to the exaltation of humility.

Chapter 7: Humility

Endnotes

1. Adalbert de Vogüé, *La Communauté et l'Abbé* (Brussels: Desclée des Brouwer, 1961), 207–211; 221–228; 251–264. ET: *Community and Abbot* (Kalamazoo, MI: Cistercian, 1979 [I] and 1988 [II]).

2. Compare the methodical commentary of Psalm 38:2–3 (RM 8.31–34 and 9.35–38) with that of Psalm 130:1–2 (RM 10.3 = RB 7.3; RM 10.8. Cf. RB 7.8).

3. Perhaps, in accordance with E* and RB, this second *omnis* should be omitted, conforming to Luke 14:11 and 18:4. In fact, one finds nothing that corresponds to it in RM 10.5–9, whereas the first *omnis* is repeated in RM 10.2 (*omnem exaltationem*). Cf. also RM 93.55 and 73.

4. Cf. RM Ths 40 = RB Prol 40: *corda nostra et corpora*.

5. And also by *aspectibus* (cf. 8.19 and 26).

6. And the heart is the "seat of the soul" (8.7).

7. By it, this step is inserted into both body and soul (RM 10.9). See nn. 14 and 15 below.

8. RM 10.75. The tongue is a "corporal branch" (8.8).

9. Not only do these two steps employ the same terms as the introduction, but they also reproduce them in the same order: first the heart, then the eyes and head.

10. Certainly, considering the parts of the human person enumerated in this step, it seems that its focus is both corporal (tongue, hands, feet) and spiritual (thoughts, will, desires). But this review of the parts of the human person is made only to convince the disciple of the divine presence and gaze (RM 10.13: *extimet*; 10.20, 23, 24: *agnoscimus*; 10.34: *credimus*). Thus the first step is clearly entirely a matter of interior conviction. Although the "heart" is mentioned only in regard to thoughts (10.14, 18–19), the Master undoubtedly references it throughout, speaking of "fleeing forgetfulness," "being constantly mindful," "reviewing in the mind" (10.10–12), "being attentive" (10.19), "being vigilant" (10.32, 35, 40), and "dreading" (10.33). Consequently, the first step could be placed before the seventh, where its *non est exaltatum cor meum* is realized. One is all the more tempted to view it as the step of humility "of the heart," as we will see that it is closely connected with the twelfth step, that of humility "of the body." The statements made in RM 10.3 and 8 both seem to allude to these two connected symmetrical steps, which are the creation of the Master.

11. Note in particular the direct reference to the "body" in the twelfth step (RM 10.82).

12. These two allude to the body and soul respectively, the two elements following the order designated by RM 10.9.

13. With a return to the interior aspect (10.30–36: will and desires).

14. As we have shown above in n. 10, the division is ostensible in the first step. In reality, the entire step is situated in the realm of the soul. But it is not impossible that the Master thinks of this superficial aspect of the first step when writing the end of his introduction (10.9). The twelfth step includes an obvious interior aspect (see n. 7 above) although the exterior attitude is especially emphasized.

15. In this case, the first step would be understood differently in the first two statements (10.3 and 8) than in the third (10.9). In 10.3 and 8, it would be considered

a step "of the heart," according to its essence (n. 10 above). In contrast, in 10.9, it would be considered as a spiritual and corporal whole, as it appears on the surface. Likewise, the twelfth step would certainly be considered corporal in the first two statements, while in the third it would concern uniting internal conviction with external bearing.

16   A. Borias, "Nouveaux cas de répétition dans la Règle de S. Benoît," *Revue Bénédictine* 75 (1965): 321–325. Cf. my remarks in *La Communauté et l'Abbé* (cited above in n. 1), 212, n. 2.

17   *Semper* reappears ten times, *omni hora* four, if not five times (following E* and RB in RM 10.13 = RB 7.13).

18   *Semper*: three times; *omni hora*: once, in a much shorter text. Cf. also *omni loco* in the first step (10.13) and *ubicumque* in the twelfth (10.83).

19   RM 10.71. Cf. 10.67, citing Psalm 72:23.

20   RM 10.13 (*extimet*) and 84 (*existimans ... existimet*).

21   RM 10.19 and 85. Cf. 10.67 (only *dicens sibi*).

22   In the sense of "divine judgment": RM 10.41 and 84.

23   RM 10.10 alludes to Psalm 35.2. Drawing inspiration from this psalm text, the Master strays from Cassian, who is inspired by other scriptural formulas (Prov 9:10; Ps 110:10). Nonetheless, it remains certain that it is Cassian who influences the Master to speak of the fear of God here. In similar fashion, at the end of the chapter (RM 10.88), the Master will modify Cassian to make the allusion to 1 John 4:18 more explicit (nn. 134–135 below). In both cases, the Master receives a scriptural concept from Cassian (the "fear of the Lord" or the "charity that knows no fear") and modifies it by drawing inspiration from a closely related scriptural formula ("the fear of God before one's eyes") or the same Scripture passage followed more faithfully ("the perfect charity that casts out fear").

24   If the theme is "only heard muted" (A. Borias, 225 [cited in n. 16]), fear is nonetheless the atmosphere that envelops the entire first step. Admittedly, the words *timor* and *timentibus* each appear only once at the beginning (10.10–11), but they are conveyed by *custodiens se* (10.12), *sollicitus sit* (10.19), *cauemus* (10.32), *pauemus* (10.33), and *cauendum* (10.35 and 40), which all express different nuances of the same sentiment. And while this "defense" is marshaled against sin, in the last analysis, the fear of sin stems from the fear of God who hates and punishes it.

25   RM 10.33: *pauemus illud* (Ps 13:1).

26   RM 10.91. Phrase added by the Master to the conclusion of Cassian.

27   This must nuance the remarks made in *La Communauté et l'Abbé*, 223–226 (cited in n. 1), on the haphazard character of the paragraphs that deal with the will and desires. Focused on the current redaction, some of these remarks do not apply to the original redaction reconstructed here.

28   It will be the same in the second step (RM 10.42). The strings of citations in RM 7.39–40 (Ps 13:1 + Prov 16:25) and 7.45–46 (*Pass. Seb.* 14 + *Sir* 18:30) also conform to the order that these citations follow in the current redaction of RM 10 although Sirach 18:30 is cited in its entirety in 7.46. In this respect, we note that the demonstration of the antecedence of RM 7 over RM 10 in *La Communauté et l'Abbé*, 222–226 must also be reviewed in light of the facts presented here.

Chapter 7: Humility

29 At least in regard to the theme of death itself because *ante oculos* is found both in 3.53 and 10.10.

30 At least in the section that we are examining because one later reads: *Praecepta Dei factis cottidie adimplere* (3.69).

31 *La Communauté et l'Abbé* (cited in n. 1), 223–228 (steps 1–4 and RM 7).

32 By replacing *et Hierusalem sanctam* with *omni concupiscentia spirituali*, Benedict adds five syllables and destroys the effect (RB 4.46).

33 RM 3.53 and 55. Cf. RM 3.9 and 3.57.

34 The maximum that the dactylic hexameter can reach is seventeen syllables (minimum: thirteen). The return to the number seventeen is thus probably explained by an academic recollection.

35 Needless to say, *expauescere* is stronger.

36 Of course, "eternal life" and "holy Jerusalem" are not defined as "judgment and hell," which are successive realities, but the beatitude is considered first from the viewpoint of duration, then from that of place. Note that the first stich has two verbs, the second, two attributive adjectives. In RB 4.46, the second stich is not only longer than the previous, but has also lost the bipartite structure that made it similar to it.

37 *La Communauté et l'Abbé*, 223–228.

38 On this integration of fear into humility, see above pp. 230–244.

39 The substitution of actions for statements occurs from the beginning of the first step. The Master changes *timor Domini est* to *timorem Dei ante oculos sibi semper ponens*.

40 Nothing obliges one to put a period after *reuoluat* (10.11). The phrase continues without interruption (10.12: *et custodiens se ...*) until the end of 10.13. One can therefore attach *extimet* to *si* (10.10). See also n. 46 below.

41 On the other hand, this grammatical construction does not seem to correspond very exactly to the sequence of ideas. See n. 45 below. It is particularly hard to see why the Master writes *ut* (10.11): Is meditation on the last things the goal or the consequence of meditation on the divine commands? It is true that, here as elsewhere, *ut* could have been written mistakenly for *et*. See Adalbert de Vogüé, *La Règle du Maître*, Sources Chrétiennes 105–107 (Paris: Cerf, 1964–65) I.448–449: critical note on RM 1.29.

42 See, however, n. 23 above.

43 Forgetfulness of what? God? The fear of God, which has just been mentioned? The divine precepts that will be mentioned next?

44 Cassian speaks only of virtues and vices. To speak of the precepts of God is less philosophical and more biblical.

45 This relationship is clearly indicated in the developments on the thoughts and desires (10.14–19 and 34–36) and in the conclusion (10.37–40): cognizance of the divine gaze precedes and inspires vigilance over oneself. In contrast, the introduction (10.12–13) presents the matter in reverse: *custodiens se ... extimet se discipulus a Deo semper de caelis respici* (cf. n. 41 above).

46 If one puts a period after *reuoluat* at the end of 10.11, the following phrase (10.12–13) no longer appears as a second conditional clause dependent on *si* (10.10) but as an independent clause in which the verb is in the jussive (*extimet*). But this punctuation is questionable (see n. 40), especially as the symmetry of the verbs (*custodiens* corresponds to *ponens* and *extimet* to *fugiat*) suggests the close correlation of the two phrases.

47 Cf. 10.19: *dicat*; 10.35: *cauendum*. It is a matter of the first and last paragraphs forming an inclusion.

48 The Master is content to affirm the fourth point (10.30) without a proof-text (*praesente Domino*).

49 Is it found elsewhere in Cassian? In any case, he cites neither Proverbs 15:3 nor Psalm 13:2. In *Conl.* 12.8, *ineuitabilis ille oculus* seems to designate the gaze of the conscience (cf. *Conl.* 11.8) rather than that of God.

50 RM 3.55. Cf. Proverbs 15:3; Psalm 13:2.

51 A. Borias (cited in n. 16) 325–326.

52 Basil, *Regula* 46, 66, 79. Cf. 34. In *Regula* 108, it is only a question of the gaze.

53 Basil, *Regula* 34 and 46. Cf. RM 10.34: *credimus*.

54 Basil, *Regula* 60, 66, 79, 108. Cf. RM 3.55: *pro certo scire*; 10.13: *extimet*; 10.20, 23, 24: *agnoscimus*.

55 Basil, *Regula* 46 (*semper intueatur*) and 86 (*semper habere et cogitare*).

56 This allusion to Psalm 7:10 (cf. RM 10.14) is found in Basil, *Regula* 34, 79, 108.

57 Basil, *Regula* 34, 46, 60, 66, 79.

58 Basil, *Regula* 2 (*PL* 103.492b–493a) and 55, 57, 58.

59 See Adalbert de Vogüé, "La Règle de Saint Benoît et la vie contemplative," *Collectanea Cisterciensia* 27 (1965) 104, n. 55. ET: Adalbert de Vogüé, "The Rule of Saint Benedict and the Contemplative Life," *Cistercian Studies Quarterly* 1.1 (1966): 54–73.

60 Basil, *Regula* 2, *PL* 103.492a.

61 See Adalbert de Vogüé, *The Rule of Saint Benedict: A Doctrinal and Spiritual Commentary* (Kalamazoo, MI: Cistercian, 1983), 122–124.

62 One finds it in RM 11.38–39, 18.6 (cf. 21.9; 82.22; 87.23), and RB 19.1. This last text, which alone brings together all the aspects of the theme, is particularly remarkable. It can be compared with RB 3.6, 63.13, and other passages where Benedict evidences such familiarity with the shared text that one is tempted to see him as its author. He may have borrowed the expression *uoluntas propria* from Basil. See *La Communauté et l'Abbé*, 225, n. 1.

63 Basil, *Regula* 86. It is a matter of indicating awareness that one is in the presence of God.

64 Thought precedes speech although *oris* is mentioned before *cordis* (8.21–23).

65 The thoughts-speech sequence is found in RM 3.56–57, completed by the desires-will couplet (3.65–66. Cf. 10.30–36). This last is missing in RM 8–9, closer to the *Ars Sancta* than to the first step in this instance.

Chapter 7: Humility

66 RM 10.23: *in opera uero manuum nostrarum*, instead of *tactus manuum* (8.24). Although the technical term designating manual labor is *opus laboris* (used more than twenty times in RM), one sometimes finds *labor manuum* (3.49; 50.52; 83.17. Cf. 11.95–96; 83.15) and *opera manuum* (50.7. Cf. 50.32 and 38).

67 *Inperfectum meum uiderunt oculi tui* (Ps 138:16). Cf. RM 7.8 (*inperfectum derelinquentes*), where the "incompletion" inspired by obedience is viewed favorably; 17.18. In these two cases, it is a matter of a job.

68 According to RM 8.25, the faults of the feet are flight and perhaps homicide (see Chapter Six, n. 3). In RM 10.24, the Master probably thinks of the trips of monks sent on errands, an occupation that sometimes replaces manual labor (50.72–74; 57.14–16; 78.4; 86.27) and requires special precautions (11.37–39; 15.48–56).

69 RM 8.17–20. See Chapter Six, n. 3.

70 RM 9.21–24. Does *uultus* (9.23) mean "face" (cf. Thp 14 and 41–42) or "gaze" (9.15; 87.49)? Even if one maintains that the first sense is more probable (cf. *inclinato*), the fact remains that the twelfth step associates head and eyes (cf. also 10.3 and 8).

71 Cf. RM 11.85–90, where frivolity, an attitude incompatible with the twelfth step, is reprimanded with the help of texts borrowed from the first. See n. 112 below.

72 RM 9.23. On the meaning of *uultus*, see n. 70 above.

73 The place of the twelfth step is better understood if one takes into account the fact that it undoubtedly originally followed the tenth. See n. 114 below.

74 *La Communauté et l'Abbé*, 251–264 (cited in n. 1).

75 *La Communauté et l'Abbé*, 265, n. 2 and 266, n. 2. If three good ninth-century manuscripts of Cassian attest to *et indignum*, it may be that this reading comes from a recollection of RB, which must have been well known to copyists.

76 *Celauerit seniorem*: cursus uelox; *iudicarit indignum*: cursus planus. This last is found in signs 3, 5, 6, 8, and 9, while the cursus velox reappears in the first sign. One also finds the cursus tardus in the fourth sign. Therefore, the whole list is very carefully thought out in this regard.

77 In the fifth step, he leaves *celauerit*, but here *iudicarit* would be more cumbersome because it follows *(contentus) sit*.

78 See *La Communauté et l'Abbé*, 262, n. 2. Note that the Master substitutes *omnibus* for *cunctis*, rare in RM. This *omnibus* echoes the *omni ... omnia* of the previous step (RM 10.66), just as *uiliorem* is reminiscent of *uilitate*.

79 *La Communauté et l'Abbé*, 252–253.

80 RM 10.80: *humiliter*.

81 Psalm 21:7; Psalm 87:16; Psalm 118:71, 73.

82 *La Communauté et l'Abbé*, 259–262 (cited in n. 1).

83 Cf. RM 10.45: *nihil suo iudicio praesumens*. See *La Communauté et l'Abbé*, 255–256 on the relationship of this text with the third sign of Cassian. On the other hand, perhaps *nihil ... praesumens* was suggested to the Master by the sixth sign.

84 "Law" designates Scripture in RM Th 19 and 23; 7.36; 11.9; 15.35. However, in RM 10.73 it may be that the "law of God" designates the Rule of the monastery (cf. 93.15). See *La Communauté et l'Abbé*, 261–262.

85 RM 9.45; 50.26 and 43. Cassian had already made the eighth sign an introduction to the signs concerning speech. See n. 88 in Chapter Six.

86 RM 7.16–18; 8.34; 9.42–44; 10.75; 11.41–43.

87 One will note that Deuteronomy 32:7 is not cited as it is (*Interroga patrem tuum*, etc.) but adapted (*cum interrogat patrem suum* ...) in a form that is not encountered in any monastic citations of the text (see *La Communauté et l'Abbé*, 262, n. 1). If the Master avoids the second person, it is undoubtedly because it would fit poorly with *dicens cum scriptura* (10.72), which puts the words in the mouth of the disciple. Moreover, in the previous citation, *tua* is addressed to God. Here, the second person would be addressed to the disciple.

88 See *La Communauté et l'Abbé*, 259.

89 One finds them reunited in RM 50.43 (*meditationem et interrogationem praeceptorum diuinorum*), but they are only authorized in the absence of the abbot. Here, on the contrary, it is the abbot that one questions. The *doctrina* of the latter can consist in examples (cf. 10.72) as well as words, as noted by RM 2.11–15. Consequently, the "inquiry" is perhaps to be interpreted broadly, including the simple gaze of the disciple silently observing the example of his abbot.

90 Beyond this connection between ideas, the eighth step is attached to the next by the uniform presentation of the citations. Cf. n. 108 below.

91 One should not exaggerate the distance between *cohibeat* and *prohibeat*. The two verbs appear alternately in the versions of Psalm 33:14 cited by RM Ths 13 = RB Prol 17. One also finds *Cohibe linguam tuam a malo* in the Roman Psalter, followed by our Rules, *Prohibe* in the Gallican. It is probable that both Cassian and the Master recall this text in writing the ninth sign/step. In the context of the psalm, *cohibe* must be taken in the strong sense, "*Forbid* your tongue to speak evil."

92 Such is certainly the thought of Cassian, as shown by *Inst*.12.29.2, which contrary to the signs of humility indicates: *facilitas in sermone, uerba passim sine ulla cordis grauitate erumpentia*. It is not the act of speaking that is blameworthy, but unrestrained speech.

93 Compare the details of the eighth step: *monasterii ... abbas* (*La Communauté et l'Abbé*, 260–262).

94 See RM 50.17, 23, 28–33, 52, 55 (cf. RM 53.38–41) as well as Chapter Six, n. 102.

95 *Leniter* (hapax) is actually the equivalent of *lente*, which is frequent in RM in the sense of "gently, in a low voice" (Ernout-Meillet, *Dictionnaire étymologique de la langue latine* [Paris: 1959], 351, notes some confusion between *lenis* and *lentus*). Yet *lente* is equivalent to *non clamosa uoce* (RM 9.43).

96 In counting up the syllables of these three members and the final phrase (8–9–11–9), one sees that *humiliter cum grauitate* is modeled on *et non sit clamosus in uoce* (nine syllables). Thus, the phrase of Cassian has left its mark on the group. One will note that the eleven syllables of the third member are reduced to the

Chapter 7: Humility

same number (8) as the first if one removes the words *et sancta*. Perhaps these words, which do not illustrate any citation, are later. See n. 117 below.

97 See n. 95 above.

98 Moreover, it is modesty of tone that Cassian himself suggests is a "sign of humility": *non clamosa in uoce*.

99 Cf. RM 11.76, where *cum grauitate* is juxtaposed with *promptus in risu*.

100 Compare the third step, repeating the second in positive form.

101 RM 3.58: *Multum loqui non amare*.

102 RM 9.31–34, citing Sextus and Proverbs 10:19.

103 *Ad loquendum … non loquatur* (ninth step); *cum loquitur … loquatur* (eleventh step).

104 *La Communauté et l'Abbé*, 257–259 (cited in n. 1).

105 Compare the prolepsis of the second step to the end of the first (*La Communauté et l'Abbé*, 225–226).

106 The sixth step is the least revised.

107 Signs three and four become steps three and four.

108 See *La Règle du Maître* I.435, note on RM 10.72 (cited in n. 41).

109 This only recurs in the sixth step.

110 Only in form because the second remark is aimed only at laughter accompanying speech.

111 See also the next section, *Origin of the Eleventh Step*.

112 Compare RM 10.37–38 and 11.86–87 (Prov 15:3; Ps 13:2); 10.40 and 11.88 (Ps 13:3). Thus, the last admonition combines elements borrowed from either the first or twelfth steps. This is new evidence of the connection between the two steps (cf. n. 71 above).

113 The relationship of the two admonitions (RM 11.46) is as clearly emphasized as that of the two steps (10.80). See more below, n. 116.

114 This paradoxical position has already been summarily explained (n. 73) by the speech-laughter-gaze sequence, which one finds in RM 9.23. In this passage, *tacitus* represents the ninth step, *tristis*, the tenth and eleventh steps, *inclinato ambulans uultu*, the twelfth step. Perhaps RM 9.23 is based on RM 10, just as RM 9.43 seems to echo the eleventh step.

115 Paradoxically, the tenth and twelfth steps, corresponding to admonitions seven and nine, do not have, like these last, the expression *cum grauitate*. The latter appears in the eleventh step, which corresponds to the second admonition. But the eleventh step is probably overloaded, as one will see in the next paragraph. The notes *sine risu … cum grauitate* have undoubtedly been introduced there for the express purpose of summarizing the tenth step and preparing for the twelfth.

116 The connection of the ninth and eleventh steps (see n. 113 above) is again confirmed by examining these citations. Proverbs 10:19 (*In multiloquio …*) and Sextus 145 (*Sapiens paucis …*) cite the ninth and eleventh steps respectively. They are also consecutive but in reverse order in RM 9.31–34. On the other

hand, Psalm 139:12 (*Vir linguosus*...), cited in the ninth step, is reemployed in the second admonition to the deans, which corresponds to the eleventh step. The 11–10 sequence of the steps is reflected as well in RM 3.57–60, where three articles corresponding to the eleventh step (words that are holy, brief, and without laughter) are followed by an article corresponding to the tenth (laughter).

117 The second admonition (RM 11.46) reproduces only this original nucleus: *ne satis clamosa uoce loquatur*. While the scriptural illustration is not taken from Sextus, but (rather awkwardly) from Psalm 139:12 (*Vir linguosus*...), it could be that *sapientes* (11.46) alludes to the Sentence of Sextus, *Sapiens paucis*... (10.81). Thus, it seems that at the time the Master writes RM 11, the eleventh step is not only previous to the tenth, but also limited to the words *pauca uerba loquatur et non sit clamosus in uoce*, followed by the Sentence, *Sapiens paucis*.... Moreover, one will note that the other elements of the eleventh step are found to some extent in the following admonition, which prohibits all speech leading to laughter (11.49, 56, 58. Cf. *cum grauitate*... *sine risu*) as well as all speech *quae ad sanctitatem non pertinet* (11.49. Cf. *sancta*, a word that I suspect is later, see n. 96). Therefore, it seems that this third admonition uses the "later" elements from the eleventh step, combined with some reminiscences of RM 3.

118 Undoubtedly also *et sancta*, which forms a third pair with *pauca* (see preceding note).

119 For Cassian, as for Saint Paul, charity elsewhere has an eternal significance (*Conl.* 1.11), but *Inst.* 4.39 only considers it in relationship to good accomplished here below.

120 He typically ends his treatises with this. See Prol 20–21; Thp 11; Ths 46; 1.90–92; 2.32–40; 3.78–94, etc.

121 *Vitae huius*... *scala* (10.87) is reminiscent of *scala*... *nostra est uita in saeculo* (10.8), which follows reference to the heavenly goal of the ladder.

122 RM 10.92, phrase closely parallel to 10.87.

123 1 Corinthians 2:9 (see n. 127 below).

124 RM 10.119: *per scalam praesentis temporis obseruantiae, gradibus humilitatis ascensis*.

125 Cf. RM 10.6, 8, 87, 92 (see nn. 121–122).

126 RM 10.119–120: *in hac regione perenni*... *eleuari, ut in perpetua cum Deo exultatione laetentur*.

127 1 Corinthians 2:9: *Quod oculus non uidit, nec auris audiuit*... *quae praeparauit Deus iis qui diligunt illum*. RM 3.83 only alludes to the end of this text (see however n. 76 in Chapter Five), while RB 4.77 cites it completely. In RM 10.120, the Master makes an actual citation but limits it to the last phrase.

128 RM 3.83: *Deum timentibus* (cf. 3.1: *timere Deum*).

129 RM 10.11: *uita aeterna*... *quid timentibus Deum praeparet*.

130 Paul modifies Isaiah 64:4, where one reads: *quae praeparasti expectantibus te*.

131 This form seems strange even if one takes into account some frequent changes of number in RM. Perhaps *peruenientes* stems from *perueniet* (cf. RM 11.89: *incipiet*), which one would wish to correct by *peruenies* (cf. *obseruabas*). The superimposition of the endings -et and -es would have led to *peruenie(n)tes*. The

Chapter 7: Humility

same result could have been attained from *peruenies*, after the insertion of the *te* (addition to *perducet* in Cassian) that the Master removed: *peruenie(n)/te/s*.

132 *Mox* (10.88) and *gehennae* (10.90), words familiar to the Master, replace *confestim* and *contemplatione supplicii*, expressions absent from RM (one finds *metus gehennae* in Cassian, *Conl.* 11.6–8). *Poena formidinis* is simplified to *formidine*, which removes the word stemming from the Johannine citation.

133 Cf. eighth sign: *non superficie pronuntiet labiorum*.

134 Cf. 1 John 4:18: *Timor non est in caritate, sed perfecta caritas foras mittit timorem, quoniam timor poenam habet*, etc. Cassian, however, is closer to the text in writing only *caritatem* (the Master adds *Domini*) and *poenam* (which the Master removes. Cf. n. 132).

135 This example shows that when two parallel texts exist, greater conformity to a shared *scriptural* source cannot serve to prove that one text is earlier than the other.

136 *Conl.* 11.6–8. One finds no more in passages such as *Conl.* 4.12.4; 6.5.1; 14.3 that deal with virtue.

137 Cassian, *Conl.* 11.6: *amor uirtutum, affectum uirtutum*; 11.7: *uirtutum amor*; 11.8: *amor castitatis, uirtutis affectum*. The idea is already latent in *delectatione uirtutum* (*Inst.* 4.39.3; *Conl.* 11.8). I do not know if the concept of the role of habit in the acquisition of virtue is present in the work of Cassian (cf. Thomas Aquinas, *Summa Theol.*, I[a]–II[ae], qu. 51, a. 3; qu. 63, a. 2). In any event, the word *consuetudo*, often employed in the sense of social "custom" (*Inst.* 3.6, 10; 4.27.1; 5.23.2; *Conl.* 21.12, etc.), does not seem to figure in the passages where Cassian treats virtue.

138 Cf. Augustine, *De diu. quaest.* LXXXIII.36.2, PL 40.25–26: it is the *consuetudo non peccandi* that causes one to advance from passing concerns (fear and hope) to love.

139 The only additions are *pro Dei amore* (7.34), *cum propheta* (7.52), *Christi et* (7.69).

140 Benedict removes nine scriptural citations. See RM 10.18 (first step); 10.45–48 and 50–51 (third step); 10.73–74 (eighth step. Cf. *La Communauté et l'Abbé*, 266); 10.79 (tenth step). The introductory formulas of the remaining citations are frequently shortened: see RB 7.15, 17, 18, 33, 37, 40, 47, 54, 66. Several citations are slightly shorter than in RM (RM 10.15, 34, 49, 70, 71 = RB 7.15, 23, 34, 53, 54).

141 Only manuscript *P* contains *caelesti* in RM 10.42 and 52.

142 RB 7.13 (*homo*); 7.67 (*monachus*). Cf. 7.66 (shortened introductory formula preceding a citation).

143 As does Cassian, *Inst.* 4.39.2 and *Conl.* 12.7 (third and fourth steps) but without the same negative consequences as in RB.

144 RB 7.34. See *La Communauté et l'Abbé*, 217, n. 3.

145 RB 7.67–70 = RM 10.87–91. The fact that the second conclusion is missing in both Cassian and RB would lead one to think that the priority belongs to RB here. But in addition to the shared introduction of the two Rules containing the announcement of this conclusion, one will note that in the fourth step, Benedict, like the Master, speaks of "the hope of divine reward" (RM 10.56 = RB 7.39: *de*

spe retributionis diuinae). Here again this is an announcement that is fulfilled in RM (RM 10.92: *retributionem Domini*), not RB.

146 RM 10.5 = RB 7.5. Cf. RM 10.8 = RB 7.8: *scala ... nostra est uita in saeculo, quae ... erigatur in caelum.*

147 RM 10.6: *erecta in caelum*, to which RM 10.8 alludes (see preceding note).

148 RM 10.8: *... in praesenti hoc tempore, exaltatum a Domino mortis exitum ...* (cf. RB 7.8).

149 The words *et capite suo* disappear at the same time. See RM 10.8 = RB 7.8.

150 Cf. nn. 121–122 above.

151 B. Capelle, "Cassien, le Maître, et S. Benoît," *Recherches de Théologie Ancienne et Médiévale* 11 (1939): 112–115. Capelle neglects the case of *obseruabas*, but it appears in the notes of G. Penco, *S. Benedicti Regula* (Florence: La Nuova Italia, 1958), 249–254.

152 This word does not constitute a redundancy pure and simple because it serves as a complement to *custodire*, while *ex consuetudine* (7.68) is linked to *uelut naturaliter*. Cf. O. Haggenmüller, "Velut naturaliter ex consuetudine," *Zeugnis des Geistes* (Beuron: 1947), 62–77. Nonetheless, the repetition of the same word in the same case, awkwardly emphasized by *ipsa*, is not graceful in the least.

153 See n. 135 above.

154 Why would the Master have removed *Christi*, so natural after *amore*?

155 B. Capelle (cited in n. 151), 115.

156 See n. 61 above.

157 Cassian, *Inst.* 4.43: *de nuditate humilitas procreatur.*

158 One finds reference to the fourth and fifth signs of humility in the lists of vices eliminated by the *abrenuntiatio secunda* (*Conl.* 3.7.7–11). This passage is inspired by 1 Corinthians 13:4–7: like humility, the *abrenuntiatio* is defined in relationship to charity, to which it leads. One of the vices eliminated is obviously pride. The second and third signs (confession of thoughts and direction from an elder) show that the humility of *Inst.* 4.39.2 implies a battle against all the vices.

159 Evagrius, *Praktikos* I.53, PG 40, 1233b: "The offshoot of *apatheia* is charity; *apatheia* is the flower of *praktikè*; *praktikè* consists in the following of the commandments; the guardian of the latter is the fear of God ... " This schema is undoubtedly the immediate source of Cassian.

160 In *Conl.* 1.6–7, "purity" and charity are even presented as equivalents and synonyms.

161 *Inst.* 4.9. Cf. *Conl.* 2.10: It is thus that one is trained in discretion, the mother of all virtues (*Conl.* 2.4).

162 See A. de Vogüé, *La Communauté et l'Abbé*, 269 (cited in n. 1).

163 Cf. *Inst.* 4.39.1: *Principium nostrae salutis*; *Inst.* 4.43: *Principium nostrae salutis ac sapientiae.*

164 It is true that the words *his qui inbuuntur ad uiam perfectionis* (*Inst.* 4.39.1) seem to designate only beginners and to exclude the perfect. On the other hand, the purification of the vices, between the *initium conuersionis* and the *uirtutum*

Chapter 7: Humility

custodia seems to designate an intermediate stage that is attached neither to servile fear nor to loving fear. However, these difficulties appear inconclusive to us. They indicate only that the distinction between the two fears, certainly underlying, is joined with other schemas here that tend to blur it.

165 Concerning the latter, note the different terms in *Inst.* 4.39.1 (*custodia uirtutum*) and *Inst.* 4.43 (*pullulatio uirtutum*). The first term is suggested by Isaiah 33:6, as we have shown.

166 In spite of the words *his qui inbuuntur* (see n. 164 above).

167 *Conl.* 11.6–12. Although hope is not mentioned in *Inst.* 4.39, it may be that Cassian thinks of it in describing the *contemptus rerum omnium*, or second stage. Compare *Conference* 11.6.2, where the effects of hope are also described in terms of "contempt for the world." As faith corresponds to fear, one would also find the three theological virtues in the schema of Pinufius that *Conference* 11 presents as the basis for good deeds.

168 At least insofar as it incites action from a simple motive of self-interest. In addition, the desire to be with God and the fear of being separated from him can only increase with charity. Cf. *Conl.* 23.5, 8–10.

169 See *The Conclusion of the Chapter* (pp. 223–227) above.

170 RM 10.87: *Ergo his omnibus humilitatis gradibus a discipulo perascensis uitae huius in timore Dei bene persubitur scala.* This cheville is almost identical to the one that introduces the eschatological epilogue (RM 10.92). See p. 224 above.

171 Evagrius, *Praktikos* I.53 (see n. 159 above): from faith to charity by *praktiké* and *apatheia*; Clement, *Strom.* 7.10–11 (PG 9.477–494): from faith to charity by gnosis.

172 RM 10.91 = RB 7.70. The word *operarium* is surprising in this last phrase, as it makes one think of a mercenary who works for a salary. Instead, one would have expected *filium*: charity is the disposition of children (Cassian, *Conl.* 11.7). But perhaps the Master has in mind the state that precedes charity. In the same phrase, *mundum a uitiis et peccatis* is reminiscent of the first step (RM 10.12 = RB 7.12). Cf. also RM 9.41, 46–47.

173 RB 7.69 = RM 10.90. On this change, see *La Communauté et l'Abbé* (cited in n. 1), 452, n. 1.

174 Which are combined with two apocryphal citations (RM 10.44 and 81).

175 Thus RM 10.77 = RB 7.58 (*Vir linguosus* ...); RM 10.78 = RB 7.59 (*Stultus in risu* ...); RM 10.81 = RB 7.61 (*Sapiens uerbis* ...); RM 10.79 (*Sicut crepitantium* ...).

176 RM 10.64–65 = RB 7.47–48; RM 10.67 = RB 7.50; RM 10.71 = RB 7.54, etc.

177 Reference to God is not absent, especially when it is a matter of obedience (*Inst.* 4.27.4: *uelut a Domino sibi esset praeceptum*), but it remains implicit throughout and is not expressed in any sign.

178 The first step also refers to the neighbor, but only implicitly when dealing with self-will and the desires of the flesh (RM 10.30–36 = RB 7.19–25), as is demonstrated by the use of the same citations in the treatise on obedience (see *La Communauté et l'Abbé*, 206 and 222). In the twelfth step, the monk "manifests his humility to all who see him." (RM 10.82 = RB 7.62).

179 Cf. *Inst.* 12.23: *humilitatem ueram quam primitus fratribus reddens Deo quoque ... exhibeat.*

180 As will be seen, in some regards, the first step has the appearance of an ideal but not in comparison with the other steps. While one cannot consider it "inferior" to those that follow (the progression of the ladder is rather artificial), it nonetheless precedes them logically as well as literarily.

181 It appears only in the last phrase of the conclusion (RM 10.90 = RB 7.70), where, however, it does not speak of "grace," but of the Lord acting by the Holy Spirit.

182 As shows *Inst.* 12.29, where the signs of carnal pride correspond, in reverse order, to the signs of humility of *Inst.* 4.39.2.

183 RM 9.41. Cf. RM 7.2–3. To so make fear and desire "perfect" attitudes is to speak as Cassian (*Conl.* 11.12) for whom fear and hope are already, although unequally and imperfectly, "perfect," charity being "more perfect" still. What is lacking in RM is the notion of a hierarchy among these three motives.

184 The only exception is RM 72.7: *caritas Christi* (subjective genitive). Cf. RM 3.23: *amori Christi* (objective genitive), which is a citation.

185 In RM 4.1 (cf. 1 Cor 13:13) *caritas* remains unspecified.

186 RM 10.88: *uitae huius in timore Dei bene persubitur scala.*

187 Benedict seems to think of it when he writes *amore Deum timeant* (RB 72.9), but the expression is inspired by Cyprian and Leo rather than Cassian.

188 See n. 171 above. One can add Romans 8:15 and 2 Timothy 1:7 to 1 John 4:18, which Cassian clearly has in mind.

189 Moreover, such is the actual meaning of the maxim *Principium* (or *Initium*) *sapientiae timor Domini* (Prov 9:10. Ps 110:10, etc.).

190 Humility commands the two other master virtues that become the object of special treatises. This is clear for obedience (RM 7.1 = RB 5.1) as well as for silence, if not in RB 6, at least according to RM 8.15; 9.3, 5–6, 9–10, 12, 14, 16–17, 20, 43). Moreover, the treatises on obedience and silence come from the meditation of *Inst.* 4.39.2 and are recapitulated in RM 10, as we have shown in *La Communauté et l'Abbé,* 207–211.

191 The only allusion to humility is the citation of Matthew 11:29, without commentary in Th 14.

192 *Humilitas* (RM 4.3) precedes *oboedientia taciturnitas* and *superbia* (RM 5.2) precedes *inoboedientia multiloquium*. Therefore, in these two chapters, the Master thinks of the bond that unites the three great virtues (cf. n. 190 above). In contrast, RM 3 does not seem to know this sequence and makes no explicit reference to humility. The only allusion to this virtue is *Non esse superbum* (RM 3.39 = RB 4.31), to which RB 4.69 adds *elationem fugere.*

193 RM 2.26–27 (cf. Mt 18:2–4 and 20:27).

194 RM 53.45; 95.14–16 (cf. Eccl 3:20).

195 RM 92.3–4; 93.54 (Mt 20:27).

196 Cf. Matthew 18:2–4 and 20:27.

Chapter 7: Humility

197 RM 92.47. This remark only aims to prohibit the creation of a "second" who would rest on his success, but it expresses well the underlying idea of the entire pedagogy of competition.

198 In RM 93.55 and 73, *Qui se humiliat exaltabitur* is only addressed to the previously chosen "second," who, according to the second citation, must remain humble under the gaze of God. But other similar *testimonia* clearly concern the competition for the abbacy, in which the abbot is the judge. In addition, the judgment of God and that of human beings are constantly linked in this treatise (cf. 93.1; 93.51, etc.).

199 RM 92.26–27, 32, 52, 62, 72, 76.

200 Cf. nn. 145–146 above.

201 RB 7.34: *pro amore Dei*. See *La Communauté et l'Abbé*, 449–452. However, Cassian, *Inst.* 12.32.2, also brings "the love of Christ" into the renunciation of exterior goods, thus, before the stage of humility and the coming of charity.

202 Except for an almost imperceptible allusion in RB 6.3: *perfectis discipulis*.

203 Benedict appeals to human "fear" in RB 48.20, and "shame" in RB 43.7, but never to ambition. Moreover, recourse to sanctions comes into play in the disciplinary section, not in the ascetical chapters.

204 While Benedict mentions "loving fear" once (see n. 187 above), he is no more concerned with the "charity that casts out fear" than the Master. Like his colleague, he sometimes proposes to "fear God" (RB 3.11; 31.2; 36.7; 53.21; 65.15; 66.1, 4); other times to "love" God (RB 4.72; 7.34; 63.13; 68.5; 72.3, 9). It would seem that the two formulas are almost equivalent.

205 Cf. Leo, *Serm.* 37.3–4: All of Christianity consists in humility. He cites Matthew 18:1–6 and Luke 14:11.

NEW CITY PRESS
of the Focolare
Hyde Park, New York

New City Press is one of more than 20 publishing houses sponsored by the Focolare, a movement founded by Chiara Lubich to help bring about the realization of Jesus' prayer: "That all may be one" (John 17:21). In view of that goal, New City Press publishes books and resources that enrich the lives of people and help all to strive toward the unity of the entire human family. We are a member of the Association of Catholic Publishers.

Other Books in this Series:

A Critical Study Of The Rule Of Benedict Volume 1: Overview
978-1-56548-480-1 $24.95

For Further Reading:

Saint Benedict: A Rule For Beginners (2nd Edition) Julian Stead, O.S.B.
978-1-56548-447-4 $14.95

15 Days Of Prayer With Saint Benedict André Gozier
978-1-56548-304-0 $12.95

Periodicals

Living City Magazine,
www.livingcitymagazine.com

Scan to join our mailing list for discounts and promotions or go to www.newcitypress.com and click on "join our email list."